Brechtian Cinemas

THE SUNY SERIES

HORIZONS OF CINEMA

MURRAY POMERANCE | EDITOR

Also in the series

William Rothman, editor, *Cavell on Film*

J. David Slocum, editor, *Rebel Without a Cause*

Joe McElhaney, *The Death of Classical Cinema*

Kirsten Moana Thompson, *Apocalyptic Dread*

Frances Gateward, editor, *Seoul Searching*

Michael Atkinson, editor, *Exile Cinema*

Paul S. Moore, *Now Playing*

Robin L. Murray and Joseph K. Heumann, *Ecology and Popular Film*

William Rothman, editor, *Three Documentary Filmmakers*

Sean Griffin, editor, *Hetero*

Jean-Michel Frodon, editor, *Cinema and the Shoah*

Carolyn Jess-Cooke and Constantine Verevis, editors, *Second Takes*

Matthew Solomon, editor, *Fantastic Voyages of the Cinematic Imagination*

R. Barton Palmer and David Boyd, editors, *Hitchcock at the Source*

William Rothman, *Hitchcock: The Murderous Gaze, Second Edition*

Joanna Hearne, *Native Recognition*

Marc Raymond, *Hollywood's New Yorker*

Steven Rybin and Will Scheibel, editors, *Lonely Places, Dangerous Ground*

Claire Perkins and Constantine Verevis, editors, *B Is for Bad Cinema*

Dominic Lennard, *Bad Seeds and Holy Terrors*

Rosie Thomas, *Bombay before Bollywood*

Scott M. MacDonald, *Binghamton Babylon*

Sudhir Mahadevan, *A Very Old Machine*

David Greven, *Ghost Faces*

James S. Williams, *Encounters with Godard*

William H. Epstein and R. Barton Palmer, editors, *Invented Lives, Imagined Communities*

Lee Carruthers, *Doing Time*

Rebecca Meyers, William Rothman, and Charles Warren, editors, *Looking with Robert Gardner*

Belinda Smaill, *Regarding Life*

Douglas McFarland and Wesley King, editors, *John Huston as Adaptor*

R. Barton Palmer, Homer B. Pettey, and Steven M. Sanders, editors, *Hitchcock's Moral Gaze*

Will Scheibel, *American Stranger*

Brechtian Cinemas

Montage and Theatricality in Jean-Marie Straub and Danièle Huillet, Peter Watkins, and Lars von Trier

Nenad Jovanovic

SUNY PRESS

Published by State University of New York Press, Albany

Printed in the United States of America

For information, contact State University of New York Press, Albany, NY
www.sunypress.edu

Production, Ryan Morris
Marketing, Kate R. Seburyamo

Library of Congress Cataloging-in-Publication Data

Names: Jovanovic, Nenad, 1973– author.
Title: Brechtian cinemas : montage and theatricality in Jean-Marie Straub and Danièle Huillet, Peter Watkins, and Lars von Trier / Nenad Jovanovic.
Description: Albany : State University of New York Press, [2017] | Series: SUNY series, horizons of cinema | Includes bibliographical references and index.
Identifiers: LCCN 2016021651 (print) | LCCN 2016035070 (ebook) | ISBN 9781438463636 (hardcover : alk. paper) | ISBN 9781438463643 (pbk : alk. paper) | ISBN 9781438463650 (e-book)
Subjects: LCSH: Brecht, Bertolt, 1898–1956—Influence. | Straub, Jean-Marie—Criticism and interpretation. | Huillet, Danièle—Criticism and interpretation. | Watkins, Peter, 1935—Criticism and interpretation. | Trier, Lars von, 1956—Criticism and interpretation. | Motion pictures—History.
Classification: LCC PT2603.R397 Z1475 2017 (print) | LCC PT2603.R397 (ebook) | DDC 832/.912—dc23
LC record available at https://lccn.loc.gov/2016021651

10 9 8 7 6 5 4 3 2 1

In memoriam Martin Walsh

Contents

Illustrations

Acknowledgments

Parts of this book have appeared previously in different form. I thank the publishers for permission to reuse the material from the following articles: "Montage and Theatricality as Sources of Estrangement: A Tendency in Contemporary Brechtian Cinema" (*Theatre Symposium* 19 [2011]), "Estranging the Postmodern: Brechtian Resonances in Lars von Trier" (*The Brecht Yearbook* 37 [2012]), and "Between the Poles of Eisensteinian Aesthetics: Editing Patterns in Peter Watkins' Biographical Films" (*Journal of Scandinavian Cinema* 4.1 [2014]).

My gratitude goes next to the people most closely involved in this study since its inception: Charlie Keil, Stefan Soldovieri, Veronika Ambros, and Marc Silberman. All of them generously lent their expertise and insights over the years, helping me refine my ideas and formulations. I am especially indebted to Charlie, who stayed with the project until its completion, tirelessly reading revisions and offering suggestions.

Thanks are due also to Ontario's Ministry of Training, Colleges and Universities, for supporting the initial stage of my research by awarding me the Ontario Graduate Scholarship, and to the Joint Initiative in German and European Studies program, which funded my multiple visits to the Brecht Archive in Berlin. I acknowledge the help of the Archive's staff members Helgrid Streidt and Uta Kohl in locating some of the material consulted.

I extend my gratitude to Mohamed Sakr and the other students in my Political Cinema class, which I taught at the American University in Cairo in the spring of 2013. Their enthusiastic and intelligent responses to Brechtian concepts and films motivated me to persist in this endeavor.

Veljko Jankovic provided me with lodging during four months of my life as an intercontinental academic nomad, for which I am forever thankful. I also cordially thank Vladislav Mijic for helping me translate more than one knotty Brechtian passage.

Listing all the people whose emotional support helped me realize this project would require more space than is available to me. Those who must be mentioned are Jean Glasgow, Lazar Rajic, and—above all—Ivana Nesovic. Thank you from the bottom of my heart.

Finally, I am most grateful to the anonymous reviewers for their benevolent criticism; to James Peltz and Ryan Morris of SUNY Press, for their patient guidance; to Eric Schramm, for his expert copyediting; and to Murray Pomerance, the editor of the Horizons of Cinemas series, for his shrewdness, wit, and belief in this project.

1

Introduction

Revisiting Brecht and Cinema

> One of the most abused critical terms we have is "Brechtian."
>
> —Jonathan Rosenbaum

GIVEN THAT BERTOLT BRECHT'S dealings with cinema were only intermittent, resulting in comparatively few films and writings on the medium, the ubiquity of his name in film criticism is astounding. One encounters it in discussions of practitioners as diverse as the Brothers Taviani (*Padre Padrone* [Father and Master; 1977], *La notte di San Lorenzo* [The Night of the Shooting Stars; 1982]), Apichatpong Weerasethakul (*Tropical Malady* [2004], *Uncle Boonmee Who Can Recall His Past Lives* [2010]), and Russ Meyer (*Faster, Pussycat! Kill! Kill!* [1965], *Beneath the Valley of the Ultra-Vixens* [1979]), and throughout the decades spanned by their careers. The continued and varied relevance of Brecht for film practice and theory has been joined by an increasing breadth of meanings that Brecht's name connotes, the fact that inspired Rosenbaum's quote above. This book at once narrows the term "Brechtian," so as to help enhance the scientific rigor of Brecht-inflected film scholarship, and expands it, so as to reflect the diversity of ways in which Brecht has impacted cinema.

The term "Brechtian" can have at least three broad meanings in the context of theater and film studies. The most obvious of these is historical: a play by Brecht is Brechtian just as *King Lear* is a Shakespearean play. The least ambiguous sense of the adjective, this is also the least common of the three. One is more likely to encounter the word "Brechtian" in a commentary of a play by Peter Weiss or Naomi Wallace, or—potentially more confusingly—of any theater production that opposes the narrative and/or stylistic norms of Aristotelian realism (which illustrates the word's second usage), than in a discussion of *Der gute Mensch von Sezuan* (The Good Person of Szechwan, 1939).

There is a conundrum posed by the practice of applying the same term "Brechtian" to the works that display narrative, stylistic, and political differences as great as are those between, for instance, Weiss's *The Investigation* (1965) and Takashi Miike's *Big Bang Love, Juvenile A* (2006), or between Wallace's *In the Heart of America* (2001) and *Beneath the Valley of the Ultra-Vixens*. *The Investigation* is a documentary-drama based on the 1963–1965 Frankfurt Auschwitz Trials, employing the contradictions among the witnesses to the genocide as a principal structural feature, while *Big Bang Love* focuses on the erotic attraction between two murderers in a juvenile detention center. Wallace's play bitterly criticizes the American Gulf War, paralleling it with the war in Vietnam, whereas Meyer's film is a minimally plotted spectacle of campy humor and large bosoms. Both *Big Bang Love* and *Ultra-Vixens* are, then, at odds with the partisan politics of all Brecht's mature works. What allows for their comparisons with Brecht (albeit problematically) are their formal operations: the former film flaunts its artificiality through a minimal setting and lighting scheme and through scenes whose claims to objectivity are uncertain, while the latter refrains from continuity editing and uses reflexivity (exemplified by Meyer's appearance in one scene carrying a film camera around the set).

A third usage of "Brechtian" applies to discussion of editing stylization, where an attempt is made to cinematically adjust Brecht's theatrical strategy of foregrounding the constructedness of a presentation to aid the spectator in creating a critical distance from it. Those to whom the term is applied in this way emphasize in various manners the "spaces" between shots, as smallest units of the filmic chain, instead of aiming for the impression of unity between discrete segments of the spaces that those shots represent, as do filmmakers who work within the continuity editing system.

These varied senses of the term "Brechtian" can serve as the lines along which to divide the existing scholarship on Brecht and cinema. One group of texts employs historiographic approaches to the topic, highlighting Brecht's writings on specific films and the medium in general, and the films on which he creatively collaborated: Martin Brady's "Brecht and Film" (2006), Angela Curran's "Bertolt Brecht" (2009), Wolfgang Gersch's *Film bei Brecht* (Brecht at Film, 1975), Walter Hinck's "Kamera als Soziologe" (Camera as a Sociologist, 1971), Thomas Elsaesser's "From Anti-Illusionism to Hyper-realism: Bertolt Brecht and Contemporary Film" (1990), Roswitha Mueller's *Bertolt Brecht and the Theory of Media* (1989), Marc Silberman's "Brecht and Film" (1997), John Willett's "Brecht and the Motion Pictures" (1998), "The Lessons of Brecht" section of Robert Stam's *Reflexivity in Film and Literature* (1995), Karsten Witte's "Brecht und der Film" ("Brecht and Film," 2006), and certain portions of Maia Turovskaia's *Na granit͟se iskusstv: Brekht i kino* (At the Border of Art: Brecht and Film, 1985) and Martin Walsh's *The Brechtian Aspect of Radical Cinema* (1981). The texts vary chiefly in their respective emphases, but commonly reflect upon the cinematic influences on Brecht, and point to the impact of his ideas and techniques on film studies (manifested most persistently in the version of psychosemiotics proposed by the contributors to the British journal *Screen* in the early 1970s) and film practice (shown in a range of cinemas and film movements, most distinctly in certain films of the French *Nouvelle vague*, Brazilian *Cinema Novo*, and New German Cinema). The other group of texts is informed by what David Bordwell disparagingly refers to as "SLAB" theory (the initials of Ferdinand de Saussure, Jacques Lacan, Louis Althusser, and Roland Barthes, writers whose ideas—linked by their use of semiotics—the theory amalgamates). Dominant in film studies until the rise of Bordwell's and Carroll's oppositional "cognitivism" in the 1980s, the "SLAB" discourse has produced numerous texts, the most influential of which (Jean-Louis Baudry's "Ideological Effects of the Basic Cinematographic Apparatus" [1999 (1970)], Peter Wollen's "Godard and Counter Cinema: *Vent d'est*" [1999 (1972)], Colin MacCabe's "Realism and the Cinema: Notes on some Brechtian theses" [1974], and Stephen Heath's "Lessons from Brecht" [1974]) are summarized and critically commented upon in chapter 1, along with Dana Polan's and Murray Smith's critiques of it ("Brecht and the Politics of Self-Reflexive Cinema" [1974], "A Brechtian Cinema? Towards a Politics of Self-Reflexive Film" [1985] and "The Logic and Legacy of Brechtianism" [1996], respectively). The lack of a recent book-length study that employs a phenomenological perspective to tackle the broader subject of Brechtian cinemas (as opposed to any one filmmaker's Brechtianisms) provided a further impetus for writing this volume.

Our era of unbridled liberalism has seen a proliferation of versions of Brecht that downplay his politics to one level or another, regarding them as fish bones that have to be removed for the dramatic or interpretive meal to become edible. A more holistic approach to Brecht considers not only his theories but also his Marxist agenda. This choice finds its rationale in the ongoing relevance of Brecht's work for the cinematic practices that acknowledge his dramatic theory as a decisive influence. As John J. White suggests, Brecht's thinking about theater developed in a linear fashion, becoming increasingly informed by Marxism in the mid-1920s. According to White, the change of emphasis from political to artistic radicalism that occurred in the middle phase of Brecht's work as a theorist of theater, and the decreased presence of recognizably Marxist ideas in his work from the period, should both be attributed to the circumstances of exile: in his countries of asylum, Scandinavia and the United States, Brecht was required to refrain from political activity, even in the aesthetic realm (White 79). This book, then, regards *Verfremdung* and related Brechtian concepts as possessing a political function.

Brecht's politics and the best examples of his film practice intersect at the notion of dialectics. The filmmakers who constitute this book's focus are selected for the diversity of formal ways in which their work uses his method as a structural principle, and for the cultural diversity they represent. The choice of Lars von Trier, a Dane, and Jean-Marie Straub and Danièle Huillet and Peter Watkins, filmmakers who worked in different European countries and the United States, illustrates that the phenomenon of Brechtian cinema is not exclusive to the German cultural context, where Brecht has long enjoyed the status of a canonical writer.

Some readers might expect to encounter additional case studies in a book bearing a title that promises a degree of comprehensiveness. Alexander Kluge and Harun Farocki, two major filmmakers who have eloquently expressed their indebtedness to Brecht, are excluded from this consideration because the prevalence of the nonfictional mode in Kluge's later works and in most of Farocki's oeuvre does not fit the book's concern with stage-like stylization. The careers of two other influential practitioners in relation to whom Brecht is often mentioned, Glauber Rocha and Rainer Werner Fassbinder, ended too long ago for their films to exemplify Brechtian filmmaking today, as one of this volume's central concerns. Lastly, Jean-Luc Godard, whose several 1960s and 1970s films nod to Brecht's literary and theoretical output, is left outside the scope of my investigation owing to the abundance of scholarship on his work.[1] (Nonetheless, he is frequently invoked in these pages, as a good specter).

Of course, the filmmakers discussed here at length are worthy of exploration for more reasons than their relation to Brecht. This book's secondary goal is to delineate the formal characteristics of Straub and Huillet's, Watkins's, and von Trier's cinemas as they have developed against a backdrop of changing cultural and social circumstances, and to update the rich critical dialogue the filmmakers have elicited. Huillet died two years after the appearance of the last English-language study on her and her artistic and life partner, Ursula Böser's *The Art of Seeing, the Art of Listening* (2004), but Straub continued to produce prolifically (often in various collaborations). Since the appearance of the only book in this language dedicated solely to his work, Joseph A. Gomez's *Peter Watkins* (1979), Watkins has produced *Resan* (The Journey, 1985) and *La commune (Paris, 1871)* (2000), ambitious films that have largely fallen under the public radar. On Lars von Trier there is not a scarcity of commentaries, but the filmmaker's rapid production rate and the polarized views on his relationship to Brecht[2] merit this addition to the existing literature.

The four filmmakers increasingly use the profilmic event as a source of Brechtian estrangement, at the expense of such specifically cinematic techniques as camerawork and editing. This trend seems conditioned by the ongoing shift of Hollywood as a globally dominant film industry from its ideal of stylistic transparency to the use of attention-grabbing cinematography and cutting as defining characteristics. To offer but one among abundant examples, the James Bond installment *Quantum of Solace* (Marc Forster, 2008) establishes a narrative connection between the scene of a horse race and the sequence of an interrogation turning into a chase only after it has crosscut between the two lines of action for a good minute. For the indicated duration, the viewer is kept perplexed about the race scene's connection to the story world.

Bordwell considers the described changes of Hollywood style sufficiently extensive to be given a distinct name: "intensified continuity." He identifies the following four strategies as characteristic of the evolved Hollywood style: (1) increasingly rapid editing; (2) "forcing the perspective" through the use of bipolar extremes of lens lengths; (3) reliance on close shots; and (4) wide-ranging camera movements (*Way* 121). All these strategies aim at distorting the everyday perception of "reality," or—in the words of the Russian Formalists and, in a modified form, Brecht—at making the familiar strange. Mainstream cinema's adoption of a language that does *not* want to be overlooked—to invert the linguist Berthe Siertsema's oft-quoted observation—necessitated the change of emphasis of Brechtian filmmakers, with their aim to estrange. As a logical consequence of their opposition to verisimilitude (in the sense of what Brecht terms "surface realism"), these filmmakers' later works are progressively more theatrical.[3]

The Titular and Other Key Terms

As Tracy C. Davis and Thomas Postlewait suggest, *theatricality* is often used interchangeably with a variety of related but distinct concepts—from mimesis to *theatrum mundi*, from ritual behavior to performativity (33). The writers do not identify the context in which the term was first used in 1837, but the assumption seems safe that the original usage was restricted to theater as an art, and that the word originally denoted the medium's various contemporary conventions. The term acquires a decidedly more complex meaning with its appearance in Russian as *teatralnost*. It is widely considered that Nikolai Evreinov, the theorist and practitioner who coined that term (Féral, "Theatricality" 95), found inspiration in the concept of literariness (*literarnost*), introduced into critical discourse by the Russian Formalist school of literary criticism. Presumably because theater addresses different senses, Evreinov's definition of the former concept is much broader than the Russian Formalists' literariness, that peculiar quality of literature separating it from other artistic forms and extra-artistic reality (Jestrovic, "Theatricality" 55). Evreinov attributed the principle to all actions resulting in transformation of the elements of the subject's environment or to those actions themselves, as well as to the human beings' will for transformation (which he referred to as "theatrical instinct"). The array of meanings attached to "theatricality" was broadened yet further with the term's 1990s penetration into the international critical discourse.[4] Three overlapping approaches to theatricality can be discerned in the literature on the subject: a predominantly historical one, which aims to elucidate the notion by tracing the changes of its negative connotations across the millennia of theater history; a predominantly phenomenological approach, which associates theatricality with not only the medium itself but also other kinds of human endeavor; and a predominantly semiotic approach, which focuses on the notion within the context of theater per se.

The historical line of inquiry into theatricality typically starts with that part of its etymological history that links it to such negatively marked traits as fakeness, superficiality, and extravagance. Representatives of this methodology—among others, Jonas Barish (*The Antitheatrical Prejudice*, 1981), Marvin Carlson ("The Resistance to Theatricality," 2002), and Davis and Postlewait (*Theatricality*, 2003)—are engaged in a dialogue with the tradition of Western theater detractors running from Plato, Tertullian, Rousseau, and Nietzsche to Sartre on the one hand and to Michael Fried on the other.[5]

The phenomenological approach to theatricality might be called "expansionist," as it involves transferring the idea of theatricality from the context of the medium into the totality of social activities. Starting in the 1950s with the work of the anthropologists Milton Singer and Victor Turner, the move necessitated a new vocabulary: instead of theatricality—one of whose connotations concerns the institutional aspect of theater, irrelevant for the variety of disciplines that were adopting the idea—the more general term "performance" was embraced. It has been used, as Janelle Reinelt writes, "to differentiate certain processes of performing from the products of theatrical performance, and in its most narrow usage, to identify performance art as that which, unlike "regular" theatrical performances, stages the subject in process, the making and fashioning of certain materials, especially the body, and in the exploration of the limits of representation-ability" (201). The dissemination of the terms theatricality and performance into the realms of anthropology, ethnography, sociology, psychology, and linguistics did not leave unaffected the studies of theater. Among the key contributors to the transformed discourse on theatricality, the first that proved relevant for the field was J. L. Austin, who in *How to Do Things with Words* (1962) remarks that performative utterances (such as "I swear" and "I bequeath") do not simply describe the reality of the acts to which they refer, but—being the sole location of the mentioned acts' truthfulness—help create that reality. Another influential writer who uses the theatrical metaphor is Erving Goffman, whose *The Presentation of Self in Everyday Life* (1959) views the individual's interaction with others as a performance aimed at creating impressions favorable for the individual's purposes.

The semiotic approach to theatricality seems a reaction to what Elin Diamond describes as the dominance of performance discourse to the point of stupefaction (qtd. in Davis and Postlewait 31), a view that seems informed by Erika Fischer-Lichte's observation that "if everything is 'theater,' the concept becomes so wide that it loses any distinctive or cognitive capacity" (qtd. in Reinelt 207). The semioticians critique the "expansionist" approach because it disregards the differences between the signs used in theater and outside of it. Eli Rozik enumerates them all in a critique of the line of thought that connects such writers as Austin, Goffmann, and Richard Schechner:

> 1) The semiotic systems employed in action and enacting an action are different: Whereas action is fundamentally indexical, enacting an action is iconic. (114)[6]
>
> 2) The ways action and enacting an action refer to a world are fundamentally different: while action is self-referent, enacting an action is both self-referential to the actor,

in producing signs, and deflects reference to a character. (115)

3) Although indexicality is shared by action and enacting an action, there is an essential difference. In real action, indexes refer to the doers, and are only self-referential. (115)

Rozik defines theatricality at once broadly and precisely: to him, the fundamental principle of theater is acting, "imprinting images of indexes and deflection of reference" (122). This refers to not only human acting, but "enacting" in the sense of "representing and describing" an object in a real or fictional world by any real onstage object (110)—a process inherent also to most of cinema.

While Rozik's notion of theatricality is too broad to be applicable here, Jacques Gerstenkorn's focus on theatricality as it relates to cinema provides a suitable framework. Gerstenkorn distinguishes between (1) theatricality as it appears in films that explicitly reference theatrical practice (theater as a content); (2) as it is produced by a film's use of a characteristically theatrical mode (theater as a form within form); (3) as it is achieved through a process he calls recycling (*recyclage*), using a distinctly theatrical convention (for example, addressing the camera in a Woody Allen film) to divest it of its aura of medium-specificity and fully assimilate it within the cinematic context (16–17). In this last context, the term pertains strictly to those aspects of a film that are semiotically marked as derivatives of theater. Because of my focus on how film borrows from theatrical conventions that are foregrounded as such, and on the implications of that strategy as it relates to a given film's use of Brecht, Gerstenkorn's third category is of particular importance here.

Montage denotes the formal principle of works of different arts, whereby heterogeneous parts are assembled to produce a fundamentally new relationship with each other (Bordwell, "Idea" 10). Theodor Adorno in *Aesthetic Theory* succinctly identifies two dialectically opposed tendencies underwriting the principle: "Montage . . . disavows unity through the emerging disparateness of the parts at the same time that, as a principle of form, it reaffirms unity" (202). The connections established can be purely abstract (as in Eisenstein's intellectual editing, explicated below), or can result in a semblance of spatial or temporal coherence (as in the canvases of the Renaissance painter Arcimboldo, which convey recognizable human portraits through the compositional arrangement of realistically depicted everyday objects) (Figure 1.1).

Figure 1.1. Montage in Renaissance Painting: "Vertumnus—Portrait of Rudolph II" (Giuseppe Arcimboldo, 1590). Digital frame enlargement.

As can be inferred from this example, montage before the letter can be traced to a distant past in art history. However, it is the twentieth century—and in particular the era of the historical avant-gardes (1910–1933)—when the technique saw its most prolific application. The period's development of mechanical reproduction changed the understanding and practice of montage, facilitating its use and allowing for the artist's subjectivity to recede, as the basic constituents of a montage were no longer necessarily a result of her work. Examples of montage exist in the novels *St. Petersburg* (1922) by Andrei Biely and *Ulysses* (1922) by Joyce, the Cubist poetry of Reverdy and Apollinaire, the Surrealist collages of Max Ernst, the satirical photomontages of John Heartfield, and the theater of Ernst Toller and Meyerhold. Finally, montage is employed in the cinematic traditions of both the West (for example, in D. W. Griffith's 1916 *Intolerance*) and East (most notably, in the works of 1920s Soviet filmmakers).

The development of montage-based art was brought to a halt at the turn of the 1920s and 1930s as a result of the sociopolitical occurrences in some of the period's leading artistic centers, the Soviet Union and Germany. Following Stalin's succession of Lenin in 1924, the First Five Year Plan was implemented in 1928, which centralized all sectors of social life, including cultural production. Prominent revolutionary artists such as the poet Vladimir Mayakovsky and most montage filmmakers were not in favor with the new government and increasingly faced accusations of "formalism." By announcing the decree "On the Reconstruction of Literary and Art Organizations" in 1932, Stalin unofficially inaugurated the doctrine of socialist realism, which sought to represent the real in its revolutionary development using the conventions of nineteenth-century realism. The gap that separates the artistic experiments of the early post-revolutionary years and socialist realism is well illustrated by the comparison between the Vasilyev brothers' socialist realist film *Chapaev* (1934) and the eponymous book by Dmitri Furtanov upon which it is based (1923). The book belongs to the mixed genre of factograph, promoted by *LEF* (the Mayakovsky-edited journal of the loose association of Soviet cultural workers Levy Front Iskusstv [Left Front of the Arts]), and uses a fragmentary structure whose different parts integrate the conventions of diverse forms, including the diary and journalism. In contrast, the screen adaptation follows the rules of continuity editing and other norms of cinematic classicism, thereby approaching Hollywood's ideal of stylistic transparency. Although the influence of the Soviet montage filmmakers is evident in one of the best known cultural artifacts from Hitler's Germany, Leni Riefenstahl's *Triumph des Willens* (Triumph of the Will, 1934), the

Third Reich's film industry likewise came to favor a style comparable to Hollywood's, after condemning much of modernist art as degenerate.[7]

Despite the umbrella term "montage filmmakers" used to describe them, the Soviet montage cinema displays a great formal diversity. David Bordwell adopts Luda and Jean Schnitzer's classification of the most prominent Soviet montage filmmakers according to the aesthetic implications of their respective politics. He associates Kuleshov with Pudovkin as conservative cineastes, and—on the other—Eisenstein with Vertov as extreme leftists ("Idea" 11). Kuleshov is today remembered less for his films than for the montage experiments he conducted between 1919 and 1924, all of which highlighted the dual nature of the film image: representational (what it shows) and relational (what inferences the joined shots leads to). The other three filmmakers are briefly addressed in reverse order of their importance for Brecht. Vertov, like Brecht and their many other contemporaries, had a fascination with the epoch's scientific developments and relativity theory in particular. The 1922 manifesto of the film collective "*Kinoki*" (cinema eyes), where Vertov was the leading figure, quotes as an aesthetic mandate the application of "the theory of relativity on the screen" (Vertov 9). As did Kuleshov in his "creative geography" experiment, which produces an impression of continuous time and space by joining together shots taken in different locations, Vertov created in *Chelovek s kino-apparatom* (Man with a Movie Camera [1929]) a semblance of a single city by combining images photographed in various parts of the country, thereby "conquering space and time" (87–88).

The metaphoric parallel between the described example and relativity theory seems apt, but Vertov's trust in the revelatory power of sight precludes further comparisons with Einstein as a subatomic physicist. Vertov's aesthetic is based on the syllogism where the camera equals an improved human eye. The task he sets for the instrument can be compared to that which the microscope or telescope has in science—to enhance perception and, thereby, also knowledge (Möbius 398). Unlike Eisenstein, however, whose intellectual montage is a means for rendering visible the truth beyond the observable phenomena, Vertov sets as a goal of his cinema "showing life as it is" (Vertov 45), "caught unawares" (41). Antagonistic to mimesis (in the sense of "representation" versus "presentation") as a heritage of the obsolete bourgeois form he sees theater to be, Vertov is unique among the Soviet montage filmmakers as a militant devotee of the documentary mode. He conceives of his cinema as "the FACTORY OF FACTS" (59), to which he contrasts popular genre films together with Eisenstein, a filmmaker with an eclectic style that borrows from the other art forms and builds extensively upon the past traditions.

Vertov conceives of montage as a broad notion that underlies all cinema's formal operations from photography to projection, as well as the cognitive processes that govern film viewing.

The implications of Brecht's special liking of Pudovkin, the least avant-garde of the identified Soviet filmmakers, have been largely ignored. As the country's other contemporary cineastes, he considers montage "the basic process of filmic creation" (Pudovkin 93). Still, the more crucial term in Pudovkin's system is neither Eisenstein's "idea" nor Vertov's "fact," but plot (in the sense of narrative).[8] Pudovkin distinguishes between constructive montage (which provides a scene, episode, reel, and the script with verisimilitudinous coherence) and montage as an expressive instrument (which influences the viewer's state of mind [62] through the use of such medium-specific devices as parallel editing). By suggesting that the expressive function of montage is mainly to enhance the viewer's emotions as opposed to advancing the narrative, Pudovkin implicitly ascribes primacy to constructive montage as a principally dramaturgical device. This appears the first reason for Pudovkin's appeal to Brecht, in whose system *Fabel* (fable, myth, or story) occupies a central place. The second reason probably concerns the Soviet filmmaker's special interest in acting. Pudovkin rejects Eisenstein's notion of type casting and acting (responsible for the former's assessment of the roles in *The Battleship Potemkin* [Eisenstein, 1925] as "depressingly banal" [22]), advocating instead the use of Stanislavski's method adjusted for film, with the close-up and the breakup of the performance into separate shots as the technology's defining characteristics.

Sergei Eisenstein, in "The Cinematographic Principle," equates montage with conflict not only between the elements in adjoining shots and between the elements within the shots: conflict of graphic directions ("*lines—either static or dynamic*," either actual or implied through the movement of an object in the shot); the conflict of scales (the relative size of objects in the shot); conflict of volumes (the absolute size and shape of objects in the shot); conflict of masses ("*volumes filled with various intensities of light*"); and conflict of depths (the positions of objects in the photographed space and in the film frame) (39). He distinguishes between several strains of the technique, of which intellectual editing is the most complex. Eisenstein describes it as "combining shots that are *depictive*, single in meaning, neutral in content—into *intellectual* contexts and series" (30). Using the example of Japanese ideograms, Eisenstein demonstrates the viability of a cinema whose formal operations would be based on the Hegelian dialectical triad, whereby synthesis arises from the opposition between thesis and antithesis (45). Among the examples he gives of images combined within the ideograms to create new meanings are water and an eye (signifying weeping), a mouth and a bird (signifying singing), and a knife and a heart (signifying sorrow). Relevant here are both this sense of the term "montage," aphoristically described by Hans-Joachim Schlegel as "denotation through connotation" (qtd. in Bogdal 263) and the sense the term usually has in English: to describe more conventional disruptions of continuity of space and time between scenes, and/or of coherent spatial and temporal relationships among the profilmic events within scenes.

Montage figures prominently even in Brecht's earliest systematic articulation of the epic/dialectic theater concept, "Anmerkungen zur Oper Aufstieg und Fall der Stadt Mahagonny" ("Notes to the Opera 'Rise and Fall of the City of Mahagonny,'" 1930).[9] The table of contrasts between dramatic and epic theater—reproduced in its entirety later in the chapter—juxtaposes montage to growth. As John J. White notes in *Bertolt Brecht's Dramatic Theory*, the three pairs of terms surrounding the cited one help clarify the sense in which "montage" is used in the context (56):

Dramatic Theater	Epic Theater
one scene makes another	each scene for itself
linear development	in curves
evolutionary determinism	jumps

All three contrasts pertain to narrative structure, rather than the other codes of a performance, inscribed in the playtext or added in staging. Elsewhere in his writings, however, Brecht uses the term "montage" more broadly, to describe the opposition to the classical and Romantic idea of stylistic organicity (Friedrich, "On Brecht" 156), which entails art's concealment of artifice through imitation of nature.[10] Brecht sometimes refers to montage also in relation to realms other than artistic, a possibility suggested by the term's inherent possession in German of such connotations as construction and assemblage.

The last titular word that needs defining is *Brechtian*. In the context of this book, it describes something substantially influenced by Brecht's theory of epic/dialectic theater, as acknowledged by the filmmakers themselves. The following few pages briefly survey the theory's main terms.

All Brecht's major theatrical and filmic concepts converge toward *dialectics*. As defined in *The Oxford Dictionary of Philosophy*, dialectics is "the process of reasoning to obtain truth and knowledge on any topic" (Blackburn 99). Traceable back to the Socratics, it acquired distinct meanings in various subsequent Western philosophies, and is today associated especially with Hegel and with Marx and Engels. The "Great Method," as Brecht often refers to dialectics, informs his 1927 "Schwierigkeiten des Epischen Theaters" ("Difficulties of Epic Theater"; *Werke* 21: 209–10) and figures prominently as a term in a wide range of later writings, from the 1931 "Notizen über die dialektische Dramatik" ("Notes on Dialectical Dramatic Art"; *Werke* 21: 431–43) to the 1951–1956 series of writings under the common title "Die Dialektik auf dem Theater" ("Dialectics in the Theater"; *Werke* 23: 386–413). To Brecht, dialectics is

> a practical doctrine of alliances and of the dissolution of alliances, of the exploitation of changes and the dependency on change, of the instigation of change and the changing of the instigators, the separation and emergence of unities, the unselfsufficiency of oppositions without each other, the unification of mutually exclusive oppositions. The Great Method makes it possible to recognize processes within things and to use them. It teaches us to ask questions which enable activity. (qtd. in Jameson 117)

Applied to the realm of art, dialectics then refers to the practice that can instigate a societal change, an expression of what Brecht calls interventionist thinking (*eingreifendes Denken*).

This links Brecht's understanding of dialectics to his original concept of *Verfremdung*. Each of the existing translations of the term to English—alienation, distantiation, defamiliarization, and estrangement—is only partly adequate. The first of these implicitly collapses the boundary between the Brechtian term and *Entfremdung*, used by Marx to describe the effects on man of the capitalist mode of production: his separation from his labor and its products, as well as from his fellow man.[11] The other English translations of the Brechtian term fail to reflect *Verfremdung's* intended purpose: to provide a new understanding of a given situation enacted onstage, thus closing the dialectical triad whose first two constituents are "to understand" and "to not understand" (*Werke* 22.1: 401; translation mine). This is what distinguishes Brecht's project from such modernist avant-garde movements of the twentieth century as Surrealism, which likewise sought to astonish the recipient but often did not aim for more than a mere destruction of the mundanely familiar (Oh 180).[12] In its political slant, *Verfremdung* differs also from the related Russian Formalist concept of *priem ostranenia* (device of making strange). Unlike Brecht, Russian Formalism presumes the ability of art to attain a relative independence from the other social realms, and sets as its ultimate goal a recovery of "the sensation of life," "[making] one feel things, [making] the stone stony" (Shklovsky, "Art" 12). *Ostranenie*, then, refers not to cognition but only to perception.[13]

Verfremdung has been developed in contrast to the principle of empathy (*Einfühlung*), a central term of Aristotle's *Poetics* (335 BC), which summarizes the formal procedures of the theater in the writer's epoch. Brecht sees Aristotelian theater as an "artistic device of an era in which the people are changeable, and their environment invariable" (*Werke* 22.1: 553; translation mine). Late capitalism's reversal of the described relationship calls for an alternative model, based on *Verfremdung* in its epistemological and practical aspects. The following definition of the concept touches upon both: "To defamiliarize an event or character means first, simply, to take away what is taken for granted, what is familiar and obvious, and instead generate astonishment and curiosity. . . . To estrange means also to historicize, to represent the events and persons as historical and transient" (554–55; translation mine). These words merit Klaus-Detlef Müller's view of historicizing (*Historisierung*) as an "encompassing substantial term of the tech3nique of *Verfremdung*, . . . its most important formal characteristic" (29; translation mine). Besides representing a dramatic event as if it has already transpired, *Historisierung* involves depicting the dramatic events as changeable (Knopf 1980, 386), whereby the spectator herself is conceived as "a great modifier, able to intervene in the natural and social processes" (*Werke* 22.1: 554–55; translation mine).[14]

While Brecht tends to discuss the broader notions of his aesthetic vocabulary in terms of each other, his definition of *Gestus*—as another *Verfremdung* technique—is self-standing. Fredric Jameson translates the original verb, *gerere*, as "to carry on," to wear, to bear, and to wage (99)—whereas Marc Silberman traces *Gestus* back to the Greek *bastos*, the root of which, *bas*, "indicates coming or going in a specific, intentional direction" ("Brecht's Gestus" 320). In 1767, Lessing referred to *Gestus* as "an actor's tool that can make moral symbolism or general moral principles perceptible and comprehensible" (qtd. in Silberman, "Brecht's Gestus" 321)—a sense similar to *Gestus* for Brecht. His earliest written reference to *Gestus* is from 1929, slightly postdating the use of the term by the composer, Brecht's collaborator Kurt Weill.

To John Willett, *Gestus* is "at once gesture and gist, attitude and point: one aspect of the two people, studied singly, cut to essentials and physically or verbally expressed" (*Theatre of Brecht* 175). Patrice Pavis's definition of the concept as "the social relationship which the actor establishes between his character and the other characters" ("Brechtian" 177) highlights its communal significance. From the late 1930s onward, Brecht used the term almost invariably in the sense of "social Gestus" (Silberman, "Brecht's Gestus" 325), and in 1951 he made a statement closest to a definition: "As a social gestus, we should understand the mimical and gestural expression of social relationships, in which the people of a certain era stand together" (qtd. in Becker 34; translation mine). The examples of *Gestus* in Brecht's theater include the use of masks to convey the changes of Peter Lorre's Galy Gay in the 1931 production of *Man Equals Man*, the beggar teaching a rich man how to eat like the poor in *The Caucasian Chalk Circle*, and the lack of Courage's emotional reaction to the death of Kattrin in the twelfth scene of *Mother Courage and Her Children*. Brecht uses also the term *Grundgestus* to refer to what Silberman describes as "surprising reversals or the unexpected identity of opposites" ("Brecht's Gestus" 326). *Grundgestus* comprises various, typically contradictory gestic material, such as Richard Gloucester courting his victim's widow, Azdak using a chalk circle to identify Michael's true mother, God betting with the Devil for the soul of Dr. Faustus, and Woyzeck buying a cheap knife in order to murder his wife (*Werke* 23: 200).[15]

Gestus and *Historisierung* are but two devices in the inventory of Brecht's *epic* theater. Erwin Piscator—the one twentieth-century theater practitioner besides Brecht with whom the term is widely associated, attributes the term's coinage to the poet, novelist, and dramatist Alfons Paquet—who allegedly used it in 1924 to describe his play *Fahnen* (Flags [1923]) (Knopf 1980, 394). For Piscator, the epic denotes primarily the disruption of the conventional theatrical models by borrowing from the other media, and especially those that rely on contemporary technologies. Brecht likewise does not describe the term as a strictly determined form, but as a quality that can be recognized in a variety of those forms (Knopf 1980, 396). He associates it with critical observation, with rejecting the notion of destiny and awakening of social activism, with demonstrating the dependence of thinking and language on the sociohistorical processes, transmitting the materialistic thinking, and democratism (reflected in the attempts to lift the boundary between the spectator and performance) (396).

The aforementioned epic/dialectic theater's characteristics can be understood even better from Brecht's own writings. The below schema, which originally appeared in "The Notes to 'Mahagonny' " (1930), concisely juxtaposes dramatic (Aristotelian) and epic (Brechtian) theater:

Dramatic Theater	Epic Theater
plot	narrative
implicates the spectator	turns the spectator into an observer, but in a stage situation
wears down his capacity for action	arouses his capacity for action
provides him with sensations	forces him to take decisions
experience	picture of the world
the spectator is involved into something	he is made to face something
suggestion	argument
instinctive feelings are preserved	brought to the point of recognition
the spectator is in the thick of it, shares the experience	the spectator stands outside, studies
the human being is taken for granted	the human being is the object of the inquiry
he is unalterable	he is alterable and able to alter
eyes on the finish	eyes on the course
one scene makes another	each scene for itself
growth	montage
linear development	in curves
evolutionary determinism	jumps
man as a fixed point	man as a process
thought determines being	social being determines thought
feeling	reason (*Brecht on Theatre* 37)

The schema invites the reader to alternate between vertical and horizontal readings, and varies its focus from dramatic structure to dramatic spectatorship. Both its formal peculiarity and its political inflection appealed to the late 1960s generation of filmmakers and critics, crucially concerned with the spectatorial agency and its transposition to the "real world." It is mainly on the basis of the schema that practitioners and commentators alike have constructed their understandings of Brecht.

Brecht's Dramatic Theory in Film Studies: From the Apparatus to Cognitive Film Theory

In terms of its scope and longevity, the influence of Brecht's concept of epic/dialectic theater on film studies surpasses that of all other theories of the stage. Evident already in the 1950s, this impact took hold two decades later—an occurrence that Sylvia Harvey and Nöel Carroll explain by Brecht's influence on Godard (Harvey 49; Carroll, *Mystifying* 91) as one of the most prominent and innovative filmmakers of the previous decade. Carroll notes also that the influence Brecht's ideas exerted on Roland Barthes, "*the* exemplary cultural critic of contemporary theorists" (91), was another factor in leading film theorists and critics to appropriate Brecht's ideas in the 1970s. Harvey also explains the phenomenon by the contemporary appearance of Benjamin's "Conversations with Brecht," Brecht's "Against Lukács," and texts by Russian Formalists and futurists hitherto unavailable in English (50), while Silberman mentions in a similar context the 1969 publication of Brecht's *Texte für Filme* (Texts for Films) ("Brecht and Film" 198). Finally, Harvey quotes as an additional reason for the return to Brecht during this period the growing interest in the relationship between cultural production and social change, and the accompanying search for the protocols of a radical art (49).

Although this book's main argument bases itself neither on the "SLAB" theory's appropriation of Brecht nor on the cognitivist critique of it, it is worthwhile to summarize, and offer a critique of, the key articulations of the two strands of thinking that continue to impact how Brecht is understood in film studies: Baudry (1999), Wollen (1999), MacCabe (1974), Heath (1974), Polan (1974, 1985) (representative of the former), and Smith (1996) (indicative of the latter). Both of these strands of thinking about Brecht are problematic insofar as they place an exceeding emphasis on his formally subversive aspect, configuring him as the rejector of past techniques and traditions and—in turn—obscuring such defining features of his art theory and practice as dialectics and narration. The second reason is the complexity of much of "SLAB" theory, and its often opaque articulations. The following few pages clarify and question "SLAB" theorists' and cognitivists' view of Brecht and further illustrate the position of importance that Brecht has occupied in film studies for the past several decades.

Since the advent of digital technologies in the early 1990s, the question of cinema's uncertain future informed discourses on moving image media with increasing frequency. Long before the now seemingly irreversible death of celluloid and photographic emulsion, with the crisis of indexicality as its corollary, Godard proclaimed cinema dead in

Week-End (1967). The film was released nearly a decade after Godard's feature-length debut, *À bout de souffle* (Breathless [1959]), which had performed the acrobatic act of simultaneously celebrating Hollywood cinema and deconstructing its "language." The former impulse was expressed in the film's numerous and earnest homages to various symbols of America, from revolvers to convertible cars and from Humphrey Bogart to William Faulkner, whereas the latter impulse manifested itself in the film's rejection of the transparency associated with the classical style. Namely, *Breathless* replaces the standard combination of three-point lighting and slow stock with available lighting and fast stock, smooth tracking shots with jittery handheld ones, and—most (in)famously—continuity editing with jump cuts. Produced at a time when the techniques of Godard's first feature had already petrified into conventions, *Week-End*'s announcement of cinema's demise did not concern merely the death of "invisible style." The problems of filmic signification, which by then had preoccupied theorists and theoretically conscious practitioners alike, were now being transposed from the terrain of industry (cinema as a product of any and all film companies from "Hollywood" to "Mosfilm") to that of ontology (cinema as a medium of photography, and therefore of representation). Also in 1967, Marxist critical theorist and filmmaker Guy Debord launched *Society of the Spectacle*, a book that diagnosed the Western obsession with spectacles of representation and identified—in words strongly reminiscent of Brecht—the supplantation of genuine activity by passive identification with spectacle (12).

The West's pre-1968 revolutionary optimism allowed for Godard's proclamation of cinema's death to be interpreted as a tongue-in-cheek rewording of Louis Lumière's description of his own invention as one without future. Similarly, Debord's indictment of representation could then still have been dismissed as an extremist exaggeration. But these expressions acquired a different tenor in the atmosphere of disappointment that marked the intellectual circles at the left side of the political spectrum in the years following the demise of the students and workers' protests. Increasingly unable to determine the aesthetic path to an efficacious progressive cinema, film theorists were now questioning not only specific "forms" and/or "contents," but also the medium itself.

The earliest text to apply Debord's ideas specifically to cinema was also an inaugural one in the corpus of texts known as apparatus theory, which decisively introduced Brecht in the context of film studies: Jean-Louis Baudry's "The Ideological Effects of the Basic Cinematographic Apparatus." Imbued with a dark outlook that Brecht would probably designate as retrograde, the article draws on diverse philosophical sources from Plato to Jacques Lacan to interrogate the possibility of attaining the real through representational art. Baudry adopts the ancient Roman *perspectiva naturalis / perspectiva artificialis* binary, which refers to the difference between the way most of us perceive the world visually (with two moving, concave-shaped eyes) and the way the results of visual perception are represented with the use of *perspectiva artificialis*, a fourteenth-century convention of visual representation that implies the hypothetical observer's fixity and monocularity, and a mathematical adjustment for flat surfaces. He implies a parallel between the two kinds of perspective and the opposites of the real and its appearances, as they appear in Plato's cave parable. The immobile slaves who confuse the shadows on the wall that they are facing with real things serve in this account as a link to the cinematographic apparatus, a term encompassing the entire film-making technology. Baudry charges the invention with being inherently conventionalized through its deployment of *perspectiva artificialis*, thereby functioning as a barrier from the real while disguising itself as a pathway to it. In addition, he indicts such agents of cinematic continuity as narrative procedures, framing, camera movements, and editing for helping subjectify the viewer, the meaning of which verb varies according to the philosophical tradition Baudry refers to in a given section of the article.

Lacan, for whom perspective is a means of man's reduction to an eye and of an eye to a point (qtd. in Damisch 45), helps Baudry advance his anti-cinematic argument by expanding the prisoner-spectator analogy to include the infant in the mirror stage. According to Lacan, the infant recognizes itself in this phase of development as an entity separate from its surroundings. This recognition leads to the formation of its unconscious and—because the unconscious is for Lacan structured like language—to the infant's entry into the realm of the symbolic. Cinema's ideological effect that Baudry refers to, following Althusser, involves configuring the domain of the spectator's natural existence as secondary in importance to that of the transcendental, of "the beyond," which ultimately hinders her possibility of acting in the world politically. While not referring to Brecht, Baudry evokes him by placing his focus—and critique—on the process of spectatorial identification (with both the characters represented and the cinematographic apparatus itself) that the medium supposedly encourages.

The period's earliest major piece of film criticism in English to draw substantially on Brecht was Peter Wollen's "Godard and Counter Cinema: *Vent d'est*" (1985 [1972]), which discusses Godard's body of work in general and the titular film in particular in terms reminiscent of the epic versus dramatic theater schema. Wollen juxtaposes the "seven deadly sins" of cinema (the left column of the schema reproduced below) with "the seven cardinal virtues" of counter-cinema (the right column):

NARRATIVE TRANSITIVITY	NARRATIVE INTRANSITIVITY
Identification	Estrangement
Transparency	Foregrounding
Single diegesis	Multiple diegesis
Closure	Aperture
Pleasure	Unpleasure
Fiction	Reality (501)

Lacking the transparency of Brecht's schema, Wollen's binaries require explanation. He defines narrative transitivity in terms of establishing causal relations among the represented events, which entails the arrangement of "function[s] that chang[e] the course of the narrative" (501) so as to produce the impression of "one thing following another" and to conform to the structure of "equilibrium—equilibrium disrupted—equilibrium restored" (501) as a version of Aristotle's "beginning—middle—end."[16] In contrast, narrative intransitivity involves "gaps and interruptions, episodic construction [and] undigested digression" (501). The second dichotomy explicitly reveals its indebtedness to Brecht.[17] Wollen's explanation of the next pair of terms, transparency and foregrounding, notes the lineage of the style of dominant cinema in the Renaissance and post-Renaissance approach to language and representation as self-effacing instruments for "showing" the world, as opposed to making it "readable." The latter approach is exemplified by what Wollen calls Godard's pictography, an assemblage of techniques that endow images with genuine semantic codes and illustrate the problem of representing the abstract through the concrete.

The fourth "deadly sin" and "cardinal virtue," single diegesis and multiple diegesis, pertain to a film's depiction of homogeneous versus heterogeneous worlds. A conventional film is a coherent "story," whose elements belong to the same space and time, whereas a counter-film can feature elements purposely incongruous in those two respects. This dichotomy bears a close relationship to that of closure and aperture, descriptively defined by Wollen as "a self-contained object, harmonized within its own bounds, v. open-endedness, overspill, intertextuality—allusion, quotation and parody" (505). The first term in the next pair of binaries, pleasure, refers to the aspiration of the cinema as a commercial enterprise to satisfy the viewer, which Wollen sees as occurring at the cost of distracting the masses from the stern tasks that are their true destiny (506). The counter-cinema should therefore provide "unpleasure," which could help mobilize the viewer toward recognizing and achieving her political goals. Wollen uses the Freudian terms of desire and fantasy to describe the principles underlying conventional filmic representation. While Brecht, following Horace, strove to both "delight and instruct," Wollen sees Godard in *Vent d'est* (Wind from the East, 1969) falling short of constructing fantasy, a condition necessary for revolutionary politics, in ways other than those of sadomasochistic provocation (507) and, therefore, of "unpleasure." Contrary to what one might expect from the penetration of psychoanalytic terms toward the end of the article, Wollen defines the last binary—"fiction" and "reality"—not in terms of Lacanian psychoanalytic orders of the Symbolic, Real, and Imaginary, but in terms of the difference between the fictional and nonfictional mode and the results of combining their respective conventions.[18]

Wollen's article provided the context for the appearance of the first Brecht-dedicated issue of *Screen* (1974). Arguably most influential among the contributions have been Colin MacCabe's and Stephen Heath's articles, both of which downplay the importance of fantasy (in the sense of pleasure) for revolutionary cinema. In his "Realism and the Cinema: Notes on Some Brechtian Theses," MacCabe notes that the classic realist text (a term he applies to both literature and film) is partly defined by its use of metalanguage, which creates an impression of allowing reality to (merely) appear, and denies its own status as articulation (9). MacCabe illustrates his point with a short excerpt from George Eliot's novel *Middlemarch* (1871–1872), where the omniscient narrator—whose status is concealed by the narrative's use of the third person—problematizes a character's attitude to his neighbors' opinions about him. According to MacCabe, the metanarrative confirms its claim to be axiomatically truthful by implicitly inviting the reader to evaluate the veracity of the juxtaposed characters' views of each other. However, the metalanguage "cannot deal with the real as contradictory" (12) as it is necessarily ideological, ensuring "the position of the subject in a relation of dominant specularity" (12).

MacCabe introduces into the discourse Lacan's concept of *méconnaissance*, which refers to both the subject's self-knowledge and misunderstanding, involved in the successful use of language or any other similarly structured area of the symbolic (18). As a result of *méconnaissance*, the subject is "continually ignored as being caught up in a process of articulation to be taken as a fixed place founding the discourse" (18). MacCabe further develops the idea of the individual's inevitable transformation into a subject (through each and every social institution in the broadest sense of the term) with the help of Althusser's view of ideology. According to Althusser in MacCabe's interpretation, the subject falsely "holds out the promise that the victorious conclusion to the class struggle will result in the arrival of the new and true ideology which will correspond to the real" (23).

MacCabe links the above thinkers to Brecht via the latter's view of the film spectator, as expounded in his article "The Threepenny Lawsuit" (1931, published 1932). As MacCabe summarizes Brecht's position on the medium, the cinema possesses the "ability to place the spectator in the position of a unified subject that ensures the contradiction between his working activity which is productive and the leisure activity in which he is constantly placed as consumer" (24). Finally, he acknowledges Roberto Rossellini (*Rome, Open City* [1945], *Journey to Italy* [1954]) for shaking the metalanguage by replacing one dominant discourse with a multitude thereof (19). But the only examples MacCabe gives of films that fully oppose the metalanguage are *Tout va bien* (Jean-Luc Godard and Jean-Pierre Gorin, 1972) and *Kuhle Wampe*, works he designates as revolutionary (21) or progressive realist texts (22). In his view, the two films resist privileging the narrative against the characters and use it as "the method by which various situations can be articulated together" (24).

The main theses of the article indeed strongly evoke Brecht and his position on realism in art as evidenced in his contributions to the debate on the topic with György Lukács in the 1930s. But MacCabe's unreserved embrace of this position is hardly congruous with his commentary on Eisenstein. MacCabe does not work from any of Eisenstein's definitions of montage, instead inferring one from the dichotomy the Soviet theorist establishes between montage and "affidavit-exposition"—"representation shot from a single set-up" (qtd. in MacCabe 14). This definition, according to which "montage is the showing of the same representation from different points of view" (14), slights the difference between continuity editing and nonlinear editing patterns that won international fame for Eisenstein and other Soviet filmmakers of his generation.

MacCabe goes on to correctly conclude that there is no possible language of "affidavit-exposition" that could convey such abstract concepts as widowhood (to give the example from Eisenstein that MacCabe uses), thus pointing to the incompatibility of the theorist's supposed definition of montage and Eisenstein's example. He objects to Eisenstein's conception of montage as exemplified by the definition provided, because it falsely presumes a stability of meaning for "the raw material of the montage" (13)—the images and sounds that comprise it. In effect, MacCabe argues, this conception obscures the contradictions of the "raw material" while attempting to illuminate those between individual constituents of the montage. As a remedy, he proposes a modified view of montage "as the effect generated by a conflict of discourse in which the opposition available in the juxtaposed discourses are contradictory and in conflict" (16).

MacCabe does not demonstrate the practical viability of cinematic signification without representation, which the above proposal appears to advocate. And indeed, even the attempts at departure from mimeticism in film as radical as Eisenstein's own projected screen adaptation of Marx's *Capital* illustrate the importance for a film to retain a degree of representational verisimilitude in order to convey a meaning. Consider, for example, the importance of naturalistically representing the texture of the silk stockings from a test scene for the film—their smoothness, shininess, etc.—for Marx's idea of this object's transformation into a fetishistic commodity to be effectively communicated. Second, MacCabe's emphasis on the convergences between Brecht's and Eisenstein's theories comes at the expense of Brecht's preference for Pudovkin, closest among the Soviet montage filmmakers to Hollywood's style and narrative. Pertinently, neither MacCabe nor Heath acknowledge the centrality of *Fabel* in Brecht's dramatic system. This allows MacCabe to proclaim *Tout va bien* (where the narrative has arguably receded further into the background than in *Kuhle Wampe*) more Brechtian than Brecht and Dudow's own film (25).

Heath radicalizes MacCabe's ideas, bringing together Freud (fetishism), Althusser (interpellation), and Brecht (the passivity of the spectator in Aristotelian theater). All these ideas converge into a metaphorical diagnosis of human position in society: we are all dominated subjects, "set in position" (106). Heath opens his explanation of Brecht's relevance for cinema by noting Godard's use of distancing formal strategies, whereby "the reality of our struggle in ideology against the representations it produces and the positions of the subject they hold" (104)—or, more broadly, the relationship between reality and its representations—receives a thematic treatment. The commentary on Godard announces two of the sources for the article's main ideas: Louis Althusser, the key terms of whose concept of Ideological State Apparatuses Heath adopts (ideology, the subject, and interpellation), and Freud, upon whose trope of sight as used in "Fetishism" he draws. Freud's article describes the case of his patient, for whom the condition of sexual satisfaction was the appearance of "a shine on the nose." The analysis transformed "shine" (*Glanz*) into "glance" in English (the patient's mother tongue, which he had nearly forgotten in Germany), and concluded that the patient alleviated anxiety from castration by glancing at the woman's nose—the substitute for the penis whose lack in women the patient had recognized as a child.

Heath takes up both "glance" and its displacement to German in the following parable of mainstream film spectatorship. The implicitly male Heathen viewer casts his glance at the photograph projected onto the film screen, which "[holds] him pleasurably in the safety of disavowal; at once a knowledge—this exists—and a perspective of reassurance—but I am outside of this existence" (107). Heath uses the term "*Glanz*" to link the fetish with representation of the latter notion as "a brilliance, something lit up, heightened, depicted, as under an arc light, a point of (theatrical) representation" (107). His view of the photograph's structure as fetishistic, capable of "[subliming] anything into the security of beauty" (107) receives support in a reference to the historic resistance to sound in cinema in the name of sublimity and beauty. Behind Heath's failure to acknowledge that the development of the microphone and the speaker was likewise governed by the purpose of verisimilitude, one can detect a view of sound as the formal aspect of cinema especially suitable for Brechtian interventions. Such a view can be accounted for by the fact that the material typically constituting the main element of film sound track—dialogue—operates with arbitrary signifiers. The filmmaker can foreground their arbitrariness, thereby exposing the viewer's interpellation through language.

Heath connects fetishism with interpellation via the fixity of the subject, posited by both Freud and Althusser: "ideology" (embodied in ideological state apparatuses such as "family, school, church, press, art, etc.") (107) "takes up individuals" and "subjects them" (114).[19] Distantiation requires breaking the separation down, repositioning the spectator so that she can adopt a critical (multi-) perspective. Heath extends the insight to Brecht by concluding that most of Brecht's criticism of Aristotelian theater concerns the type of spectatorial identification (*Einfühlung*) it promotes. For him, fetishism and interpellation are related processes, operating at the levels of both narrative and style. These processes are supported by the adherence of the medium's optical apparatus to Renaissance perspective and the architectural setup of conventional theater and cinema. Their concomitants are empathy and catharsis, the effects on the viewer fostered by Aristotelian theater and mainstream cinema through an array of formal characteristics associated with realism as a style (not "the illusion as reality," but "the illusion of reality") (113).[20]

Heath goes on to establish a parallel between the fourth wall, one of the stylistic conventions of Aristotelian theater, and mainstream cinema's stylistic operations that emulate ostensibly objective and neutral third-person narration, through a metaphor based on Barthes's remark that "Aristotelian theater and cinema are held together in this bond according to a series of shared aims (the effect of 'Reality') and devices" (117). Both media "dispos[e]— . . . la[y] out—the coherence of a subject-spectator whom [they] hol[d] in position" (117). Being itself an ideological state apparatus, cinema cannot demolish ideology but can attempt to displace its formations by posing the specific relations of those formations in the mode of production (124). More succinctly, cinema can complement the unavoidable interpellation with its opposite: disinterpellation through distantiation, defined as a work of demonstrating contradictions (119)—fundamental elements of the real. Brechtian form thus becomes "the form . . . of the domination of reality" (123), a term Heath distinguishes from "Reality" (121), as the subject's faulty impression of the real.

Heath's discussion of the three broad strategies used to achieve distantiation in film—(1) self-reflexivity; (2) montage; (3) theatricalization (narrative references to the medium and the use of its stylistic conventions)—collapses the distinctions between montage and the other two. The examples of self-reflexivity he provides entail a process essential to montage: juxtaposing (the representation with its account of itself), and one of the definitions of theatricalization is "critical heterogeneity" (119) (in other words, a montage of styles). By proposing both montage and theatricality as viable techniques of cinematic estrangement, Heath treats their compatibility as a given, disregarding the problems in blending the two modes from the standpoint of perception. Namely, if the intercutting between two or more images that represent objects of indeterminate mutual spatial and temporal relations alternates at such a speed that the purported theatricality of those images is rendered inconspicuous, then the perceptually challenging rapid editing will take precedence over mise-en-scène techniques.

Between narrative and so-called Brechtian form (which Heath sees as predicated on montage and related principles), Heath posits a contrast. In support of this position, he refers to Brecht's note of narrative interruption as essential (122) (thereby blurring the distinction between linear and nonlinear narrative forms), and interprets Brecht's remark on movement as a basic unit of film structure to be a tacit suggestion that film needs to "hold back the narrative" (125). The "narrative/montage" dichotomy (121) that Heath attributes to Brecht disregards the centrality of the notion of narrating (*erzählen*) in both of Brecht's schemas that contrast dramatic and epic theater.

Finally, Heath establishes a link between the Freudian-Althusserian parable of the processes underlying dominant (mainstream) cinema and the project of counter-cinema theory and practice through a passing reference to fetishism as a concept in Karl Marx. The Marxist aspect of the reform of cinema that he calls for further manifests itself through the resonance between the eleventh of Marx's "Theses on Feuerbach" ("the point is to change the world") (qtd. in Heath 110) and an argument from the article's final segment, that "the real work is the attempt at a ceaseless transformation [of cinema]" (126).

During the same period as these essays, Dana Polan lightened the serious apparatus discourse by offering a made-in-Hollywood example of reflexivity and deconstruction: Bugs Bunny and Daffy Duck cartoons in which the characters address the camera and comment on the act of filmmaking. Following Shklovsky, Polan notes that all art is distanced, that the formal operations the 1970s contributors to *Screen* hail as radical can in fact be readily encountered in mainstream cinema, and that the notion of "classic realist text" and its vicissitudes delineated by MacCabe are questionable in light of such works as *Tristram Shandy* (1759–1767). The eighteenth-century novel, notes Polan, foregrounds its artifice no less than *Tout va bien*. Shklovsky's description of the novel as "the most typical [one] in world literature" ("Tristram" 57) comes in handy to advance an argument against the *Screen* critics. But the Warner Bros. cartoons and *Tristram Shandy* possess another key commonality, on which Polan is silent: they are prominently humorous. And if all art requires distantiation, this is especially so with comedy. If it were not for the slapstick's jocose stylization, the genre's violent content would unsettle us rather than make us laugh. The emotional and intellectual distance promoted by literary works and films that aim primarily—or at least importantly—to incite amusement enables us to accept and justify the reflexive commentaries suffusing such texts. In Mel Brooks's *Robin Hood: Men in Tights* (1993), the title character (Cary Elwes) objects to a narrative development as untrue to the script, an element that would constitute an intolerable transgression in an "earnest" rendition of the tale.

As to Shklovsky and *Tristram Shandy*, the Russian critic's view of the novel differs from what the decontextualized quote Polan uses may lead one to infer. For Shklovsky, *Tristram Shandy* destroys before the letter the conventions of the nineteenth-century novel by laying them bare. It is the novel's parodic inventorization of techniques that later came to be associated with the genre that makes *Tristram Shandy* typical. The novel's similarities to such contemporary works as *Tom Jones* (which Polan compares with and contrasts to Laurence Sterne's novel) are, then, homologous rather than analogous: its shared traits serve different aesthetic functions, much like *Robin Hood: Men in Tights* and such non-comedic renditions of the legend about the Sherwood forest archer as *The Adventures of Robin Hood* (1938). Accordingly, Shklovsky's argument would better support MacCabe's view than Polan's.

As importantly, Polan's cinematic examples come from animated films, the kind to which many of the issues apparatus theorists advance do not apply. Baudry and the others would hardly refute that it is perfectly feasible to *draw* a scene that defies the rules of *perspectiva artificialis*, and to reproduce it via the cinematographic apparatus so as to maintain intact the perspectival relations among the scene's elements. What they would deny instead is the possibility of "bypassing" the Renaissance discovery when *photographing* a three-dimensional object, as the entire lineage of optical instruments from the *laterna magica* to the movie projector base themselves on the principles of Brunelleschian perspective. Notwithstanding the youthful bravado of his prose, Polan's article thus cuts the Gordian knot: it dismisses the problems identified by apparatus theorists as irrelevant by ignoring some of their crucial postulates.

The cybernetic revolution of the 1980s spurred the ascent of cognitive science,[21] and a band of film scholars—perhaps most notably David Bordwell and Nöel Carroll—soon rode the tide of the new discipline. The proliferation of computer technologies during the period was not the sole reason that the word "revolution" was less and less associated with politics: the economic downfall and the suppression of democratizing currents in communist Europe now seemed irreversible; Jerry Rubin had completed his transition from a hippie into a yuppie; and Francis Fukuyama was about to proclaim the free market as the ultimate point of humanity's development. The Freudian-Althusserian visions of the mind and society as a labyrinth without an exit, which had pervaded film theory in the preceding couple of decades, were now being replaced by sobriety-exuding discourses predicated on the analogy between the mind and the computer. Whereas apparatus theorists understood the experience of film viewing as entailing an interpellation of passive subjects, the cognitivists regarded that experience as an active engagement with cues provided to the viewers. The process sees the viewer making inferences and formulating hypotheses by comparing the cues against the schemata—different kinds of knowledge relevant to the processing of cues.

Carroll was the first critic of cognitivist orientation to offer a lasting commentary of pertinence to the application of Brecht to film. In *Mystifying Movies* (1988), he attacks Brecht for setting the ground for "SLAB" theory's conflation of illusionism and representation (91). The former term is, he notes, inadequate to describe the effect on the spectator of a mimetic representation, as it—unlike visual illusions proper—does not rest on deceiving the recipient (93). Building upon that, Murray Smith notes in his "The Logic and Legacy of Brechtianism" (1996) the causality poststructuralist film theorists posit between the illusionism of mainstream films and spectatorial empathy. He traces the conjecture back to Brecht, from whom he derives the following two premises:

> *Premise 1*: Emotional response of the emphatic type requires that the spectator mistake the representation for reality.
>
> *Premise 2*: Having an emotional response of the emphatic type deadens our rational and critical faculties (132).

As a proof that Brecht saw theater as capable of inducing the confusion referred to in the first premise, Smith offers a quote from "A Small Organon," which proposes that "too much heightening of the illusion in the setting, together with a "magnetic" way of acting . . . gives the spectator the illusion of being present at a fleeting, accidental, 'real' event" (qtd. in M. Smith, "Logic" 132). He then proceeds to dispute the premise, noting that "spectators do not behave as if they mistook represented actions for real ones—for if they did, they would in many instances flee or intervene, rather than weep and laugh" (132).

The observation, which Smith describes as "damning" (132), is itself questionable. First, it carries the unwanted implication that spectatorial responses of weeping and laughter belong to an order essentially different from that represented by leaving the theater house in panic or interacting with the people and objects onstage. Of course, reality proves otherwise: the former kind of reactions are no more characteristic of artwork reception than of other contexts, and we respond to everyday life phenomena in a wide range of ways, often merely observing situations that allow—and call for—direct involvement. This being obvious, it is difficult to infer what criterion has led Smith to implicitly establish the two categories of responses once the possibility is dismissed that they were meant to correspond to the spectatorial "passivity"/"activity" involved (the dichotomy, prominent in Brecht and his poststructuralist followers, neither serves Smith's specific argument nor fits the general cognitivist conception of the viewer as producer of meaning).

Even if we disregard the inadequate proof Smith uses to demonstrate that viewers do not mistake onstage representations for real events, the assumption underlying his point—that Brecht equated the effects on the viewer of a "surface realist" stage representation and of an actual event—remains hard to accept. The multiple hints in the article that *Verfremdung* is indebted to *ostranenie* indicate that Smith assumes Brecht's familiarity with Shklovsky, and therefore also with Shklovsky's view that estrangement is the essential condition of all art. But Smith's discussion implies that it somehow escaped Brecht that the average theater spectator with some knowledge of everyday matters will *not* mistake a stage event for a real one. Heath, a representative of the poststructuralist school of thinking against which Smith mobilizes his insights, did not miss the quotation marks surrounding the word "real" in the quotation of Brecht that Smith offers. In "Lessons from Brecht," he reminds us that Brecht maintains that "the spectator never loses consciousness of the fact that he is at the theater," but "remains conscious of the fact that the illusion from which he derives his pleasure is an illusion" (113).

That is precisely where lies much of the appeal of illusions, at least in the sense Brecht uses the word. For instance, optical illusions would not be perceived as such if they did not flaunt their operations (the Müller-Lyer arrows, for example, become just two figures of different length if they are not accompanied by the explanation that their length is actually equal).[22] Optical illusions, then, are defined by their persistence in spite of our cognitive correction of our faulty perception of them. Tom Gunning's description of the push and pull between belief and disbelief that one feels when watching a manipulated photographic image teetering on the verge of plausibility ("What's" 45) applies to all media that lend themselves to creating verisimilitude.[23] This impression can occur if we see from the right spot the fresco on the flat ceiling of the Church of St. Ignazio in Rome, where the painting's use of linear perspective helps convey the impression that the structure possesses a dome, or a photographic image whose properties emphasize its similarity to the object it represents. That an artwork's verisimilitude can vary from that of a *Peanuts* comic strip frame to a frame of a documentary in 3D is a key question here, to reverse Smith's remark that "the force of defamiliarization is, of course, variable, but that is another question" (134).

Smith downplays the difference between arbitrary signs (such as linguistic ones) and non-arbitrary signs (such as the iconic and indexical signs used in much of theater and cinema). To that end, he uses an example from literature in a discussion of how an aesthetic context transforms the perceiver's emotions into "quasi-emotions" (133). He quotes the Russian Formalist critic Victor Erlich, for whom the word "blood"—when used in a poem—"becomes an object of esthetic contemplation rather than a catalyst of fear, hatred, or enthusiasm" (qtd. on 133). In Smith's account, Erlich's "poetic" context is conflated with a broader, aesthetic one. This allows his argument to advance, but only at the expense of a fact for which no other example needs to be sought than Erlich's, when adapted for theater and cinema. Many viewers are disturbed by convincing visual representations of blood even when they do not understand the narrative context of the latter's appearance, and when they are aware of the artifice typically involved by such representations.

Smith identifies two problems with Premise 2: first, its assumption of a dichotomous relationship between emotion and reason, contrary to the dominant position in contemporary cognitive science and philosophy of mind that no emotion can arise without a preceding cognitive evaluation. Second, combining the insights of Kendall Walton and Victor Erlich, Smith argues that the aesthetic context—with which Brecht and his followers are concerned—transforms emotions into "pseudo-emotions," thereby defamiliarizing them. We are thus led to infer that the strategies of *Verfremdung* Brecht advocates are already embedded even in those artworks that Brecht would see as addressing our emotions rather than our reason, which makes his techniques superfluous.

A few points need to be made about this postulate and Smith's commentary on it. First, by stressing the Brechtian term *Einfühlung* ("identification") in the introductory paragraph of his article, Smith neglects to acknowledge the development of Brecht's own understanding of the relationship between "feeling" (*Gefühl*) and "reason," reflected by Brecht's replacement of the binary with that of "identification" (*Einfühlung*) and "reason" (*Ratio*) in the revised version of the dramatic/epic theater schema. Second, given that what Smith refers to as "Brechtianism" was propelled by an opposition to dominant cinema, it seems ironic that he criticizes the discourse partly in the name of another discourse's *dominance*, without attempting to explain the positive connotation he implicitly assigns to the term. Pertinent to the second point is also the question of whether the position Smith uses against "Brechtianism" really is dominant, given the existence of important dissenting voices in cognitive science, such as Greg M. Smith. The latter film scholar has convincingly built the case for the independence of emotion from conscious condition, following the insights by Cannon (who noted that emotional behavior may manifest itself even when the cerebral cortex has been anesthetized), Normansell, and Panksepp (who reported that play behaviors in decorticated animals do not completely cease), and Pylyshyn (who noted the impossibility of eliciting and extinguishing emotions through purely cognitive efforts) (G. M. Smith 20–21).

Murray Smith thus attacks "Brechtianism" for its lack of scientific rigor, while the discipline he uses for the endeavor is itself fraught with uncertainties and contradictions, and frequently denigrated as a "soft" science. Even if it were otherwise, a troubling question would remain: does the attempt of Murray Smith and some other writers working within the framework of cognitive science to overturn the feeling/reason dichotomy seem viable, given the global epistemological stability the dichotomy had enjoyed since long before both they and Brecht came along? And does not the persistence of both terms in cognitive science itself indicate a degree of the dichotomy's continued usefulness? Also, does not the fact that "emotion is [normally] integrated with perception, attention, and cognition" (133) add relevance to the contrasting comparison (rather than detract from it), much as the color green, for example, can be productively compared with yellow precisely because of their possession of a common element? Finally, Walton's sound argument that Murray Smith adopts is valid in the context of "Brechtianism" only if we substitute

Brecht's understanding of illusion for that of Murray Smith. The reasons against that move have been explained.

Despite the authority of Murray Smith's deprecating assessment of Brecht's legacy in cinema, the concepts of epic/dialectic theater continue to inspire film practitioners. Before looking at some examples in detail, Brecht's own practical and theoretical dealings with the medium need to be examined.

2

Brecht the Filmmaker

The "Great Method" Adjusted

> A priori l'oeuvre de Brecht n'a pas affaire avec le cinema. Je dirais plus: elle repousse, elle refuse violement le cinema. [Brecht's oeuvre has nothing to do with cinema. I would say even more: he rejects, he violently refuses cinema.]
>
> —Bernard Dort

BRECHT'S PROLIFIC LITERARY OUTPUT includes poems, short stories, novels, and journals, in addition to dozens of plays. Blurring the low art / high art dichotomy well before the advent of postmodernism, he also embraced the proliferating mass media as his expressive outlets. Among the results of such ventures are his recordings of some of the Kurt Weill–composed songs for which he was the lyricist, and the rhymes for an automobile newspaper ad. Brecht likewise periodically forayed into cinema as a writer and director, provided bases for several films in whose production he did not participate, and served as a model artist for a great number of major filmmakers from the 1960s onward. What could then have prompted Bernard Dort to make the above statement (in Witte 62)? This chapter pursues that question, approaching Brecht's relationship to cinema from historical, aesthetic, and theoretical standpoints.

Brecht's articles and journal entries show that he remained a frequent moviegoer throughout his life. We know that he saw such major German films of the silent period as *Golem* (Paul Wegener, 1920), *Das Kabinett des Doktor Caligari* (Cabinet of Doctor Caligari; Robert Wiene, 1920), and *Die Abenteuer des Prinzen Achmed* (The Adventures of Prince Ahmed; Lotte Reiniger, 1926). Crucial cinematic influences on Brecht, however, came from outside of his native country: Charlie Chaplin, a darling also of such avant-garde movements of the period as Dada and Surrealism, and the Soviet montage cinema, a major cultural export of the new nation and an emblem of the October Revolution's triumph. Brecht's praise of the contrast between the comedic style and the tragic narrative in Chaplin's *The Face on the Bar Room Floor* (1914) anticipates his later-developed views on dialectical form. In a note from 1936, Brecht characterizes Chaplin's "eating the boot (with proper table manners)" (Brecht 2000: 10) in *Gold Rush* (1925) as a *Verfremdung* effect, an homage to which is included in the scene of *The Caucasian Chalk Circle* where the beggar teaches a rich man how to eat like the poor. *Herr Puntila und sein Knecht Matti* (Puntila and His Man Mati, 1940) offers another example of Chaplin's influence, the dynamic between the play's wealthy protagonist, who is affectionate with his servant when intoxicated and cruel with him when sober, being comparable to that between the millionaire and the tramp in *City Lights* (1931). Brecht's *Der Aufthaltsame Aufstieg des Arturo Ui* (The Resistible Rise of Arturo Ui, 1941), a parable on the Nazi regime set in the 1930s America, bears a comparison with *The Great Dictator* (Chaplin, 1940), but owes also to American gangster films, such as *Public Enemy* (William Wellman, 1931) and *Scarface* (Howard Hawks, 1932) (Witte 65).

Chaplin's cinema, American gangster films, and the revolutionary Soviet dramas of the 1920s and early 1930s appealed to Brecht presumably because of their potentially subversive politics (one of them, *Scarface*, was banned in the United States at the time Brecht saw it) and their character portrayal, comparable to Brecht's anti-Aristotelian view of people's inner selves as determined by the sociohistorical circumstances of their lives. This conception of character in early Soviet cinema, with its shift of emphasis from the individual to the collective, comes together in the following words from Brecht's programmatic play *Dialoge aus dem Messingkauf* (The Messingkauf Dialogues, 1939–56): "In the Soviet film *The Battleship Potemkin*, there were even some bourgeois who joined in the workers' applause when the sailors threw their officer persecutors overboard" (93). But Brecht's focus on the commonalities in the behavior of different social classes does not preclude an interest in the individual's uniqueness. In "On Film Music," he praises *Mother* (Vsevolod Pudovkin, 1926), *The Youth of Maxim* (Grigori Kozintsev and Leonid Trauberg, 1935), and *Baltic Deputy* (Iosif Kheifits and Aleksandr Zarkhi, 1937) as films "with real individuals," contrasted to the characters in the cinema of the United States, a nation whose cinema has no individuals despite the nation's pride in their individualism (Silberman, *Brecht on Film* 13).

References to cinema are a comparatively small part of Brecht's body of work. Twenty-two of his shorter notes and essays on cinema, spanning nearly Brecht's entire literary career (1919–56), occupy thirty pages in *Brecht on Film and Radio*, a compilation of his writings on the titular media translated and edited by Marc Silberman. Yet Brecht's enthusiasm for cinema seems striking when compared to the medium's dismissal by such other preeminent modernists as Gertrude Stein and Virginia Woolf. Stein referred to cinema's photographic nature as "the trouble" (117), whereas Woolf described its procedures as "inherently parasitic" (168–69). In contrast, Brecht positively inflects his observation that R. L. Stevenson and Rimbaud use "the filmic optic" (*Werke* 21, 107) (thereby promoting the questionable notion of cinema's origin as a teleology).

The majority of Brecht's texts on cinema focus on particular films and film projects, several of which are screen adaptations of Brecht's own plays. One such film, G. W. Pabst's *Die Dreigroschen Oper* (The Threepenny Opera, 1931), caused Brecht and Weill—the composer of the original score—to file a lawsuit against the production company for its failure to protect the integrity of the artists' work (Silberman, *Brecht on Film* 147). That case motivated the writing of Brecht's only essay on cinema of considerable ambition and length, "The Threepenny Lawsuit." The essay consists of five parts of uneven length, and includes documents of and newspaper articles on the trial, followed by Brecht's polemical comments. In the introduction, he explains that the screen adaptation of *The Threepenny Opera* offered an occasion to challenge ideas that "are characteristic of the current state of bourgeois ideology" (Silberman, *Brecht on Film* 148). He summarizes the history of his and Weill's involvement with the film project, the court's verdict, and the reactions of the press to the trial before proceeding to critique the fourteen ideological assumptions purportedly underlying the trial (Silberman, "Brecht and Film" 207), of which the following are most salient: "The cinema needs art" (Silberman, *Brecht on Film* 163); "Film is a commodity" (168); "A film can be regressive in content and progressive in form" (172); and "Capitalism's contradictions are like the snow of yesteryear" (180). The following passage of the essay addresses all of these ideas:

> To understand the situation we must free ourselves from the widespread idea that only one part of art needs to be concerned with the battles for the modern institutions and apparatuses. According to this idea there is a part of art, true art, that—completely untouched by these new possibilities of transmission (radio, cinema, book clubs, etc.)— uses the old ones (the freely marketed, printed book, the stage, etc.). In other words this true art remains completely free from all influence of modern industry. According to this idea the other part, the technological art, is something else altogether, creations precisely of these apparatuses, something completely new, whose very existence, however, is in the first place beholden to certain financial expectations and therefore bound to them forever. If works of the former sort are handed over to the apparatuses, they immediately become *commodities.* (Silberman, *Brecht on Film* 163)

In the concluding part of the essay, Brecht delineates the goals of the lawsuit, which Silberman summarizes with precision in the following few words: "To analyze how culture functions . . . and to construct a controlled public framework in order to trigger a collective thought process" ("Brecht and Film" 207).

Most of the points in Brecht's texts on cinema written after 1930, the year that saw publication of the "Notes to 'Mahagonny,'" discuss film in relation to the precepts of epic/dialectic theater, usually emphasizing that the latter are equally applicable to the newer medium. To avoid repetition, the rest of this survey of Brecht's thinking on cinema focuses not on the many parallels he makes between the epic/dialectic and mainstream cinema dramaturgy, but on his ideas about the properties of film that distinguish it most from other art forms: its combined use of images and temporal montage.

The Brechtian Image

Brecht came of age as an artist in the era of the historical avant-gardes of the 1910s and the following two decades, whose collective ambition to probe the arts' limits brought about a great number of aesthetic innovations within the relatively short span of the movements' existence. Whereas the antecedent Impressionism revolutionized art by according the status of a primary thematic concern to light, hitherto considered as but a means to loftier painterly ends, Marcel Duchamp—an artist associated with various twentieth-century "-isms"—did so by proclaiming a signed urinal an object of his creation (*Fountain*, 1917). The former movement's contemporary radicalism notwithstanding, its products still belong to the genre of easel painting whose lineage can be traced back all the way to the Renaissance. Exploring such boundaries as those that separate art from non-art, expressiveness from inexpressiveness, and good from bad taste, Duchamp and others were breaking from a centuries-long tradition that postulated a transcendence of the quotidian as the mandate of artistic creation. One would expect the irreverent mischief and populist impulse that underlay much of the historical avant-garde's practice (for example, respectively, that of Dada and both Soviet and Italian Futurism) to have appealed to Brecht. Yet one finds no praise for such artists as Duchamp among Brecht's references to painting. Instead, it is a late Renaissance painter whom Brecht frequently lauds: Pieter Bruegel the Elder.

Brecht refers to Bruegel in a descriptive definition of naïveté (*Naivität*)—a notion Karl-Heinz Schoeps usefully renders as "directness," "intuitiveness," "naturalness," "freshness," and "vitality" (190):

> Naïve is the representation of the entire population of Rouen by a small group of seven persons. Naïve is the altered course of the third scene in the *Commune.*
>
> Naïve is the appearance of a character, when one can say: that and that is coming right now. Or: that and that is happening right now.
>
> The representation of historical processes in Brueghel is naïve, for example The Fall of Icarus.
>
> The opposite of naïve representation is naturalism. (190)[1]

Most of the purported *Verfremdungseffekte* of the Flemish master's images concern their thematic contrasts, such as that between the titular event in "Icarus" and the serenity of the painting's other figures, oblivious to the tragedy taking place in the depicted moment. Brecht's use of juxtaposition as an organizational principle, previously indicated, has led Joachim Schacherreiter (1988) to describe his episodic dramaturgy in terms applicable also to Bruegel: those of "*Bilderbogen*," the hand-painted prints showing thematically connected images of popular subjects, widespread in Europe of the eighteenth and nineteenth centuries. The referents of "*Bilderbogen*" follow the norms of the contemporary realism, but their arrangement does not suggest a coherent, credible, realistic space. Just as the pinned insects in the entomologist's collection do not reveal how the animals use space in their habitat, the motifs of "*Bilderbogen*" do not reveal how their referents might relate to each other in actual geographic space: on a colored print depicting a village, for instance, one sees a pig placed next to a windmill of the animal's size, and a cow whose apparent dimensions equal those of the stable adjacent to it. Schacherreiter's analogy can be profitably used as a link between Brecht's remarks about contradictions and naïveté, that is, between "content" and "form" in Bruegel as his favorite painter. The compositional policentrality in Bruegel's canvases forces the observer to search for a center of interest and thematic connections among the relatively independent microcompositions the paintings display, a procedure comparable to that invited by "*Bilderbogen*." Brecht's use of "The Fall of Icarus" as an illustration of naiveté seems to owe partly also to the inconspicuousness of the titular figure, and its focusing instead on the historical—but "small"—man, the plowman dominating the composition (Figure 2.1).

From the standpoint of society, which the politically minded Brecht strove to adopt, Icarus is an idealist overreacher, the futility of whose ambition to transcend Earth is inscribed in his fall. In contradistinction, the plowman—whose effort is of the materialist provenance, directed

Figure 2.1. A "naïve" image: "The Fall of Icarus" (Pieter Bruegel the Elder, c. 1558). Digital frame enlargement.

toward the soil—is *nützlich* (useful), to invoke the term Jameson uses as a starting point for his investigation into Brecht and dialectics (1998). The other feature of Bruegel's art that makes it "naïve" is its challenging of the rules of perspective as known in Western art since Brunelleschi. The combination of the perceptual cue lent by the title "The Fall of Icarus" and the high angle the canvas employs suggest a singular vantage point, but the pattern in which the depicted objects decrease in size with distance does not systematically follow linear perspective. The painting thus simultaneously uses and rejects the convention, combining contrasts at the levels of both subject matter and style in a manner that Brecht would qualify as dialectical.

But whereas a painting can escape the use of *perspectiva artificialis*, a photograph is denied that possibility, the convention being intrinsic to the medium. The reality effect the photograph produces seems the reason for Brecht's reservation about its artistic usefulness. He writes: "The simple 'reproduction of reality' says less than ever about that reality. A photograph of the Krupp workers or the AEG reveals almost nothing about these institutions" (Silberman, *Brecht on Film* 164). The argument is put into more overtly political terms in an article published in the *Arbeiter-Illustrierten-Zeitung*, where Brecht notes: "The truth regarding the prevailing conditions in the world has profited little from the frightening development of photo-journalism: photography has become a terrible weapon against the truth in the hands of the bourgeoisie. The immense amount of photo-material that the presses spew out on a daily basis and which does not have the appearance of truth really only serves to obscure the facts. The camera can lie just like the typesetting machine" (qtd. in Soldovieri 143). Embedded in the latter statement is an analogy between verbal (arbitrary) and visual (non-arbitrary) signs. As such, Brecht's view can be described as anti-Bazinian: it proposes that a photograph is not a death mask, an asymptote, or a mirror of the real—to mention some of André Bazin's metaphors for the medium—but its distortion.

An earlier remark, however, suggests an opposite view of photography. Writing about the contemporary German poets, Brecht criticizes their "wholly unabashedly romantic products . . . into which nothing photographic thrusts and which, significantly, fit splendidly and walloppingly the petty-bourgeois notion that these were made out of thin air" (*Werke* 21: 163).[2] Here, Brecht posits photography's potential to reveal the sociohistorical factors of which it is a result. As Bazin does overtly in such essays as "The Ontology of the Photographic Image" (1945), Brecht implicitly praises photography's semi-automatic operations and positively contrasts it to the position of the poet as a demiurgic creator, able to transcend this world and fashion new ones. As we will see, Brecht regards montage as capable of countering the "surface realist" properties common to all representational media, and especially to the photographic ones, with their inherent Vertovian promise of showing life "as it is."

The Brechtian Montage

We have seen that the "*Mahagonny*" table contrasts montage to growth as a property of organic art, and the discussion of the titular and other key terms noted that Brecht's understandings of montage on the one hand and of dialectics on the other are related. And indeed, every salient element of the Brechtian stage production stands in a dialectical relationship with another: the bare stage and painstakingly detailed props; the ephemerality of performance and the fixedness of the cinematic images and titles that often accompany it; the stage and the auditorium, at once connected and separated by a half-curtain. The language of Brecht's drama can likewise be regarded as a montage of different styles, borrowed from sources as diverse as Luther's *Bible*, German street ballads, the songs of the comedian Karl Valentin, the plays of Elizabethan dramatists, Georg Büchner, and Frank Wedekind, the novels of Rudyard Kipling, Jonathan Swift, Upton Sinclair, the Danish novelist J. V. Jensen, and Charles Dickens, as well as gangster films (Esslin, *Brecht: Choice* 96). Brecht's plays frequently combine "high" and "low" speech styles, the goal of which strategy is—as Martin Esslin observes—"to reveal to us the discrepancy between the endeavoured lofty appearance and the real, low being" (*Brecht: Paradox* 158; translation mine). The case in point is *Die heilige Johanna der Schlachthöfe* (Saint Joan of the Stockyards, 1932), whose characters speak in a quasi-Shakespearean blank verse. *The Caucasian Chalk Circle* offers an opposite example, with Grushe's use of an elevated language that reveals the discrepancy between the socially imposed low appearance and real, lofty being.

Similarly, songs and music, featured in a great number of Brecht's plays, do not merge with the dramatic action to enhance its emotional undertone, but to distance it and foreground the constructedness of the text and performance. Sometimes, these elements punctuate the scene where a major dramatic change occurs (as they do throughout *Die Tage der Commune* [The Days of the Commune, 1957], to give but one example), and are elsewhere used as a point of contrast and/or irony. For instance, in *Trommeln in der Nacht* (Drums in the Night, 1920), a play set in the aftermath of the disastrous 1914–1918 war, a stage direction calls for the anthem "Deutschland über Alles" (Germany Above All) to be played on the gramophone. A twofold function is performed also by Brecht's scene titles: they facilitate the spectator's comprehension of the narrative by reducing it to its essence and draw her attention to the "how" of the theatrical representation (Knopf 1980, 396). Reminiscent of chapter introductions in eighteenth-century novels and silent film intertitles, the device is intended to relieve the viewer of the emotional tension of anticipation and enable her a cool analysis of the event represented. Finally, the idea of a dialectical duality underlies the acting style Brecht used as a theater director. Inspired largely by the Chinese actor Mei Lan-fang, the style runs counter to the contemporaneous tendency in the German theater of valuing a performer for her intensity and ability to "disappear" in the role. Through epic acting, "the showing one becomes shown." The actor "is not Lear, Harpagon, Schweik; he *shows* them" (*Brecht on Theatre* 137). To facilitate the actor's split into a dramatic figure and herself as a person, a narrator of the events and a participant in them (Schacherreiter 76), Brecht the director employs such exercises for her as narrating in the third person and in the past, quoting the dramatist's scene instructions and commentaries, and "*Fixieren des Nicht-Sondern*" ("fixing the not, but")—the actor acknowledging the alternatives to the manner of representation that she has chosen.

Showing that the individual "is alterable and able to alter" (the act that goes against the Aristotelian "continuity of soul" [Oh 194; translation mine]) requires breaking the unities of space, time, and action. Thus during the twelve years spanned by the dramatic action of *Mother Courage*, the spectator sees the characters in Sweden, Poland, Saxony, Bavaria, and Alsace. The unity of action is here violated as a corollary of the shift of the dramatic foci from the characters and their actions (central in the works of "surface realism") to the social context by which the characters are conditioned. Brecht does not abandon an interest in causality, but focuses on its "deeper" manifestations: just as the physicist of the contemporary, subatomic era transcends the limits of our sensory apparatus and makes the invisible apparent, Brecht—a dramatist of "the scientific age"—uncovers the relations between phenomena that would otherwise pass unnoticed (Knopf 1980, 406). Like the identified stylistic devices, Brecht's implicit removal of the hero from the center of the dramatic universe as its consequence makes obvious the "knots" in the production's structure.

While certain stylistic patterns in Brecht's plays and theatrical productions recur, the existence of a truly Brechtian form would be difficult to prove. Neither of the genres that Knopf identifies as characteristic of the playwright (parable and historical drama) (405) are associated with distinct formal procedures. In addition, Brecht's own classification of *Galileo* among his parables (Fradkin 367)—a play widely regarded by the commentators as a historical drama—renders questionable Knopf's division of Brecht's body of dramatic work into two basic genres.[3] More relevant to his theater than the moral or religious precept or truth that the parable conceals (Pavis, *Dictionary* 48) is the two-level structure associated with the genre. At the first level is the immediate narrative, and at the second, the hidden one, "whose 'soul' must be discovered by the [perceiver]" (248). As such, the parable is connected to the double goal of instruction and entertainment that links epic/dialectic theater to Diderot and Horace. This opposition of aims represents yet another example of dialectical montage in Brecht.

Let us now consider more closely two instances of Brecht's use of montage as a dramaturgical device, corresponding to cinematic time compression and flashback. In scene 4 of *The Caucasian Chalk Circle*, Grushe brings the baby Michael to the home of her brother Lavrenti's family. After Lavrenti tells her that she cannot stay long, the singer conveys through a song that "the autumn passed" and "the winter came." Later, Grushe tells the baby Michael that if the two of them make themselves small, like cockroaches, the sister-in-law will forget that they are in house and their shelter for the winter will be secured. During the ensuing dialogue between Lavrenti and Grushe, sounds of the melting snow's drops from the roof become prominent. The play thus compresses six months of the story time into a few minutes of the performance.

Scene 8 of *The Good Person of Szechwan*—whose breakdown by Joachim Lang is quoted below in full—represents a more complicated example, at once eliding story time and subverting the narrative's linearity in the manner of the cinematic flashback.

1. Madame Yang addresses the audience and announces an account about Sun, her son, that will depict how a "dissipated" person was transformed into a "model" one.
2. The first "illustration" takes place three months prior to the announcement, when Madame Yang took her son to Shui Ta's factory.
3. In the dramatic present, Madame Yang narrates about her son's difficult beginning there.
4. The second "illustration" of the account depicts the period following Sun's first three weeks in the factory. Sun pushes himself to the fore at the expense of a coworker. Madame Yang comments on this.
5. One day in the past is skipped with Madame Yang's short interruption in the present.

6. The third "illustration" of the account shows how Sun advanced through his ruthless behavior.
7. Madame Yang talks about the "true miracles" that her son accomplished.
8. The fourth flashback shows Sun as a slave driver.
9. Madame Yang narrates further that none of her son's hostilities could deter her from fulfilling her duty.
10. The workers sing "The Song of Eight Elephants."
11. The account ends: Madame Yang praises the progress of her son, whom Shui Ta "compelled to more honest work" (32; translation mine).

A comparison between the above scenes and those comprising Eisenstein's staging of *Enough Simplicity for Every Wise Man* (1923) can serve as a segue into a discussion of the similarities and differences between his and Brecht's uses of montage. Below reproduced are the descriptions of the first ten segments of the show's epilogue, prepared by surviving creative contributors to the production, and included in Eisenstein's selected writings.

1. On stage (in the arena) we see Glumov who, in an ("explanatory") monologue, recounts how his diary has been stolen and he has been threatened with exposure. Glumov decides to marry Mashenka immediately and so he summons Manefa the clown onto the stage and asks him to play the part of the priest.

2. The lights go down. On the screen we see Glumov's diary being stolen by a man in a black mask—Golutvin. A parody of the American detective film.

3. The lights go up. Mashenka appears, dressed as a racing driver in a bridal veil. She is followed by her three rejected suitors, officers (in Ostrovsky's play there is just one: Kurchayev) who are to be the best men at her wedding to Glumov. They act out a separation scene ("melancholy"). Mashenka sings the "cruel" romance, "May I be punished by the grave." The officers, parodying Vertinsky, perform "Your hands smell of incense." (It was Eisenstein's original intention that this scene should

be regarded as an eccentric music-hall number ["xylophone"], with Mashenka playing on the bells sewn as buttons on to the officers' coats.)

4, 5, 6. Exit Mashenka and the three officers. Enter Glumov. Three clowns—Goroudin, Joffre, Mamilyukov—run out from the auditorium toward him. Each performs his own curious turn (juggling with balls, acrobatic jumps, etc.) and asks for his payment. Glumov refuses and leaves. (The "two-phrased clowning entrées": for each exit there are two phrases of text, the clowns and Glumov's rejoinder.)

7. Mamayeva appears, dressed in extravagant luxury (a "star"), carrying a ringmaster's whip. She is followed by three officers. Mamayeva wants to disrupt Glumov's wedding. She comforts the rejected suitors, and after their rejoinder about the horse ("My friendly mare is neighing") she cracks the whip and the officers scamper around the arena. Two imitate a horse while the third is the rider.

8. On stage the priest (Manefa) begins the wedding ceremony. Everyone present sings, "There was a priest who had a dog." Manefa performs a circus turn (the "rubber priest"), imitating a dog.

9. Through a megaphone we hear the paper boy shouting. Glumov, abandoning the wedding, escapes to find out whether his diary has appeared in print.

10. The man who stole the diary appears. He is a man in a black mask (Gollutvin). The lights go out. On the screen we see Glumov's diary. The film tells us of his behavior in front of his great patrons and accordingly of his transmogrifications into various conventional figures (into a donkey in front of Mamaev, a tank driver in front of Joffre, and so on). ("Montage" 37)

Eisenstein exaggerates the play's farcical dimension by writing into the scene the wedding, which makes Glumov's decision to marry Mashenka appear more abrupt, and by using conventions of the circus: the song, the film, and the enacted action as relatively independent "attractions" (a method corresponding to Brecht's *Prinzip der Trennung* [principle of separation]). These scenes announce some of his cinematic techniques. It is apt to elaborate on intellectual editing as the most complex among those, as a point of comparison with Brecht's understanding of photography and montage.

The technique breaks with the tradition of the previous major innovator of film editing, D. W. Griffith, the spatio-temporal relationships of whose shots are invariably subordinate to the narrative. Eisenstein's intellectual editing, by contrast, often combines nondiegetic images with diegetic ones. A practical application of the concept can be found in *October*, which juxtaposes the image of a bridge—being opened to kill the protesters against the tsarist regime—with a close-up of an Egyptian pharaoh's stone bust that adorns the structure. The idea of the regime's autocracy and obsolescence thereby suggested is not a sum, but a sublation of the two consecutive images (or *Aufhebung*, to use Hegel's original term). Schematically, the difference between Griffith and Eisenstein can be represented as follows. Griffith's editing conforms to the formula a + b = ab (for instance, the chaser, nearing the prey throughout a sequence, eventually catches her, thus bringing two parallel narrative lines together);[4] Eisenstein's intellectual editing, on the other hand, follows the formula a + b = c (for example, the image of the bridge in *October*, followed by that of a pharaoh, equals the notion that the tsarist regime is autocratic and obsolete).

But the two images lend themselves to more than one viable interpretation, not in the least because cinema's visual signs—with their intrinsic richness of detail—denote and connote multiple things at once. Recognizing the pharaoh as a concrete ruler of a concrete Ancient Egyptian dynasty, or simply as an ornament noticeable in the background of a wide shot seen previously in the sequence, are but two possible ways of seeing the image that would likely distract the viewer from the meaning Eisenstein intended for the shot. Hence the contradiction Dudley Andrew notes about Eisenstein's theorizing of editing, reflected in his vacillation between the view of the artwork as the "art machine" and the "art organism" (89). The former model requires what Andrew terms neutralization—"decomposing reality into usable blocks or units" (73), whereas the "art organism" model is undergirded by an understanding of those blocks and units as related and imbued by a general theme (109) that makes the artwork appear self-sufficient and self-sustaining (96), organism-like. This appearance owes to the "noise" previously mentioned in relation to the photograph but present in all images. As Barthes notes, all images are polysemous, each implying a "floating chain" of signifieds, and allowing the perceiver to choose some and ignore others (*Image* 39). Recognizing how this complicates the feasibility of intellectual editing, which presupposes that the meaning of film shots in particular combinations with each other is single and fixed, Eisenstein resorted to Roman Jakobson's concept of the dominant—"the focusing component of a work of art [which] rules, determines, and transforms the remaining components" (751). This borrowing from literary theory, however, did not eliminate the problem of diversity of interpretations to which every image lends itself, a problem that seems to inform also Brecht's critique of the photograph's reality effect. Despite his wording ("the simple 'reproduction of reality' says less than ever about that reality" [Silberman, *Brecht on Film* 164]), Brecht objects not only to what a photograph fails to "say," but also what it manages to "say"—which is invariably more than "a mouth," "water," or "knife"—to refer again to some of the examples Eisenstein uses in his discussion of intellectual editing.

Verfremdung pertains to understanding a meaning and *Naivität* to perception, as an escape from what Barthes calls the "tyranny of meaning" (*Image* 185). If the image allows the escape, it does so courtesy of its excessive elements, which refuse to be subsumed among the image's codes. But *Naivität* stands in relation to *Verfremdung* at once as a precondition and a result. To be able to perceive an artwork and progress from "understanding" to "not understanding"—the middle stage in the dialectical process entailed by *Verfremdung*—one needs to possess perceptual freshness, the quality that occurs also as a result of one's reaching the final stage of the mentioned process: different understanding. Thus Eisenstein's vacillation between the view of the (photographic) image as a representation of reality—corresponding to the "art machine" trope—and the view of it as a creation of a new reality—corresponding to the trope of the "art organism"—applies to Brecht, too. Perhaps no simpler and clearer example can be found than the nonfictional film scenes he used in two different productions of *Mother* (1932, 1952), and in the 1952 production of *Die Gewehre der Frau Carrar* (Senora Carrara's Rifles, 1937). The documentary scenes suggested the objectivity of the artistic vision to which they had been made subservient, while the combination of different media the productions exemplified served as a reminder of their constructedness, and therefore of the limits of the productions' objectivity. In the remaining parts of the chapter, we will see how similar paradoxes play themselves out in Brecht's practice as a filmmaker.

Toward Kuhle Wampe: Early Scripts and a Short

Brecht realized few of his film projects. His unproduced scripts comprise over forty texts, of which most of the extant ones date from 1921. Commentators explain Brecht's unusual productiveness that year by financial need,[5] and assess the screen writings it yielded— *Robinsonade auf Assuncion* (Robinsonade on Assuncion), *Das Mysterium der Jamaika-Bar* (The Mystery of the Jamaica Bar), *Der Brilliantenfresser* (The Jewel Eater), and *Drei im Turm* (Three in the Tower)—mostly favorably.[6]

In addition to being more suggestive of Brecht's view of the contemporary cinema than his theoretical writings, these texts are valuable as sole examples of the application of young Brecht's dramaturgy into an image-based medium. Thematically, they can be separated into two pairs: the first and the last use the motif of rivalry between men for the same woman, whereas the other two are detective stories, each featuring an unusual criminal gang. Set on Assuncion Island after the volcanic eruption, with a hungry tiger scouring its streets, *Robinsonade*—as Maia Turovskaia observes—literalizes the central metaphor of *Im Dickicht der Städte* (In the Jungle of the Cities, 1921–24), the play Brecht wrote immediately after the script (37). The narrative of *Three in the Tower* is widely seen to be drawn from Strindberg's *Dance of Death* (Gersch; Hinck; Silberman *Brecht on Film*), which Brecht saw in Munich two years prior to writing the script. Focusing on a captain who, upon discovering that his wife is having an affair with his lieutenant, commits suicide in a cupboard and continues to haunt the couple with the odor of his decaying corpse, the narrative is replete with trademarks of the Expressionist style. A focus on lighting (the script contains several references to lanterns and candles, as well as allusions to Goya's paintings) and the architecture of the setting (throughout the script, there are references to winding staircases and narrow corridors) betrays the painterly hand of Caspar Neher, who collaborated on Brecht's theater productions as a set designer. As Walter Hinck observes, the film conveys its ironic stance toward the Expressionist style mainly through intertitles, such as the announcements of each of the five "acts" (" 'Toiletries in the house of death' or 'Lime is not enough' or 'A corpse in the lovers' bed' " [Silberman, *Brecht on Film* 106]). The intertitles, notes Hinck, "kill off all cinematic sentimentality" (70; translation mine) in a manner similar to the stage direction "gawk not that romantically" from *Drums in the Night* (70). *The Mystery of the Jamaica Bar* has a convoluted storyline that involves vanishing guests of a party. While this script, too, suggests the use of broad gestures and mannerisms associated with Expressionist theater and film (it describes the playfulness of a group of gentlemen in club rooms as "exaggerated" [Silberman, *Brecht on Film* 52] and Paduk's gesticulation as "wild" [57]), the script rejects Expressionism's interest in interiority. The characters are flat and functional, as befits the detective series on Stuart Webb for which the project was intended.

Turovskaia explains Brecht's attraction to the criminal film—a category in which the last three mentioned films can be classified—by its opposition to psychologism, compatible with Brecht's understanding of realism (42). The same applies to *The Jewel Eater*, which stands out from the four projects for its numerous comedic elements, and the reliance of its narrative on a medium-specific trick: at a turning point, a character's body is rendered transparent to reveal a swallowed jewel.

An important later project, the screen adaptation of *The Threepenny Opera* entitled *Die Beule* (The Bruise; 1930), written for "Nero-Film" in collaboration with Caspar Neher, Slatan Dudow, and Leo Lania, resonates with the *Lehrstück* theory Brecht was developing at the time. It was conceived in the climate of inflation, joblessness, and class struggle that had intensified since the play's original production in 1928, and brings the mentioned issues further to the thematic fore. *The Bruise* transforms Macheath and his gangsters into bank owners, thereby glossing the equation between the ruling class and the criminals, present already in John Gay's versions of the play. The titular motif appears on the head of one of the beggars, a result of a thrashing by Macheath's gangsters for informing the police about them. Bringing about a series of further dramatic turns, the motif of the bruise acquires causal agency, thereby epically/dialectically minimizing the characters' function as such. The narrative culminates in a dream sequence showing the miserable march into the cultural, judiciary, and political institutions, and ends with Macheath's, Peachum's, and Tiger Brown's realization of their interdependence in the threat of the beggars' rebellion. *The Bruise* was to utilize cinema's potential for spectacle: the gang numbers would number 120 people, roasted oxen would be prepared for the wedding banquet meal in the hall that holds 150 guests, and the sequence of Tiger Brown's dream would feature tanks rolling the streets of London. In addition, each of the film's planned three "chapters" was to employ

> its own technique in terms of photography, rhythm of events and images, and the particular camera shots they require, etc. The first chapter should flow without editing and cuts. (The spectator does not see Polly Peachum's face before Macheath does.) The second chapter introduces two regularly alternating and mutually qualifying activities: the falling-in-love (soft focus, indolent) and the organising of the trousseau (sharp, montage editing). The third chapter shows single, unconnected still lives; the camera searches for motives, it is a sociologist. (Silberman, *Brecht on Film* 135)

The narrative parallels the juxtaposition of stylistic conventions associated with melodrama (for example, soft focus) to those of a documentary (vaguely suggested by the equation of camera with a sociologist). As much as the cinematographic style intended for the third "chapter" was to foreground the artificiality of the representation of Macheath's romance with Polly, the vividness and epic scope of the oneiric sequence was to render the "happy end" intentionally unconvincing.

Having realized that Brecht failed to fulfill the contractual obligation of adhering to the play, the producer attempted an accommodation. Brecht refused the offer, but the production continued nonetheless with a new version of the script, authored by Béla Balász and Ladislaus Vajda. The resulting film—widely seen as betrayal by Brecht scholars (Turovskaia; Elsaesser *Weimar*; Silberman *Brecht on Film*)—downplays the play's satirical aspect, emphasizing instead the role of erotic attraction in power relations (Silberman,"Brecht and Film" 205). While the director Georg Wilhelm Pabst retained the Weill-composed songs, he eliminated the contrast between their intentional sentimentality and the irony that underlies the play's parallel between the Victorian England's underworld and its judicial system. As a result, the original production's separation of elements and the formal tension it produced has given way to a uniformly romantic vision of the milieu of poverty and crime that eclipses the narrative's topicality.

The group of films on which Brecht collaborated as a co-director comprises a mere two titles: *Mysteries of a Hairdressing Salon* (with Erich Engel, 1923), a short comedy featuring Karl Valentin, a Bavarian cabaret and film comedian, and *Kuhle Wampe*.[7] The films contrast with each other in terms of their respective stylistic dominants: the short emulates the contemporary Western cinema fare, while *Kuhle Wampe* is fashioned after the period's Soviet films. Narratively, *Mysteries* evokes the works of the caricaturist and poet Wilhelm Busch, with his dark humor of violent pranks. Within the span of approximately twenty minutes, the viewer witnesses a stylist give electroshocks to the wife of a professor with whom she is infatuated, another stylist blow the professor's hat away with a blast of soda, a restaurant guest challenge the professor to a duel over a stolen hat, and a stylist accidentally decapitate the restaurant guest while shaving him (Figure 2.2).

Crude in terms of editing rhythm and spatial organization, *Mysteries* still does not deserve Knopf's near-dismissal on account of its failure to utilize the medium's unique expressive possibilities.[8] The film's use of such techniques as parallel editing and animation (one scene has the restaurant guest's severed head crawl along the floor) testify to a fascination with the specificities of cinema, manifested more systematically and forcefully in *Kuhle Wampe*. Rather than its structural flaws, the reasons for the film's problematic status in Brecht's oeuvre seem to be its modest

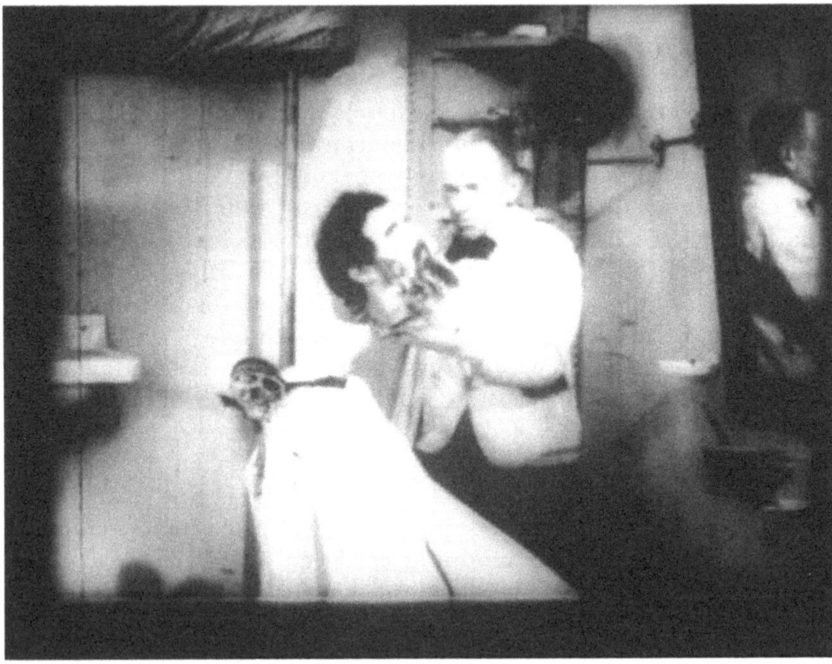

Figure 2.2. Dark humor in *Mysteries of a Hairdressing Salon* (Bertolt Brecht and Erich Engel, Kuprofilm, 1923). Digital frame enlargement.

ambition and a thematic and stylistic discontinuity from the artist's best-known works.

Kuhle Wampe: A Montage Film?

Unlike *Mysteries*, *Kuhle Wampe* roots itself in the peculiar political milieu of the Weimar Republic, a fact that calls for the film's historical contextualization. The October 1929 stock market crash had a harsher impact on Germany than it did on other Western European countries. The United States' credits, on which the fragile economy had been dependent, were now increasingly unavailable. Between 1929 and 1932, the industrial production dropped by 40 percent, and the number of unemployed is conservatively estimated to have reached seven million in the latter year. A dispute between the liberal nationalist DVP and the social democratic SPD over state support for the jobless led to the collapse of the Grand Coalition. The chancellor Hermann Müller of the SPD was replaced by Heinrich Brüning, a Center Party politician who secretly aimed to restore the Hohenzollern monarchy. President von Hindenburg, a self-professed hater of the republic, had promised Brüning to use the power the constitution gave him and issue an emergency decree whenever a bill he supported was voted down. Hindenburg's and Brüning's anti-democratic stance notwithstanding, the mathematical assignment of Reichstag seats and the rise of splinter Communist (KPD) and National Socialist (NSDP) parties during the period made the achievement of a parliamentary majority virtually impossible. The parliament's proper functioning was further hampered by the regular interruptions of the debates by the KPD and NDSP representatives.

The Communists considered the SPD an enemy as fierce as the NSDAP. In the summer of 1931, the KPD followed the instructions from Moscow to join forces with the right-wing parties by participating in the popular vote the latter organized against the Prussian government, under the slogan "All party forces must be thrown into the battle against social democracy." Due to the SPD's collaboration with certain reactionary politicians in the Clerical Center Party and the Bavarian People's Party, the Communists denounced them as "socialist fascists." On the 1928 May Day demonstration, the police force controlled by the Socialists fired on the demonstrators, killing thirty-one persons and wounding hundreds more. Between March 1931 and March 1932, fifty-four Communists were killed and 677 arrested. The working class answered to this oppression by further mobilizing itself.

Such was the political climate in which *Kuhle Wampe* was conceived by Slatan Dudow, a Bulgarian émigré who had worked as an assistant director for Lang's *Metropolis*, collaborated in different capacities on a series of Brecht's didactic plays and *The Bruise* screenplay, and directed a short documentary entitled *Wie der Berliner Arbeiter wohnt* (How the Berlin Worker Lives, 1930). In 1931, he approached "Prometheus Films," an independent company founded in 1926 by Willi Münzerberg, a KPD representative in the parliament, with a synopsis for a feature-length film involving the suicide of an unemployed Berlin worker. Once a successful distributor of Soviet films and a producer in its own right (perhaps most notably of Piel Jutzi's *Mutter Krausens Fahrt ins Glück* [Mother Krausen's Journey to Happiness], 1929), the company was now at the verge of bankruptcy. Averaging fifteen productions a year between 1927 and 1930, "Prometheus" made only four shorts in 1931. *Kuhle Wampe*, the company's final film, could not have been completed without the financial assistance of an entrepreneur who provided the bulk of the film's modest budget on condition that Brecht write a song for him, and the Swiss company "Praesens-Film," which bought the unfinished production and enabled its completion after the bankruptcy of "Prometheus" in 1932 (Brewster and MacCabe).

Along with the extraordinary financial difficulties, which demanded that about a quarter of the footage be shot within the period of two days, the production was plagued by a dispute with the "Tobis-Klangfilm" concern over the use of sound technology, as well as by censorship. After reviewing the film twice, on April 9, 1932, Berlin's Film Inspection Board proclaimed *Kuhle Wampe* unsuitable for public release because of its propagandistic tendencies (Silberman, *Brecht on Film* 203). As a result of the ensuing protest meetings, petitions, newspaper debates, and the readiness of "Praesens Film" to cut the scenes found inappropriate by the Board, the film eventually received a release permission. Perhaps as a result partly of the heated debate that preceded its German premiere (Turovskaia 99), *Kuhle Wampe* attracted 14,000 spectators during the first week of its run in fifteen Berlin cinemas, but was withdrawn from circulation immediately after the Nazis' seizure of power in March 1933.

While the original idea came from Dudow, its development is the work of a collective including also Brecht, Hanns Eisler, and Ernst Ottwalt. The first three men had previously worked together on the staging of *Die Maßnahme* (The Measures Taken). Ottwalt, a proletarian-revolutionary playwright and novelist, was brought into the creative team by Brecht, on account of his firsthand knowledge of the working class milieu. Dudow was principally responsible for the shooting script, while it was chiefly Brecht who determined the performance style.

The film's three parts, divided by montage sequences showing "images of apartment buildings, factories and natural landscapes" (Silberman, *Brecht on Film* 205) and accompanying songs, form a hierarchy that can be designated as dialectical.[9] The first part, centering on a laborer who commits suicide after a vain job hunt, represents one answer to a manifestation of the crisis of the capitalist system (suicide as thesis). The second episode, where the dead laborer's family—upon their eviction from their Berlin home due to unpaid rent—moves to the film's eponymous tent colony, represents another answer (eviction as antithesis). While the first two parts center on the concerns of the individual, the third one, showing a leftist sports festival, focuses on the collective. It is constructed as the only viable answer to the problem of the crisis of capitalism established in the film's exposition (the workers' mobilization as a synthesis). All formal operations assisting the dialectics of the content can be safely associated with montage and "documentariness," once we broaden the former concept to include the sound-image relationship (as in Eisenstein's "vertical montage"),[10] and the latter to include all elements of the film that oppose the principles of Aristotelian dramaturgy. This is not to imply that montage, as applied in *Kuhle Wampe*, does not interact with the film's dramaturgy, and that it does not have a role in the process of thwarting the viewer's identification with the characters. (Brecht himself leaves no doubt about this, when he contrasts the Aristotelian growth to epic/dialectic theater's montage in his *Mahagonny* schema.) Neither is the conjecture about the dialectical relationship between montage and "documentariness" in *Kuhle Wampe* to imply that the applications in the film of the two concepts do not coincide. But while the two are inseparable from each other and often share a narrative function, their purposes are diametrically opposed. The potential of montage to denote through connoting (to once again refer to Schlegel's idea) limits the potential of "documentariness" to connote through denoting, and—in the cases when it is applied together with the former concept—suggests its purpose within a narrative form. Silberman's observation that the film's rhetorical effects counterbalance its narrative continuity (*German* 41) applies also to the relationship between the "documentariness" and montage in *Kuhle Wampe*.

The film opens with a brief shot of the Brandenburg Gate, which locates the narrative in Germany's capital. This image is followed by four shots that gradually shift the focus from the public to the private sphere: factories dominate the first two, while the third depicts a train moving toward the camera, the smoke of its engine surrounding the apartment building in the background. Connecting an industrial motif with a residential one, the shot announces the next series of images, which show the buildings and back courtyards of the city's working-class area. James Pettifer is right to conclude that the cluster of shots of newspaper headlines showing the disastrous effects on the unemployed of the economic crisis, which follow the expository sequence, represents an important *Gestus* (57),[11] but the rest of his discussion of the montage appears tenuous. In interpreting the emphasis in the film on the newspaper "as a means of communication among the unemployed" (57)—which observation is further supported by the remark that "few were likely to own radios" (57)—he disregards the relative prominence in the film of the motifs of the radio and gramophone. In the sequence that shows the Bönike family's arrival to the tent colony inhabited mostly by unemployed workers, military marches and a radio voice that announces them are heard, while the engagement party sequence shows Anni winding up a gramophone and playing yet another march: Fucik's "Entry of the Gladiators." More importantly, Pettifer's remark that the headlines sequence reveals its problematic through the absence of politics—which makes the effect of the collage methodology synthetic rather than analytic (57)—ignores the shift in emphasis within its course from the political to the purely economic: "Westfalia South splits off," reads one of the headlines in the montage sequence's first part. Finally, Pettifer does not take into account the political connotations of the shot of the Brandenburg Gate as the historic site of battles between soldiers and revolutionaries in 1849 and 1919. Crucially positioned at the very opening of the film, the image anchors the economic crisis—whose implications on the working class constitute the narrative's foci—to the realm of the political.

The next segment, introduced through the intertitle "the job hunt," has been insightfully commented upon by Gersch (1975), Pettifer (1974), Turovskaia (1985), Silberman (1997), and, in particularly great detail Reinhold Happel (1978) and Roswitha Mueller (1989). What immediately follows this stylistically virtuosic but narratively and structurally simple sequence bears a close examination, too. Showing the young Bönike return home after the unsuccessful attempt to find work, that sequence includes the first two instances of disrupting the diegesis through the visuals. A crossover from Eisler's unharmonic score to the diegetic sound of street music marks the beginning of the sequence, where we see the young Bönike with his bicycle at the front door of an apartment building. Upon entering the building, the young Bönike pauses in front of two musicians playing in the back yard. The two shots are separated by a low-angle image of the building's façade. Evoking the series of shots of buildings in the workers' district seen previously, the image forms an associational link between this and the segment preceding the job hunt sequence. The shot has little movement, contrasting the hectic pace of the previous sequence. Through its relatively long length (13.3 meters, compared to 5.5 and 3.1 meters, respectively, of the preceding two shots), it places an emphasis on the back yard—the space where Bönike the son will later jump to his death. The shot will also become a point of comparison with the film's other scene of a public performance—that of the agit-prop theater group "*Das rote Sprachrohr*" ("The Red Megaphone"), whose performance about the threat of eviction due to unpaid rent, significantly, mirrors the Bönike family's situation. The next shot introduces Bönike the father. Lying on the sofa with a newspaper in his hands, he declares that "the boy" will not get financial welfare any more. When his wife, occupied with setting the lunch table, fails to respond, he makes a reproachful remark on account of her alleged indifference. The unorthodox composition of the next shot, showing the young Bönike tying his bicycle's pulley rope to a nail, produces a deliberately jarring effect. Suspended in the air and occupying the foreground, the bicycle only allows for a limited view of the character. The shot's use of a wide-angle lens, which exaggerates the difference between the relative sizes of the objects in different planes, assists the composition in deemphasizing the figure. The described stylistic choices produce an impression that the character is but an accessory to the bicycle (the metonymical relation of which to the idea of job seeking has been established by the sequence of the character's and his fellow workers' anxious riding from one factory to another).

The image previously seen in the job hunt sequence interrupts the conventional editing pattern of the next five-shot segment, which shows the young Bönike's and his sister Anni's entrance into the living room and the beginning of lunch. Depicting the entire group of unemployed workers riding their bicycles toward the traveling camera, the shot is prompted by Mrs. Bönike's lines: " 'The early bird gets the worm.' If you don't try anything, how can you be surprised when things go to pot." The inserted shot, which highlights the falsity of Mrs. Bönike's remark, here appears outside of the story world's context. The absence of sound enhances its estranging quality: neither Eisler's music nor the ambiance of the Bönike home accompanies the image. In addition, the shot prevents the possibility of being interpreted as a flashback through the use of formal strategies that thwart the viewer's identification with the young Bönike. First, the character's introduction is purposely inconspicuous. He first appears in a long shot following the newspaper headlines montage, along with several other figures, at a seemingly arbitrary point. Second, close-ups of other job hunters and the distributor of the classifieds surround that of the young Bönike, thereby tempering the emphasis on the latter character provided by the mentioned shot scale. Third, none of the shots in the job-hunting sequence emulates the young Bönike's point of view. Fourth, the character is absent from some of the scenes of the film's first part. Finally, the young Bönike never speaks.

The shot of the pedaling workers punctuates the scene two more times (its appearances in the sequence equaling three—the number of cases necessary for creating a pattern). Importantly, the content of the line that prompts the cut to the second of the three inserts ("there are no jobs") contradicts the one that served the mentioned purpose in the previous instance. It is Anni who delivers the line, in reaction to her parents' citing the young Bönike's purported impoliteness as the reason he cannot find work. The insert shot here has a different function, confirming the accuracy of Anni's claim. In its final appearance, the shot of the unemployed riding bicycles is coupled with that of the young Bönike's bicycle hanging from the ceiling. The latter image, in combination with the one whose connotation of strife has already been established, thus acquires a connotation of giving up, which the young Bönike's suicide retrospectively asserts.

A scene from the film's second part further foregrounds editing as the film's dominant technique. In terms of dramatic action, it echoes with the beginning of the scene discussed previously. Set in the tent where the Bönike family now resides, the scene again shows the father reading a newspaper while Mrs. Bönike is working (Figure 2.3a). This time around, she is not preparing to serve a meal but is calculating the prices of food items. The tone of the article the father is reading aloud is sensationalistic and apolitical—a fact that resonates disturbingly in light of the link between the newspaper article the character was reading earlier in the film and the motive for his son's suicide. The slight low-angle shots of the couple, of Mrs. Bönike, and finally of her hand as it is compiling the list are interspersed with non-diegetic shots of food items with price tags, photographed through a store window (Figure 2.3b). Unlike the shot of the riding workers from the earlier example, these do not confuse the spatio-temporal relationships of the scene, as they leave Bönike's monologue uninterrupted. However, its continuity and the small scale of the shots render the inserts of food items near-abstract.[12]

It is this quality that facilitates the images' adjustment to the narrative context. The sequence contrasts the luxurious life of the dancer and courtesan Mata Hari (the article quotes her as saying that she received as much as 30,000 German Marks for her favors) to the illustration of the family's daily monetary struggle. A significant point of similarity between Mata Hari and Mrs. Bönike, their gender, facilitates the contrast. Signified as the scene's primary character by the comparatively close shot scales in which she is shown, Mrs. Bönike embodies domesticity, contrasting the exotic sex appeal of Mata Hari. The purpose of these insert shots, too, changes as the scene unfolds. The newspaper quote—"The rich connoisseurs admired her as a delicacy of the rarest kind"—acquires an ironic aspect when it coincides with an image of pickled fish, marked by the tag as "best German herring."

Imagery similar to that punctuating the "Mata Hari" sequence appears in the visions of the film's other protagonist, Anni. Upon learning that she is pregnant, the character has a distorted vision of children designed to illustrate her anxiety at the prospect of motherhood (superimposed images of children looking at the camera lens convey the distortion) (Figure 2.4). The ensuing montage sequence includes a variety of ads for baby products and the actual items they advertise, photographed—like the food items in the "Mata Hari" scene—through the store window. While the sequence stands out as the film's only attempt to convey interiority, Silberman's observation that it represents a "concession to realist conventions of psychological motivation" (*German* 45) may be somewhat overstated. Namely, the similarity between the images of baby products with the insert shots used in the "Mata Hari" sequence,

Figures 2.3a and 2.3b. Juxtaposed diegetic and nondiegetic images in *Kuhle Wampe* (Bertolt Brecht and Slatan Dudow, Prometheus / Praesens, 1932). Digital frame enlargements.

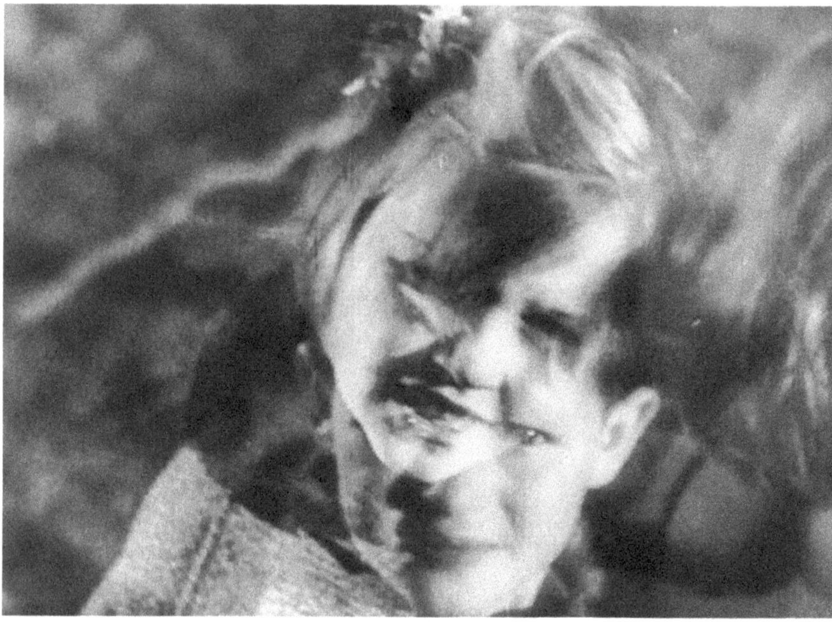

Figure 2.4. Superimposed imagery in *Kuhle Wampe* (Bertolt Brecht and Slatan Dudow, Prometheus / Praesens, 1932). Digital frame enlargement.

as well as the association of the former's content with the world of material goods, work to objectify and depersonalize Anni's vision, thereby mocking—rather than affirming—the conventions of "surface realist" art.

Kuhle Wampe uses montage not only as an editing technique, but also as a structuring dramaturgical principle, applied at the respective levels of its three parts and the scenes these consist of. The parts are relatively independent from one another, each one centering on a separate issue: the first on unemployment (suggesting that the crisis of capitalism renders futile all its methods); the second on undesired pregnancy (suggesting that dire economic circumstances cannot be transcended through marriage); the third on the agency of the dissatisfied to change the world. Significantly, each of the three parts is open-ended: the subsequent ones never refer to the death of the young Bönike, who constitutes the first part's narrative focus. Similarly, the final part drops the motif of Anni's pregnancy, central for part two. Lastly, the narrative provides a confirmation that "those who do not like the world will change it," as Kurt and Gerda say will happen in the subway scene. The end is left open, the impression of "spilling into the real" thus created functioning as a *Verfremdung* device.

The film often resists continuity also in the transitions from one scene to the next, and within the given narrative line, as illustrated by the following summary of the narrative line concerning Fritz's relationship with Anni.

1. The woods. The couple is shown walking, with the accompaniment of Helene Weigel's singing of the erotic song "On Nature in Springtime" ("The play of the sexes renews itself / Each spring. That's when the lovers / Come together. The gently caressing hand / Of her lover brings a tingle to the girl's breast. / Her fleeting glance seduces him. // The countryside in spring / Appears to the lovers in a new light. / The air is already warm. / The days are getting long and the fields // Stay light for a long time. // Boundless is the growth of tress and grasses / In spring. / Incessantly fruitful / Is the forest, are the meadows, the fields. / And the earth gives birth to the new / Heedless of caution.)

2. The "Mata Hari sequence." Toward its end, Anni appears in the tent, only to leave it after greeting her parents.

3. The couple is in front of the tent. After Mrs. Bönike makes a circle around them and goes to the back of the tent, the following exchange takes place: "Were you there?" (Fritz); "It's too dirty there. I'm not going to ruin my life" (Anni).

4. Anni and her father are at the table in the tent, eating. When he threatens to "beat [her] to a pulp" in case "anything happens," Anni angrily leaves.

5. The factory where Anni works. Women are testing electrical units. Gerda (to Anni): "Don't lie, something is the matter with you." Anni: "Don't make trouble here at work, otherwise I'll be fired tomorrow."

6. The auto repair shop where Fritz works. He is spraying an engine, while a coworker of his is greasing it. Co-worker (to Fritz): "Paying alimony and single taxes, you might as well get married." Fritz: "Nonsense. I want my freedom."[13]

While the described series of scenes provides sufficient detail on the relationship's progression, it does not exploit the emotional turns within it, as a film based on Aristotelian dramaturgy would. Instead of the viewer's emotions, the film mobilizes her intellect, by creating narrative gaps and inviting her to make the effort of filling them.

The repetition of certain actions sustains a structural unity of this narratively fragmented film. Evident already in the job hunt sequence, with its three instances of the unemployed workers' inquiring about the availability of factory work, repetition manifests itself most overtly in the film's penultimate sequence, with its elaborate montage of the workers' sports activities. The sequence, which "shows the search for work as—work" (Silberman, *Brecht on Film* 205), continues in the tent colony. The scene of the party thrown at the occasion of Fritz's and Anni's engagement repeatedly shows Fritz carrying crates of beer bottles and piling them by the tent. The three shots that show him perform the action or talk about it with his father-in-law temporally define the relationship between the interior shots, which depict different phases of the party. Photographed from the same angle and employing similar shot scales, the three shots that punctuate the party scene function also as rhythmic constants, each one marking the end of a visual cadence.

In addition to the already mentioned devices borrowed from Brecht's theatrical practice, the film employs intertitles, songs, voiceover (a form corresponding to his idea of narrating as opposed to dramatizing), and epic acting (Figure 2.5). This last stylistic feature—conveying the impression that the actors are distanced from the characters they play, and the characters' apparent emotional detachment from themselves and each other—rests in *Kuhle Wampe* to a considerable extent on the use of the actors' eyelines. Ordinarily the pivot of our focus in interactions with fellow humans, the eyelines constitute the basis for such techniques of mainstream cinemas as the 180-degree rule and shot-countershot. In *Kuhle Wampe*, however, the characters seldom look at each other. Mr. and Mrs. Bönike do not make eye contact during the "Mata Hari" sequence; Fritz's and Anni's eyes do not meet as they discuss the possibility of getting married; Fritz and Mr. Bönike do not look at each other in the scene where Fritz announces the wedding—to give but three examples. (A rare moment of a silent exchange of glances occurs in the film's first part between Bönike the son and Anni, and functions to transfer the attention to the latter character, a protagonist of the film's subsequent parts.)

With its sparse narrative and overt political agenda, *Kuhle Wampe* resembles Brecht's *Lehrstücke*—the most famous among which, *The Measures Taken*, was written shortly before the film's production (in 1930). The film's real drama, however, plays out on the level not of narrative,

Figure 2.5. Epic acting in *Kuhle Wampe* (Bertolt Brecht and Slatan Dudow, Prometheus / Praesens, 1932). Digital frame enlargement.

but of style, which combines austere dialogues and restrained acting with oneiric and humorous montages and seemingly unrehearsed, documentary scenes. In light of the wide stylistic range shown of Brecht's scripts and the occasional brilliance of *Mysteries* and *Kuhle Wampe*, Bernard Dort's statement that Brecht "violently refuses cinema" appears unfounded.[14]

Conclusion

Brecht's numerous film projects can be classified according to the originality of their scripts: some were conceived specifically for the screen, whereas the other ones derived from preexisting texts. The former are extraordinarily diverse and include projects that—had they been produced according to Brecht's planned design—would share salient characteristics with Expressionism. (That this would occur despite Brecht's dislike of the style situate these projects alongside *Baal*, a play that is—although intended as a ridicule of Expressionist drama—often regarded as its supreme example.) *Kuhle Wampe*, which belongs to the same group of film projects, is paradigmatic in being the sole Brecht film that embodies his aesthetic, production, and political principles as presented in such writings as "The Threepenny Lawsuit" and the various articulations of epic/dialectic theater theory. The most notable projects from the other group, the adaptations of *The Threepenny Opera* and *Mother Courage*, are linked also by their troublesome productions. The largely improvisational nature of the production of *Mysteries* and *Kuhle Wampe* on the one hand, and the "true to the page" nature of the play-based films on the other, makes one tempted to hypothesize about Brecht's personal role in the sharp contrast. Could it be that it was partly the success of the theater productions that thwarted the films' success, by imposing on Brecht the hard-to-reconcile imperatives of staying true to the "originals," and of ensuring the same status for the screen adaptations by making them sufficiently different from the theater productions?

Brecht's disagreement with DEFA, which was to produce a screen version of *Mother Courage*, concerned the company's intention to give the play an epic treatment (not in the sense the term has in Brecht, but in the sense of "impressively great"): the use of an international film star (Simone Signoret), intricate settings, a widescreen aspect ratio and color stock.[15] What underlies Brecht's reservations about cinema in general and the screen version of *Mother Courage* in particular (which led to his halt of the project) is the conduciveness of photographic representation to "surface realism." Both this and the problem of original versus adapted works are crucial to the film poetics of Jean-Marie Straub and Danièle Huillet.

3

Jean-Marie Straub and Danièle Huillet

The Caveman's Avant-Garde

THE EMERGENCE OF JEAN-MARIE STRAUB and Danièle Huillet as filmmakers has been situated variably in the French *nouvelle vague* and the *Neues Deutsches Kino*.[1] They belong to the former context by their original citizenship, and—in Straub's case—on account of the developmental trajectory that preceded the production of their first film, *Machorka-Muff* (1962). Like some of the other best-known *nouvelle vague* filmmakers, Straub participated in the 1950s culture of ciné-clubs, semi-formal groups of film enthusiasts organized together for the purpose of studying the medium. According to Richard Roud, Straub's decision to pursue film professionally—first as a critic and later as a practitioner—resulted from the experience of exhibiting Robert Bresson's *Les Dames du Bois de Boulogne* (Ladies of the Park, 1945) (19). Straub claimed he would never have made *Chronik der Anna Magdalena Bach* (Chronicle of Anna Magdalena Bach, 1968) had it not been for Bresson's *Journal d'un curé de campagne* (Diary of a Country Priest, 1951) (Albera 48).

Roud identifies the following commonalities between Bresson and Straub. Both base their films on literary works (Bresson, in the first three films; the latter, throughout his career); both filmmakers' screen adaptations show fidelity to the original texts; both reject the methods of "psychological acting" in favor of restrained, distanced techniques that emphasize the properties of the playscript in a manner reminiscent of

Brecht; both Bresson and Straub depart from "surface realism" by shifting the relationships between the shot's audiovisual constituents; both show a predilection for sparse, uncluttered compositions (21–23). Roud has a point in attributing the roots of Bresson's visual style to Christianity (describing it, he invokes Jansenism, Calvinism, and Protestantism), with which Bresson's entire oeuvre shows a thematic concern. Bresson is, along with Yasujiro Ozu and Carl Theodor Dreyer, a subject of Paul Schrader's study *Transcendental Style in Film* (1972), which investigates the relationship among the three filmmakers' styles and religious metaphysics. But while Straub and Huillet's films share prominent features with those of the other filmmaker on whom Schrader's study focuses, they do not seek to "express the Holy" (3)—which phrase he uses to describe the profound aim of Ozu, Bresson, and Dreyer. Straub and Huillet's perspective is materialist: it stresses the concreteness of the photographed objects as the technical basis of their images and sounds.[2]

The Algerian war and the prospect of Straub being drafted prompted the couple's exile to West Germany. Because they made their first several works there, debuting at the time of the country's introduction of the film subsidy system and the penetration of the term *Neues Deutsches Kino* into critical discourse, they are frequently classified in the German national context. When one considers the less literal sense of the adjective characterizing the French New Wave and New German Cinema—the one concerning the originality of the works in question—the placement of Straub and Huillet in both contexts appears tenuous. In their writings and interviews, the filmmakers often compare their work with that of the pioneers of film. Oft quoted is the anecdote from a screening where Alexander Kluge described the films of *Neues Deutsches Kino* as new, to which Straub stood up from the audience and furiously replied that what he does is traditional (Byg, *Landscapes* 41). Many commentators concur with this assertion. Hans Hurch describes Straub and Huillet as the last great primitives of the medium and compares them with Griffith and Stroheim (qtd. in Byg, *Landscapes* 226), while Roy Armes makes a comparison between the directorial tandem and Louis Lumière (qtd. in Byg, *Landscapes* 209). Barton Byg's observation that Straub and Huillet's cinema "evoke[s] the photographic immediacy of the early cinema" (*Landscapes* 22) may serve as an explanation of the above comparisons. Peter Handke, writing about the filmmakers' *Die Antigone des Sophokles in der hölderlinschen Übertragung für die Bühne bearbeitet von Brecht* (Sophocles' Antigone in Hölderlin's Translation as Reworked for the Stage by Brecht, 1992), takes this view further by describing Straub and Huillet's cinema entirely in terms of the older medium: "The

Straubian cinema and ancient Greek theater are for me virtually one in the same, of like form"[3] (qtd. in Byg, *Landscapes* 217).

Handke sees the presence of "Brecht's rhetoric" as aesthetically detrimental to the Hölderlin, implicitly dismissing the former's trace in the film. Yet commentaries of Straub and Huillet's work consistently invoke Brecht,[4] Martin Walsh (1981), Barton Byg (1995), and Ursula Böser being notable examples (2004). Straub and Huillet themselves acknowledge indebtedness to Brecht in their films and film projects, theoretical writings, and interviews. Brecht is one of the dedicatees of *Machorka-Muff*, and a quotation from him follows the opening credits of *Not Reconciled*. The latter film also bears a quote from *St. Joan of the Stockyards* as a subtitle: "Only violence helps where violence rules." Straub also authored "'Filmcritica,' Eisenstein, Brecht" (1973), a programmatic essay that includes an entire Brecht's dramaturgical poem. *Geschichtsunterricht* (History Lessons, 1972) is based on Brecht's novel fragment *Die Geschäfte des Herrn Julius Caesar* (The Business Affairs of Mr. Julius Caesar), *Antigone* uses Brecht's adaptation of Hölderlin's translation of the Sophoclean tragedy, and *Corneille / Brecht* (2009) combines texts by the eponymous writers. Straub and Huillet also planned a screen adaptation of *The Measures Taken*, which project remained unrealized due to copyright issues (Byg, *Landscapes* 10).

As can be inferred from the above examples, Straub and Huillet and Brecht have common political leanings. In festival announcements of *Chronicle* and *Othon*, Straub and Huillet dedicated the films to Viet Cong and French workers, respectively. In Straub's comments following the premiere of the first incarnation of his and Huillet's *Antigone* as a Berlin's Schaubühne production in May 1991, the work was dedicated to the 100,000 Iraqi victims of George H.W. Bush's "New World Order" (Byg, *Landscapes* 84). Most provocatively, *Moses und Aron* (Moses and Aaron, 1974) is dedicated to Holger Meins, a cameraman who died from a hunger strike during his imprisonment on account of his suspected involvement with the Red Army Faction.

The filmmakers' relation to the left has not been unambiguous, though, as illustrated by Straub's remark that he is uncertain whether he is a Marxist (Fairfax). Because of their refusal to render their politics in the overt manner of a Gillo Pontecorvo or Emile de Antonio, Straub and Huillet have been accused of a lack of true political involvement. Helmut Färber objected to the moderation of the political stance displayed in *Machorka-Muff* (Byg, *Landscapes* 84); Godard regarded *Chronicle* as missing relevance to contemporary problems (Reimer and Reimer 285); and Martin Walsh remarked in regard to *History Lessons* that Straub and Huillet's "claims for a specific radical content are in some respects undercut by the formal investigations of language which are aimed at the elimination of meaning" (105). Straub's response to Färber by a letter to the editorial board of *Filmkritik* appears applicable also to criticisms concerning the insufficient political explicitness of his later films: "Even supposed leftist intellectuals react to *Machorka-Muff* as if they had expected pornography and were shown a marble Venus" (qtd. in Byg, *Landscapes* 84).

Equally controversial is the filmmakers' relationship to Brecht. Straub declared that John Ford—a filmmaker of rightist politics—"is the most Brechtian of all filmmakers, because he shows things that make people think, damn it, is that true or not" (qtd. in Byg, *Landscapes* 41). Also, he detaches himself from the project of *Verfremdung*, stating that he "[does] not believe that the so-called alienation is transferable to the film" (qtd. in Byg, *Landscapes* 224).

The following pages continue the introduction by identifying the general formal characteristics of Straub and Huillet's cinema:

(1) Like Brecht, a majority of whose plays—from *Baal* to *Pauken und Trompeten* (Trumpets and Drums, 1955)—are reworkings of preexisting texts, Straub and Huillet never work from original scripts. Their films are based on artworks in different media: Bach's music in *Chronicle of Anna Magdalena Bach*, Heinrich Böll's fiction in *Machorka-Muff* and *Nicht versöhnt oder Es hilft nur Gewalt, wo Gewalt herrscht* (Not Reconciled or Only Violence Helps Where Violence Rules, 1965), and the Schönberg opera in *Von Heute auf Morgen* (From Today Till Tomorrow, 1996), to give but a few examples. Four of the twenty-four films the couple produced between 1962 and 2004 are based on unfinished artworks: *Moses and Aaron*, based on the opera by Schönberg, *Klassenverhältnisse* (Class Relations, 1983), an adaptation of Kafka's unfinished novel *Der Verschollene* (*Amerika*) (The Missing One [America]), and the films based on two versions of Hölderlin's play *Der Tod des Empedokles* (The Death of Empedocles, 1798–1799): *Der Tod des Empedokles oder Wenn dann der Erde Grün von neuem euch erglänzt* (1986) and *Schwarze Sünde* (Black Sin, 1988). Straub and Huillet have also released different cuts of their films (for example, of *Sicily!* [Sicily!, 1998]) and made segments of the same works into various films. *Cézanne* (1989) and *Une visite au Louvre* (A Visit to the Louvre, 2003) are based upon the same chapter from Joachim Gasquet's *Cézanne* (1921); *Operai, contadini* (Workers, Peasants, 2000) and *Umiliati* (The Humbled Ones, 2002) are adapted from Elio Vittorini's *Le donne di Messina* (The Women of Messina, 1949), while *Dalla nube alla resistenza* (From the Clouds to Resistance, 1979) and as many as three shorts—*Il*

Ginocchio di Artemide (Artemis' Knee, 2007), *Le streghe—Femmes entre elles* (The Witches, 2008), and *L'Inconsolable* (The Inconsolable, 2010)—derive from Cesare Pavese's *Dialoghi con Leucò* (Dialogues with Leucò, 1948). Their frequent intertextual techniques promote the view of Straub and Huillet's cinema as a singular but malleable and polyphonic text, a quality that runs counter to the notion of a coherent and distinctive authorial vision that is associated with art cinema.

(2) The narratives of Straub and Huillet films are frequently set in past epochs. Ten of the films they produced in the period between 1962 and 2004 employ historical costumes. A frequently concomitant characteristic of the filmmakers' period films is their use of anachronistic elements. Examples include the twentieth-century buildings in the background of Sicily of the fourth century B.C. in *The Death of Empedocles*, of first-century Rome in *Othon*, and—more conspicuously—the combination of a protagonist in modern-day dress and toga-clad Romans in *History Lessons*.[5]

(3) Straub and Huillet's films invariably use direct sound. The unorthodoxy of this choice becomes clear when one considers that sound re-recording and dubbing in the post-production process were technological hallmarks of the German and Italian film industries at the time when Straub and Huillet's careers were starting. As the filmmakers' use of direct sound represents a return to previous technological standards, its "avant-gardism" is comparable to that of Gregg Toland's return to deep-focus photography—a stylistic feature predominant in Hollywood of the silent era—in the 1940s films of William Wyler and Orson Welles.

(4) The filmmakers often set their scenes in nature (examples include *Othon* and *The Dialogues with Leucò* films, the *Women of Messina* films and *O somma luce* [Oh Supreme Light, 2010]). As with their other aesthetic predilections, Straub and Huillet explain this one in terms of politics: "For me," Straub remarks, "industrial society is barbarism" (qtd. in Byg, *Landscapes* 229).

(5) As a corollary of the filmmakers' penchant for exteriors, their films frequently rely on natural available lighting. Examples include *Othon*, *History Lessons*, *Moses and Aaron*, *From the Clouds to the Resistance*, *Antigone*, and the *Women of Messina* adaptations. The *nouvelle vague* filmmakers in France and direct cinema filmmakers in England typically use this lighting style to facilitate the camera's greater mobility. The former group of filmmakers employed the technique also to bring the acting closer to the naturalistic ideal, the idea being that this technological simplification facilitates the performer's immersion in the role. But neither mobile framing nor naturalistic acting characterizes Straub and Huillet's

films. Nor is the fixity of the camera position in them counteracted by an increase of figure movement, as one might intuit would be the case.

(6) With its emphasis on the aural rather than the visual aspect of performance, the acting in Straub and Huillet's films share little with the performance styles of conventional cinemas. Straub and Huillet have their actors recite their lines instead of acting them, a technique that starkly contrasts with that of psychological realism, used by Hollywood and related film industries. This aspect of the filmmakers' work evokes a diversity of theater traditions from the times when one went to hear, rather than see, a play. The other major influence on the acting style in Straub and Huillet's work is Brecht, whose credo on performance—included in the opening section of *Not Reconciled*—relates to the previous observation: "Instead of wanting to create the impression that he is improvising, the actor should rather show what the truth is: he is quoting." Putting the programmatic sentence in practice, Straub and Huillet have created an acting style more austere than that employed in, for instance, Brecht's own production of *Mother Courage*, as documented in Peter Palitzsch's and Manfred Wekwerth's film version of the play (1961).[6]

(7) Straub and Huillet's cinema frequently uses shots configured through the narrative context as empty (hence Gilberto Perez's observation that every Straub and Huillet film may be called "lacunary") (324): for example, the cloudless sky in *Machorka-Muff* and *Moses and Aaron*, or the Italian landscapes in *Fortini/Cani* (1976) and *Sicilia!* (Sicily!, 1999). These shots bring into the films' thematic scope the relationship between form and content, making the viewer ask herself not only the usual question of what they are presented *about*, but also the more rudimentary one of what it *is*. ("A film that signifies something," observed Straub in an interview, "can only be trash, since it confirms people in their clichés") (qtd. in Franklin 80). Because of its emphasis on the films' physical aspect, commentators often situate Straub and Huillet's films in the context of materialist cinema.[7]

Straub and Huillet's Brechtian affinities manifest themselves mainly in the combination of the implicitly or explicitly political content of their films, the filmmakers' thematic and stylistic concern with dialectics, and their refusal of the conventions of mainstream cinema. Often resulting in stylistic simplicity, this last characteristic merits the filmmakers' claim that their films are for "cavemen and children" (qtd. in Fairfax n.p.). The problematics of Straub and Huillet's relationship with Brecht is the subject of this chapter's remaining sections. The following analyses of *Machorka-Muff*, *History Lessons*, *Antigone*, *Cézanne* (1989), and *Sicily!* illustrate the development of Straub and Huillet's understanding of montage and theatricality.

Challenging the Language / Film Analogy: Machorka-Muff

Machorka-Muff is adapted from Heinrich Böll's short story "Haupstädtisches Journal" (Capital Diary), whose rendition into English as "Bonn Diary" somewhat diminishes the title's political resonance. The story was first published on September 15, 1957, the day of the third German federal election, which—in Barton Byg's phrase—" 'consecrated' the remilitarization of West Germany" (*Landscapes* 74). Written in the first person and in the form of five journal entries, the story follows the visit to Bonn in an unspecified postwar era of Erich von Machorka-Muff, a former Nazi major. In the course of four days spanned by the narrative, the protagonist lays a foundation stone to the Academy of Military Memoirs, his old brainchild, "where every veteran from the rank of major up is to be given the opportunity of committing his reminiscences to paper, through conversations with old comrades and cooperation with the Ministry's Department of Military History" (Böll 59). The story's other central themes are Machorka-Muff's promotion to general and his marriage to Inniga von Schekel-Pehnunz, a woman seven times married, each of her husbands a military man higher in rank than the previous.

Produced independently after Straub and Huillet's failure to raise funding for the feature-length *Chronicle of Anna Magdalena Bach* and the medium-length *Not Reconciled*, *Machorka Muff* is narratively unique in the filmmakers' oeuvre as their only work that visually depicts a character's interiority. The brevity of the scene in both the short story and the film allows it to serve as an example of Straub and Huillet's method as adapters. Entitled "Night jottings," the scene describes the dream Machorka-Muff has upon his arrival in Bonn (see Figure 3.1):

> I was walking through a forest of monuments, straight rows of them; in little clearings there were miniature parks, each with a monument in the center; all the monuments were alike, hundreds, thousands of them: a man standing 'at ease,' and officer to judge by the creases in his soft boots, yet the chest, face and pedestal of each monument were covered with a cloth—suddenly all the monuments were unveiled simultaneously, and I realized, without any particular surprise, that I was the man standing on the pedestal; I shifted my position on

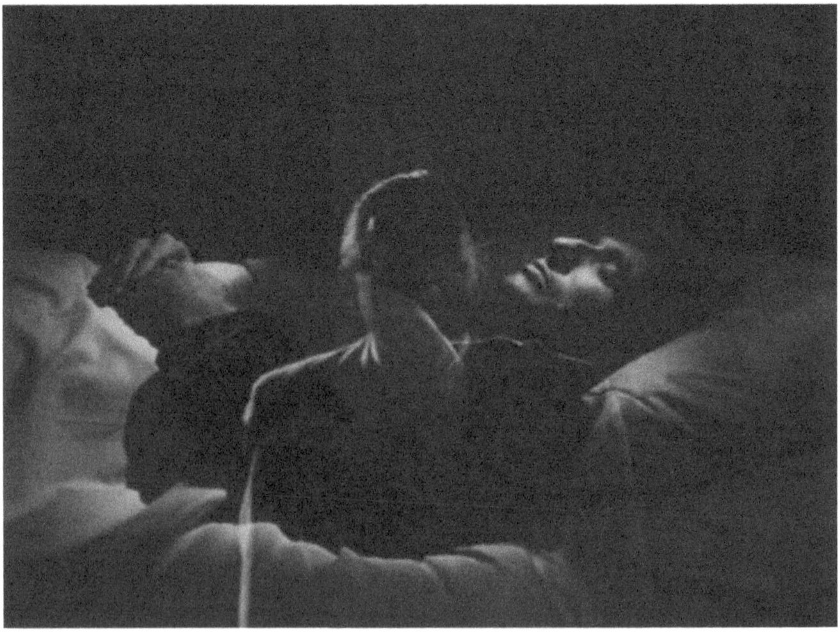

Figure 3.1a–h. Language into images: *Machorka-Muff* (Jean-Marie Straub, Atlas / Cineropa, 1962). Digital frame enlargement.

Figure 3.1a–h. *Continued.*

Figure 3.1a–h. *Continued.*

Figure 3.1a–h. *Continued.*

> the pedestal, smiled, and now that the covering had dropped off I could read my name thousands of times over: Erick von Mackarka-Muff [*sic*!]. I laughed, and the laugh echoed back to me a thousand times from my own mouth. (54–55)

The use of chiaroscuro, perhaps intended to illustrate the difference from the protagonist's perception in the wakeful state, sets off the scene from the rest of the film. The hundreds and thousands of monuments to which the narrator of the story refers are reduced to six (shown in two shots separated by a medium close-up of Machorka-Muff turning his head from one row of monuments to another). As Straub and Huillet otherwise tend to adhere to the story's minutest details, this departure from the original is probably due to budgetary constraints rather than aesthetic reasons. But it is entirely to the latter that the absence from the scene of the protagonist's laughter should be attributed. The omission appears to reflect a wariness of representing strong emotional responses, characteristic also of a range of art cinema filmmakers from Bresson to Godard. The somewhat heightened emotionality of the story's characters (of which Barton Byg [*Landscapes* 78] offers an illustration by pointing out the frequency with which Böll uses the word "ergriffen," moved) is suggested neither by the acting nor the music—often the principal sources of a dramatic situation's affectivity. The film's subdued performance style evokes Brecht and his caveat about the correlation between the arousal of the spectator's emotion and identification, this latter process posited as an impediment to understanding the social aspect of the represented event. In *Machorka-Muff*, the strategy adds to the political radicalism and subversiveness already integral to the short story. The acting distances the distance created by the satirical mode, and the narrative presents itself as earnest, to an unsettling effect.

The pause in the actor's delivery and the quick fadeout that precedes it stress a segment of the sentence that follows the description of the dream: "It is only here in the capital that one has dreams like that" (Böll 55). (Throughout its duration, the film uses the fadeout as a visual equivalent of the gaps between the entries and their titles, which graphically segment the story.) The word "dream" appears not only in the narrator's voiceover, but also in the Straub's handwritten and signed note that follows the opening credits, which describes the film as "an abstract pictorial dream, not a story." Considered in retrospect, the remark foreshadows Straub and Huillet's formal experiments, in which the exaggerated style sometimes threatens the narrative's intelligibility (a case in point are the long sections in *History Lessons* that show the protagonist riding the streets of contemporary Rome).

Written text is foregrounded also in the film's other montage sequence, which at once exemplifies Brechtian *Historisierung* and *Literarisierung*—the latter term echoing the Russian Formalists' *literaturnost*, which Brecht used to denote an array of estranging techniques that "denaturalize" a given discourse by foregrounding its semantic nature. The sequence comprises images of different national newspaper articles on West Germany's 1950s rearmament, which mark historical time as powerfully as the short story. Drawn from at least three years of time (the earliest date shown is 1951, with 1953 the latest), the articles are ordered according to the thematic links between them. The themes include the law of general compulsory service then coming into effect, as well as religion, suggesting the role played in the rearmament by the Christian Democratic Union, the party with the most representatives in the Bundestag during the era. It is in religious terms that the montage ends: "Is a Christian allowed to slay? Must a Christian slay? Why did God knock the weapons off our hand twice?"

The short story and the film also associate Christianity and military elsewhere. The protagonist reports about the multiple divorcée Inniga's skepticism about marriage as an institution, and adds that a difference in their backgrounds and outlooks separates them further: she comes from a strict Protestant family, and he from a strict Catholic one (Böll 58). What links the couple symbolically, the protagonist goes on to conclude, are the numbers: "She has been divorced seven times, I have been wounded seven times." At the wedding ceremony in church, Machorka-Muff says to the bride: "Your eighth [husband] will be a general," thus completing the line of the voiceover narration that identifies three of Inniga's former husbands as military figures. In the scene following the wedding, the priest, walking along with the newlyweds, declares that "since none of [Inniga's] former marriages was solemnized in church, there is no obstacle to you and General von Machorka." In the world of Machorka-Muff, where form is everything, everything is also merely form.

The newspaper headlines in the montage sequence are not the only example where the film recontextualizes a preexisting cultural product to transform its meaning. In the relatively long sequence where Machorka-Muff is walking the streets of Bonn, he is twice shown stopping at store windows. In one of these shots, the camera tracks toward the window where fashion garments are displayed, with the accompanying slogan: "In the style of hussars." The uniform-inspired clothing thus becomes a metaphor for rearmament. The other shot opens with a dissolve to the inscription that reads: "Grow old—stay young / that is all we want." The camera then tracks away to reveal a bearded mechanical acrobat turning on the trapeze, and bottles of the medical lotion the toy advertises.

The link between sexuality and warfare, most unequivocally established in the story by Machorka-Muff's remark that—during a walk before his romantic encounter with Inniga—he "had the impression of a sword dangling at [his] side," "although [he] was in civilians" (Böll 57), here receives a visual presentation.

In his letter to Straub sent à propos *Machorka-Muff* (a rare positive critique the film initially received), the composer Karlheinz Stockhausen praises the film for its resemblance to music (Roud 37). What makes peculiar the film's musicality is that its primary agent is not the "internal" component of acting (as is customarily the case), but the "external" elements of the interacting cinematography and editing. The editing is often independent from the narrative: no action takes place in relatively long parts of several shots. In the scene at the foundation of the Academy of Military Memoirs, the screen at one point remains occupied for seconds solely by the uniform whiteness of the sky, illustrating Straub and Huillet's broader strategy of challenging the usual dominance in narrative cinema of human (or humanlike) figures and their actions, which might be designated as "de-anthropocentrizing." The strategy may be motivated by the filmmakers' fondness of nature, as well as by their interest in exploring the limits of photographic representation. As an illustration of the latter hypothesis, consider the similarity between of the emptiness suggested by the images of the sky in *Machorka-Muff* and *Moses and Aaron*, for example, and by the "non-image" of black screen in *History Lessons* and *Einleitung zu Arnold Schönbergs Begleitmusik zu einer Lichtspielszene* (Introduction to Arnold Schoenberg's 'Accompaniment for a Cinematographic Scene,' 1972), among other films.[8]

Machorka-Muff invites a reflection on the relationship between the logic of literary and film "syntaxes." A case in point is the film's use of Böll's prose as a base for the voiceover, which the imagery attempts to illustrate. Machorka-Muff's acts of shelling a breakfast egg and drinking coffee at breakfast, for example, are separated by a few inconclusive remarks on the dream of the monuments he had, the brief series of these ending with the question: "I wonder whether the psychologists have really plumbed all the depths of the self?" The film confuses the relation between the simple events as a result of the scene's linking the imagery through dissolves, the transitions used in the period's films of Hollywood and related industries to indicate passage of longer periods of time, as well as by the track away and toward the character in its two consecutive shots, the camera movements employed in the mentioned contexts to end (i.e., open) a scene. The intended incongruity between the images and words the film employs together calls attention to the work's artifice, ultimately suggesting the arbitrariness of both. The filmmakers' investigation of the relationship continues in their feature-length films, and is carried out perhaps most radically in *History Lessons*.

The Dialectics of Image and Sound: History Lessons

In certain respects, *History Lessons* is comparable with previous Straub and Huillet films. Like *Machorka-Muff* and *Not Reconciled*, it is based on a literary text intended to be read, not performed; like *Chronicle of Anna Magdalena Bach*, it uses a (pseudo)biographic mode; like *Othon*, it is (partly) a period piece; like *The Bridegroom*, it employs materials heterogeneous in terms of both narrative and style. No earlier work of the filmmakers, however, possesses this many qualities in combination that actively impede what Brecht would refer to as passive spectatorship, allowed and promoted by mainstream cinema as heir to Aristotelian theater. Paradoxically, the film is structurally rather simple.

History Lessons is based on Brecht's unfinished novel *The Business Affairs of Mr. Julius Caesar*. Written in 1938 and 1939, the period of Hitler's infamous rise to prominence, the narrative traces Caesar's ascent to power through the accounts of his contemporaries given to the novel's narrator, a young man preparing to write a biography of the Roman political and military leader. The novel contains four books, of which the second and fourth are written in the form of a diary of Caesar's secretary Rarus. Much of the work is written in dialogue form, but its prose vastly differs from that of Brecht's plays: first, in its relatively greater density, and second, in its centering on a character absent from the novel's immediate space and time. Brecht mediates the portrayal of Caesar through others, thereby indirectly implicating anonymous people in his career, and dispelling the myth of the strong, extraordinary individual as a maker of history.

History Lessons parallels the novel's dual structure in an oblique way: it consists of the young man's interviews with representatives of different classes and professions who knew Caesar personally, and of shot-sequences showing the interviewer driving the streets of (contemporary) Rome. The latter parts are, like Rarus's diaries in the novel, marked by the contingency of everyday life as observable in public.[9]

Shot from the camera fixed in the backseat of the protagonist's convertible (see Figure 3.2), the driving scenes do not obey the logic of narrative build-up that governs mainstream narrative cinema: none of the micro-events seen in the background is configured as dominant, and none seems more important than the other. Because the linguistic and visual signs within the scenes are scarce (the audio consists entirely of street noises), one is tempted to take the image of the hammer and

Figure 3.2. A character looking ahead at the story world and back at the viewer in *History Lessons* (Jean-Marie Straub and Danièle Huillet, Janus / Straub-Huillet, 1972). Digital frame enlargement.

sickle, which appears on a wall poster in one of the three scenes, as the interpretative key for them all. But if the symbol's resonance with the dialogue recommends this move, the brevity of its onscreen presence does not: the image is legible for only a few seconds, whereas the shot's duration is close to ten minutes.[10]

While the background of the shot sequences constantly shifts, the foreground remains unchanged, save for the occasional turnings of the young man's head and the small movements of his hands at the wheel. The body of the open-windowed car, as photographed in the film, forms a grid that breaks the frame into distinct segments, its diagonals (as well as the one suggested by the driver's eyeline) pointing toward the composition's golden section. In Perez's words, "Built into photographic image are the rectangular frame and the perspective of an individual viewing point" (283).

The "frames" within the frame evoke the cinematic technique of split screen, conventionally used to suggest simultaneity of two or more narrative events. This appears relevant with regard to the organization of the film's time, incorrect from the standpoint of "surface realism." While the young man is dressed in modern clothing, his interviewees wear Roman togas. Through the former character's appearance in both groups of scenes, the film configures him as the protagonist (although his status is constantly questioned through the film's other formal operations). The interview scenes are set in spaces that do not readily reveal their contemporaneity (Roman-built structures or landscapes), thus suggesting that it is the protagonist—not the interviewees—who has access to both the Rome of fifty years after Caesar's death, and the Rome of the early 1970s. It is he who travels through time, hinting at the continuity of history, of its repeating itself. But the anachronisms of the costumes can be seen also as a signal of a fissure within the narrative space-time. Seen this way (which reading is encouraged by the mentioned allusion to split-screen technique), the young man's trajectory is simpler than it appears at first: he is traveling between the spaces where history is made, and the spaces where history has to be merely endured.

Equally ambiguous are the actions within the scenes. In the context of the film that—like Brecht—challenges the notion of history as a matter of the past, the character's simultaneous moving and resting becomes a trope for agency. Riding through the kind of Roman streets one does not see on tourist flyers, the young man's role fluctuates between that of a participant in and an observer of his surroundings.[11] The car's windshield distances him from the environment, but the turning wheels close that distance. If the prerequisite for the young man's taking political action is to synthesize the information collected from his interviewees and the sights and sounds perceived during the ride, the prerequisite for the viewer's synthesis of the film's material can be said to be a perceptual shift that will allow her to accept the ride scenes as action proper, equal in importance with the interviews.

The film invites a parallelism between the young man and the viewer, while discouraging identification. The camera shows the young man from the back, its vantage point preventing the viewer's interpretation of the sights and sounds of the streets in terms of his reactions to them. However, the rearview mirror in front of the character returns his look, reminding the viewer that what she perceives as the character is but an image, equal in flatness to the reflection in the frame's center.[12] Showing an object in a manner that would appeal to Cubist painters, from opposite directions, the composition seems to mock the Brunelleschian perspective, which the lines both present and implied by the shot otherwise emphasize. The spatial split beside the direction of the man's look (returned at the viewer) and the direction in which he is moving rhymes visually with the temporal split indicated through the combination of modern and period costumes, thus subtly connecting the two groups of scenes.

Contrary to the standards of professional narrative cinema, the scene with the peasant does not employ the sound bridge—the technique whereby a portion of the audio is carried from one shot to the next. As a result, the shots sharply cut from one to another in terms of both video and audio. It seems an intended paradox that the filmmakers' use of direct sound, whose common purpose is to facilitate a continuity in the post-production between the separately recorded video and audio channels, here becomes related also to the concepts of montage and *Prinzip der Trennung*. The example illustrates the difference between factual realism and what Stephen Prince (1996) terms perceptual realism in cinema. Focusing on the medium's visual aspect, Prince descriptively defines perceptual realism—as "[image] which structurally corresponds to the viewer's audiovisual experience of three-dimensional space" (32). Notwithstanding the definition's foible inferable from the above discussion of Renaissance perspective versus *perspectiva naturalis*, which concurs with the apparatus theorists' faulting cinema for adopting the former model, Prince's distinction is valuable. As we will see, it pertains also to Peter Watkins and Lars von Trier, whose reformulation of realism often entails crossing the boundary between the style's identified two kinds.

The film's use of the other, verbal, kind of language poses a perceptual challenge of a different kind. *History Lessons* couples the already estranging density of Brecht's prose with a relatively rapid delivery style. One understands that the dialogue consistently points to the connections between economy and politics, money and power, but is not given sufficient time to fully understand the relationships between the two realms. While the ride scenes will give the impatient viewer of the DVD edition of the film the impulse to fast-forward through them, the dialogue scenes (see Figure 3.3) will prompt her to occasionally press the pause button so that she can digest the dense material.

From the standpoint of a viewer with typical spectatorial habits, the first group of scenes can be said to contain too little and the other too much. This impression (which the film at once presumes and attempts to overthrow) points to the film's other dialectical split—that between images (which the ride scenes can be said to be primarily "about") and words (which the dialogue scenes can be said to be primarily "about"). As the film uses throughout its duration both the video and audio channels, this impression can also be challenged: is the viewer's tendency to rely

Figure 3.3. Paralleling historical epochs through costume: *History Lessons* (Jean-Marie Straub and Danièle Huillet, Janus / Straub-Huillet, 1972). Digital frame enlargement.

on her hearing during the interview scenes, and on her sight during the ride scenes, a sign of perceptual laziness? Is this why the scenes serve as an index of the unintelligibility of history, as Martin Walsh observes (65)? Would we be able to understand the workings of history if we mobilized both senses?

The challenge this poses for the viewer serves as a reminder of cinema's domination by language—verbal or visual. The verbal language is Brecht's prose; the visual one is the style of mainstream cinema. Writing about *History Lessons*, Maureen Turim invokes Jean-Pierre Oudart's concept of suture, "a primary means by which cinema binds its discourse, concealing its construction" (239). Oudart's view singles out the shot-countershot as the key element that contributes to suture. Turim notes that Straub and Huillet develop in *History Lessons* an alternative to the technique, which "calls attention to itself as system, to the process and effects of camera work and montage" ("Textuality" 240). Martin Walsh's analysis of the first scene with the banker and the one with the peasant refines the argument, showing that the film does not reject the technique entirely, but rather reformulates it. The first scene with the banker cuts back and forth between the interviewer and the interviewee facing each other, as a film made in the "invisible style" would. However, the camera's position changes between each two shots of the same character, its overall trajectories suggesting the shape of a semi-circle. This strategy subverts the technique's traditional role of aiding the viewer's orientation in the filmic space by juxtaposing complementary perspectives.

Consisting of only fifty-five shots, *History Lessons* exemplifies the strain of montage Eisenstein calls intellectual editing better than this filmmaker's own cinema and *Kuhle Wampe*. While Eisenstein uses the technique only in certain scenes, *History Lessons* juxtaposes the two kinds of material that form a dialectical relationship throughout its duration. Moreover, while Brecht and Dudow's film offers a synthesis of the dialectical opposition represented by the film's two parts (the episode showing the workers' mobilization through sport), Straub and Huillet's film is open-ended, leaving ambiguous the two opposed kinds of material and the narrative and stylistic elements within them. Byg's commentary of Straub and Huillet's *Moses and Aaron* applies here with particular force: "A parallel to Straub / Huillet and Brecht emerges here. There is no 'resolution' in their work, according to the hierarchical rules of a traditional organization of its materials to these traditional forms implies a resolution outside the work itself" (*Landscapes* 156). In no other Straub and Huillet film, however, does a narrative issue converge with that of spectatorship as tightly as in *History Lessons*: the cognitive agency that the film demands from the viewer parallels that of the various accounts requested by the young man. This agency, the film suggests, can acquire a political dimension if the comparability is understood between the two pairs of timeframes within *History Lessons*—the narrative ones (the era of Caesar's contemporaries and that of the young man) and the timeframes concerning the film's production and exhibition (the latter one being a constantly changing variable). For the societal factors to be experienced as changeable, history needs to be approached as being always in the making.

The Aristotelian Unities Applied to a Brechtian End: Antigone

With its reference to Sophocles', Hölderlin's, and Brecht's versions of the play, the title signals the film's palimpsestic character. Unlike a typical rendition of a classic literary text, which tends to justify its existence by a claim of finality, Straub and Huillet's *Antigone* configures itself not as *the* reading, but as *a* reading of the play. The title's reference to the names of three artists who have had a hand in the playtext marks the narrative's openness to interpretation rather than the extent of the tragedy's historical-cultural relevance, its canonical status. But the title does not acknowledge all the authorial voices that contributed to the work's shape: the voices of anonymous storytellers that had perpetuated the myth of Antigone before Sophocles wrote a play of it, and Straub and Huillet's own voices. Pertinent to this is the question Robert Savage raises about the authorship of Brecht's adaptation of the tragedy—whose title, too, invokes the original playwright (*The Antigone of Sophocles*):

If Sophocles owns Antigone, who owns *The Antigone of Sophocles*? Not Brecht, surely, otherwise the title would be meaningless or disingenuous; but not Sophocles, either, for then the authorship of the title would still remained unaccounted for. By invoking what Brecht once called "the question of ownership, which in the bourgeoisie, even as far as spiritual matters are concerned, plays a (quite bizarre) role," the citation of ownership in the title problematizes the ownership of citation (Savage, "Precedence" 101).

There are at least two ways to approach Savage's question in relation to the Antigones with which this discussion concerns itself—Brecht's, and Straub and Huillet's. A more obvious approach would be to align with John Fuegi's view of Brecht as essentially a plagiarist (1994), and to dismiss Brecht's words quoted by Savage as an attempt to give an entrepreneurially oriented strategy a veneer of progressive politics. Extending this view to Straub and Huillet would not be difficult: Heinrich Böll, on whose works the directorial tandem based two of their films, gives it authority by assessing the reliance of the couple's films on other artworks as a shortcoming.[13] The other possibility—which will be taken up in the following few pages—is to approach the blurred authorship of the two Antigones as unique in the artists' respective oeuvres. *Antigone* leads to different conclusions on the question of their authorship.

The Sophoclean spirit this adaptation preserves has led Hugo Schmidt to rhetorically ask whether this *Antigone* should be considered an example of epic theater, implying that there is too much of the Greek dramatist in the work for it to be considered a decisive departure from Aristotelian dramaturgy (208). But Brecht's use of the ancient Greek play foregrounds Brecht's textual interventions on the "original," inviting and facilitating—rather than discouraging and hindering—a comparison between the Aristotelian and epic/dialectic dramaturgical models. Like that of Brecht's adaptation, the title of Straub and Huillet's film announces the work's *Verfremdung* devices, referring only to the playwright who figures as an exemplary model in Aristotle's *Poetics*, the validity of whose theoretical precepts for our age Brecht denies.[14] The title distances the viewer from the narrative, while also encapsulating a partial history of the play in the German cultural context through its acknowledgment of the author of the translation from which Brecht the adaptor worked.

Brecht gives Hölderlin's translation of the play a Marxist slant, the very "unfaithfulness" to the "spirit" of the original being a rationale for the adaptation's existence. But what do Straub and Huillet aim to accomplish by transposing the adaptation to film almost without changes (the unorthodoxy of this choice becomes apparent when it is compared with, say, the many cuts in every cinematic version of *Hamlet*, including *Kenneth Branagh's William Shakespeare's Hamlet* [1996], which was nonetheless advertised as "full text")? Furthermore, what are the implications of the filmmakers' refusal of the many possibilities the medium offers (apart from those that characterize Straub and Huillet's entire oeuvre, *Antigone* is unique in relying on fixed camera)?

The adequate pursuit of these questions requires a closer look at the playtext. Written at the turn of the eighteenth and nineteenth centuries, Hölderlin's translation has been praised for its poetic use of the language and his portrayal of German sensibility (Wannamaker 342), but also criticized for its many inaccuracies. (Writing about the poet's rendition of the tragedy, Ulrich Weisstein—for instance—describes some of Hölderlin's solutions as a translator as "idiotisms" [588]). According to Brecht himself, the appeal of this translation to him lay in "swabian accents and grammar-school latin constructions" (qtd. in Wannamaker 342). Robert Savage notes that Brecht kept many localisms from the Hölderlin despite the audience's potential unfamiliarity with them (114), and goes on to suggest that Brecht was attracted to "the earthy, vernacular quality" (115) of the translation, which makes it "practically an example of the V-Effect before the letter" (Ibid.). Brecht also broke the meter of Hölderlin's verse, thus creating complex and surprising rhythmic patterns.

Brecht's version of the play uses the strategy the Czech structuralists designated as topicalization (*aktualizace*) (whose commonalities and differences with Brecht's *Verfremdung* were pointed to in chapter 1). Brecht adapts the text for the contemporary context by adding a prologue set in Berlin in April 1945.[15] The prologue features two nameless sisters who find out that their brother has been hanged for deserting the army. As they prepare to cut the brother's body from the rope (an act that was punishable by instant execution [George Steiner, qtd. in Wannamaker 338]), an officer appears. After the sisters' deny that they know each other, the officer asks: "So what's she doing with the knife, her there?" (*Collected Plays* 7). At the end of the prologue, the first sister expresses uncertainty about the second sister's next act: "Should she on pain of death go now, / And free our brother who / May be dead or no?" (7). By rejecting a closure to the scene, Brecht diverts the focus from the narrative to the question of heroism—both of the second sister and of the heroine in the play proper. He confirms the implication carried by the prologue's final line, that the second sister is complicit in her brother's death, by a remark made elsewhere: "Antigone's deed can only consist in helping the enemy . . . , which is her moral contribution; she, too, has eaten all too long of the bread which was baked in the dark" (qtd. in Savage 103).

The prologue, more than the play proper, holds true to the point about narrating versus enacting in the revised version of the epic-versus-dramatic-theater schemata. Stylistically, the text abruptly switches from the one mode to the other, from a dialogue between the two characters to a recounting of the event to the audience. For instance, the first sister's line "I didn't want you scared" is followed by one that begins with "And as we sat there saying nothing" (*Collected Plays* 4). It should be noted, though, that an element equivalent to the described one is present already in Sophocles, and Greek drama in general: the chorus. Its commentaries on the action both "epically/dialectically" interrupt the flow of the narration and distance the viewer from it.

The play proper transforms the chorus into the elders financially benefitting from Kreon's war. Their first line in the adaptation is "But victory big in booty has come / And favored the numerous chariots of Thebes / And after the war / Now let there be a forgetting" (*Collected Plays* 12). It is the elders and their hunger for profit that Kreon identifies as the reason for the war: "When I went against Argos / Who was it sent me? Metal in the spears / Went after the metal in the mountains / At your bidding. For Argos / Is rich in metals" (43). Brecht diverts focus from Argos to its exploiter Thebes by making Polynices and Eteokles soldiers of the same, Kreon's army. After seeing his brother killed on the battlefield, Polynices runs away to the desert, where Kreon himself punishes him by death. The adaptation eliminates the relatively complex backstory, which results in a concentration of the viewer's attention to the mechanism that links capitalism, war, and tyranny, as embodied in Kreon.

Straub and Huillet eliminate the prologue, thus restoring the original's Aristotelian unities. The second distinctly theatrical element is the setting: *Antigone* was shot in the Teatro de Segesta, a Greek theater in Sicily from the fourth century B.C. The film's theatricality, however, stems less from the setting than the style of delivery and blocking—both bearing traces of the production's initial incarnation as a theater show staged at Berlin's Schaubühne in 1991. Characteristically, Straub and Huillet combine actors of varying degrees of experience and ability, casting in the role of Antigone and Ismene first-time actresses (respectively, Astrid and Ursula Ofner). The figures' movements and gestures are measured and used mostly for emphasis. For example, Kreon, when faced with Hamon's criticism of his rule, asserts his power by swinging his scepter as he dismisses his son's words on the account of his ignorance of the case, and raises his arms high in the air upon receiving the news of Megareus's death (see Figure 3.4a). The fact that the identical movements are made by other actors in other Straub and Huillet films (for example, in *Sicily!* [see Figure 3.4b]) indicates that the gesture is a creation of the filmmakers rather than the performers.

Figure 3.4a and b. Gestural acting in *Antigone* (Jean-Marie Straub and Danièle Huillet, Regina Ziegler / Pierre Grise / Straub-Huillet, 1991) and *Sicily!* (Jean-Marie Straub and Danièle Huillet, Straub-Huillet / Pierre Grise / CNC / Alia / Istituto Luce, 1999). Digital frame enlargement.

Another gesture that recurs throughout the film is the turning of the characters' heads to mark a new character's appearance. Among the instances, the elders perform the gesture upon Kreon's entrance, as does the king himself upon the entrance of a guard. The entrances usually occur offscreen. If this works to alleviate the theatricality of the mise-en-scène, the actors following the caesuras of Brecht's verse, pausing at the end of each line, produce an opposite effect. To realize the peculiarity of this directorial choice, it is useful to consider again the tradition of Shakespearean directors and actors in both theater and film, whose innovativeness is often measured by the new meanings they endow to the Bard's lines through unexpected emphases and pauses. Straub and Huillet deny this possibility to their actors. Their faithfulness to the meter as inscribed in the playtext functions—like the title—as another *Literarisierung* device. The intended result of the strategy is, as Walter Benjamin summarizes it, to "make what is shown on the stage unsensational" (*Understanding* 7).[16]

The dialogue often determines the pace of the cutting, too. The beginning and ending of a shot typically coincide with the beginning and ending, respectively, of the portion of the dialogue delivered by one or more characters. As Laurence Giavarini observes, when applied to quick exchanges, this logic works to enhance the effect of stychomitia, already created by the dialogue (qtd. in Byg, *Landscapes* 223). The earliest example of this kind occurs when Kreon asks for the elders' approval to leave Polyneikes unburied. Their reply—"We do approve it" (*Collected Plays* 14)—marks the beginning of a series of seven brief shots, in all but one of which the character(s) shown in the image speak a single sentence. The shot–reverse shot technique here employed is, of course, used also in continuity editing as a staple of Hollywood and other mainstream cinemas. But while a mainstream film would smooth the cuts through the use of sound bridges, *Antigone*—like *History Lessons*—rejects this essentially illusionistic device.

Carrying to an extreme the use of offscreen space in the instances where the film refrains from cutting for a relatively long period of time produces the same effect of drawing the viewer's attention to the cinematographic apparatus. For example, for the entire section of thirteen lines of the dialogue between Kreon and Antigone that starts with the former's question— "So you think others see it as you see it?" (21)—the camera holds Kreon in close-up. A little later, it privileges Antigone for the portion of dialogue that begins with her words to the elders, "So then you let it be and keep your mouths shut for him" (*Collected Plays* 22), which in the printed version occupy over two pages. Even more overt is the use of offscreen space in the portions of shots that feature no human figures. Like several other Straub and Huillet films, *Antigone* consistently uses such compositions. Namely, all of the film's four images devoid of human figures show a stone formation in the ground that seems to represent the boundary between the ancient theater's orchestra and skene spaces (see Figure 3.5). Second, the audio accompanying such images always consists of an ode of the elders. Third, they are introduced through a pan rather than a straight cut.

Accordingly, the pan, a movement equivalent to the aversion of the theater spectator's eyes from the dramatic spectacle, further enhances the "epic/dialectic" distantiating character of the chorus (aka the elders). The scene's literary application of the idea of estrangement appears to carry a trace of irony—an impression reinforced by Straub's view of *Verfremdung* as non-transferrable to film (Byg, *Landscapes* 224).

Relevant to the described stylistic device as the film uses it is also the original function of the stones in the ground. As mentioned, the line represents the boundary between the playing space of the orchestra and the skene, the place occupied during a performance by a temporary construction with double purpose: to represent the play's location, and

Figure 3.5. Architecture of ancient theater space in *Antigone* (Jean-Marie Straub and Danièle Huillet, Regina Ziegler / Pierre Grise / Straub-Huillet, 1992). Digital frame enlargement.

to serve as the changing room for the actors. By at once temporarily abandoning the transparency of the film's style and pointing to the dividing line between the space where the actors of the theater of Segesta appeared in character and the space where they were allowed to step out of it, the film invites the viewer to a meditation on the relationship between representation and presentation, between illusion and reality.

Byg remarks that "the camera [in *Antigone*] divides the theater into three views, somewhat more than 180 degrees" (227). The semi-circle it covers informs also the camera placement and movement in other Straub and Huillet films, including *Machorka-Muff* and *History Lessons*. In the former, the semi-circle is most prominent in the short scenes that show the protagonist walking the streets of Bonn before his rendezvous with Inniga. The pans, at first configured as point-of-view shots, end on Machorka-Muff, thus denying their initial status. Martin Walsh demonstrates the centrality of the circle for the framing of *History Lessons*, too. In the scene featuring the young man and the peasant, as well as in that featuring the former character and the banker, the camera performs a "twin circling" (75) of the characters (see Figure 3.6).

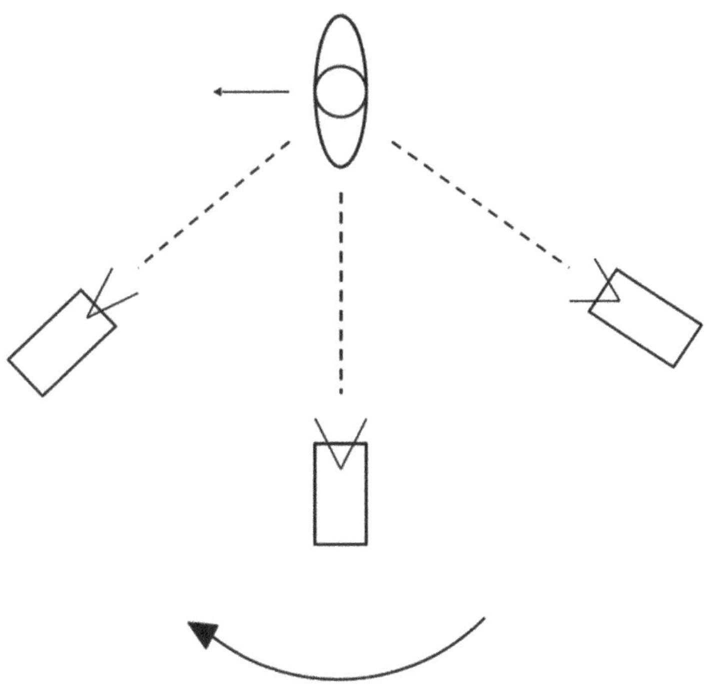

Figure 3.6. The pattern of camera movement in *History Lessons* (Jean-Marie Straub and Danièle Huillet, Janus / Straub-Huillet, 1972).

As Walsh observes, the camera as used in the two scenes is not supporting the dialogue but performing its own choreography of the profilmic event (75). If the shot-countershot syntax attempts to emulate the impression an observer gets when turning his head back and forth between two centers of attention, the reformulated version of the "syntax" Straub and Huillet use in *History Lessons* can be said to perform an opposite function. The singularity of perspective that shot-countershot ordinarily mimics is here replaced by a shifting, multiple, dialectical perspective (see Figure 3.7).

Antigone achieves its variety of angles and shot scales solely by the use of lenses with different focal lengths and horizontal movements around the axis. The many camera pans explore the diegetic space freely, while simultaneously keeping the taboo, as Byg observes, of the space where the camera stands (*Landscapes* 226). The camera's fixity invokes that of the viewer of traditional film and theater, consequently implicating them in the narrative. It is as if the theatrical fourth wall is crossed not by the actors—as was the case in Brecht's productions—but by the technological apparatus itself: the camera announces its presence by denying the spectator a view of its position within the setting.

Antigone is also linked to the anti-military world of *Machorka-Muff* and *History Lessons* thematically, as evidenced by Straub and Huillet's few additions to the textual base by Sophocles, Hölderlin, and Brecht.

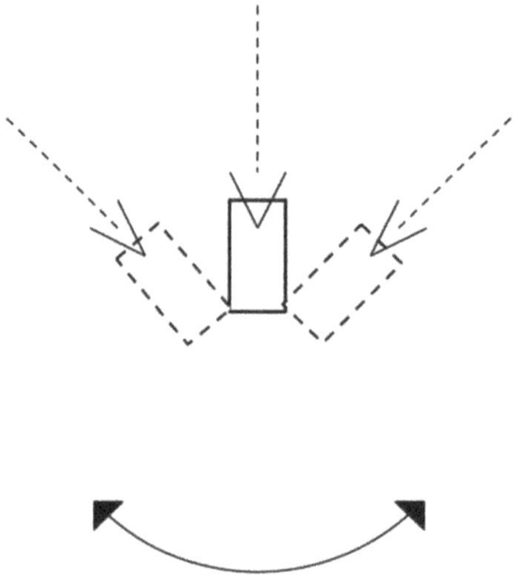

Figure 3.7. The pattern of camera movement in *Antigone* (Jean-Marie Straub and Danièle Huillet, Regina Ziegler / Pierre Grise / Straub-Huillet, 1992).

These include the collage of classical compositions that accompany the image of the Teatro de Segesta, and the 1952 pacifist and programmatic Brecht quotation that ends the film. "Mankind's memory of the endured suffering is astonishingly short," reads its beginning. "Its premonition of the suffering that is yet to come is even smaller. It is this apathy that we must fight." The sound of a helicopter that accompanies the image, combined with the most prominent part of the musical collage from the beginning—"The Ride of the Valkyries" from Richard Wagner's *Die Walküre*—produces an intertextual association to Francis Ford Coppola's *Apocalypse Now* (1979). In Coppola's film, the music theme can be heard as a squadron of helicopters is attacking a Vietnamese village.

As mentioned, Straub and Huillet's first feature was dedicated to Viet Cong workers, while the stage version of *Antigone* was dedicated to 100,000 Iraqi victims of George H.W. Bush's "New World Order." The two quotations themselves can serve as an index of the continuity of American imperialism. Commenting on the film, Byg brings up a different kind of continuity: that concerning the unification of Germany, another major political event that nearly coincided with the film's production. He rightly sees Straub and Huillet's *Antigone* as a response to the event, much like *Machorka-Muff* is a response to the rearmament of West Germany in the 1950s (*Landscapes* 231).

Straub and Huillet's minimalism, which in such films as *History Lessons* foregrounds the operations of both narrative and style, produces in *Antigone* a twofold impression of transparency and self-consciousness. As such, it merits at once Handke's comparison of the film's formal procedures with those of the cinemas of Howard Hawks and Raoul Walsh (Handke 118)—two eminent representatives of Hollywood's "invisible style"—and with avant-garde filmmakers such as Andy Warhol, whose films draw attention to their constructedness precisely through their reduction of artistic means.[17] *Antigone*'s experimentation with the emphatic use of recital, restrained figure movement, static camera, and shots of progressively long duration has been carried even further in more recent Straub and Huillet collaborations and the films Jean-Marie produced after Danièle's death. The identified combination of stylistic elements cues the ear to the spoken words and the other odd element of the soundscape such as the buzzing of insects and the babbling of water. Simultaneously, the eye is led to note the minute visual changes that occur during the course of the shots, such as the frequent shifts of natural lighting. As illustrated here in the frames from *The Witches* (see Figure 3.8), the mentioned phenomenon propels light as a theme in Straub and Huillet, thus exposing—in a characteristic manner—the questionability of the division between an artwork's content and form,

Figure 13.8a and b. Shifting natural lighting in *The Witches* (Jean-Marie Straub and Danièle Huillet, Pierre Grise / Straub-Huillet, 2009). Digital frame enlargement.

that is, narrative and style. To various degrees, the theme of light is relevant for both *Sicily!* and *Cézanne*.

Rebellion as a Conspicuous Non-Event: Sicily!

Sicily! is based on Elio Vittorini's novel *Conversazione in Sicilia* (Conversations in Sicily). Published in book form for the first time two years after its completion in 1939 under the title *Nome e lagrime* (Name and Tears), the censors withdrew the book from circulation. The edition published in 1942 in an altered version under the book's other, final title escaped the censors' attention and remained available throughout the Fascist reign. Already the fact of Vittorini's censorship problems within the historical and cultural context speaks about the writer's politics. While anti-fascist, they do not conform entirely to a Marxist program. In his study *Three Italian Novelists: Moravia, Pavese, Vittorini*, Donald Heiney describes the novelist's political position as twofold: revolutionary ("something is wrong with the world" and "something fundamental must change") and collectivist (the novelist attributes the sense of losing oneself in another to common human efforts) (153). Vittorini's belief in communion, for example, rests on a sentiment that also informs the doctrine of Fascism, but nowhere does he persuasively explain how his understanding of the notion differs from that of the politics to which he is antagonistic.

Diverging from an orthodox Communist platform, the novelist is similar to Brecht. Another point of similarity between them is their common interest in the musical aspect of language. The novel achieves the musicality of its prose largely through an unconventional use of punctuation,[18] as well as by frequent repetition and variation of phrases. Commentators have attributed the latter technique to American influences,[19] and especially to Ernest Hemingway, the author of the introduction for the English-language edition of *Conversazione, In Sicily* (1949). A remark Vittorini makes in a 1933 article, distinguishing "between two kinds of writers: those who make you think, 'Yes, that's the way it is,' and those who make you think, 'I had never supposed it could be like that,' and in this way suggest a new mode of experience, a new 'how' to existence" (152), brings Brecht to mind even more strongly.[20]

Brecht is as aesthetically and politically systematic as are the thinkers and artists with whom he engages in dialogue: from Aristotle to Wagner, from Hanns Johst (the writer of *Der Einsame* [The Lonely, 1917], the play on which *Baal* is based) to Samuel Beckett. As far as his implied theoretical position is concerned, Vittorini shows comparatively less rigor, hence the greater breadth (but also vagueness) of his classification of writers in terms of the reader's response. *Conversations in Sicily* is a tale of homecoming: the protagonist and narrator, Silvestro, who has for a long time been tormented by unidentified, "abstract furies" (Vittorini 13), receives a letter from his father stating that he left Silvestro's mother in Sicily for another woman. Answering the father's appeal to visit his mother, Silvestro ventures on a trip home, during which he engages in talks with other travelers. The topics of these conversations concern largely the islanders' cultural specificities, many of which the protagonist has forgotten during his decade-and-a half absence from Sicily. Two of these characters, Coi Baffi (Mustache) and Senza Baffi (No Mustache), express their scorn at the poor, stating that "every starving man is dangerous" (33), capable of stealing, murder, and perpetrating political crime. One can infer the characters to be police agents. Their anonymity and the tendency to finish each other's lines make them consonant with the literary tradition of deindividualized representatives of the state, of which most famous examples from the nineteenth and twentieth centuries are probably Dobchinsky and Bobchinsky from Gogol's *The Government Inspector* (1836) and the anonymous agents from Kafka's *Der Prozess* (The Trial, 1925).

The book's central part is occupied by Silvestro's reunion with his mother, Concezione, at the family house. During dinner with her, Silvestro inquires about a range of subjects, including the circumstances of his father's departure, her and other Sicilians' dietary habits, and the political and religious beliefs of his ancestors. Next, Silvestro accompanies his mother, a village nurse, in her daily visits to the sick and, often, the severely underprivileged. These scenes have an unexpected erotic undertone: the mother insists that Silvestro be present when her female patients receive injections from her, to see how "well-made" (158) they are. Having grown weary of accompanying his mother, Silvestro parts from her and meets a knife grinder, Calogero, who complains about not having much to grind in the village. Heiney notes the anti-fascist insinuation that Calogero's words carry (186) ("Ah, if only everyone always had a true blade!" [181], he exclaims at one point), strengthened by the reference to a firearm in the questions Calogero says he habitually asks the villagers: "What have you got for me to sharpen? Have you a sword? Have you a cannon?" (181). Heiney goes on to observe that an anti-fascist innuendo is made also by Ezechiele, a harness maker and the owner of an awl, whom Silvestro and Calogero subsequently visit. Ezechiele spends his days writing into a little notebook about "the terrible outrages against humanity and the world" (213). A scene at Porfirio's, a clothier who owns half a pair of scissors, follows a conversation between the three men. Together, they go to a tavern, where all those present except Silvestro get intoxicated on wine. The near-hallucinatory atmosphere created through the scattered polylogue in the tavern prepares the ground for the scene that follows, unique in its possession of magical touch. In the scene, Silvestro meets and has a conversation with the ghost of his brother Liborio, who has been killed in the war. Finally, the last scene features the mother and a crying old man hiding his face with his hand: Silvestro's father. To her question: "Don't you want to greet him?" Silvestro replies that he will greet him another time (255) and silently leaves the house.

The film does not incorporate any of the material contained in the nondialogue parts of the novel, including Silvestro's confession on the abstract furies that haunted him the winter when the narrative takes place, and their identification twenty-five chapters later as a knowledge of "profound miseries of the working class" (139). More importantly, the film eliminates the series of scenes that carry the themes of eroticism, religion, and the supernatural. As a result, the novel's symmetry (formed by the father's letter in chapter 2 on the one hand, and its writer's appearance in the epilogue) is lost. *Sicily!* is thus as open-ended as the group of Straub and Huillet films based on unfinished literary works or musical compositions. The film's narrowing of the original narrative's spatial and temporal scope adds emphasis to the characters in the included episodes, thereby bringing it closer to the Aristotelian ideal of unities of space and time.[21] But neither the novel nor the film aims at unity of action. In both, we witness the narrative's inhabitants in stasis of political biases or poverty, which gradually comes to be associated with the Fascist rule. Deprived of agency, they spend their time in alcohol-fueled conversations, their subjects varying from historical to erotic, from culinary to philosophical. When the scenes are categorized on the criterion of their primary thematic concern, a tripartite structure evocative of *Kuhle Wampe* becomes apparent.

The first part shows Silvestro's travel to Sicily and his different encounters with the locals, while the subsequent two parts show the protagonist in conversation with his mother and Calogero, respectively. The political dimension of the narrative, introduced already in the expository scenes through the characters of Mustache and No Mustache, becomes prominent in the scenes where the mother speaks of her grandfather as a Socialist who believed in St. Joseph (81). When Silvestro observes that the two positions are incongruous, Concezione makes a series of vague remarks suggesting that the grandfather's religious belief diverted from the official Church doctrine, and goes on to contradict herself repeatedly: she first says "that when the man fell ill it meant the end," and then "that when the woman fell ill it meant the end" (134); at one point, she declares that "it was better to have a touch of malaria than a touch of consumption," and at another, that "a touch of consumption was better than a touch of malaria" (134–35). The film, likewise, localizes and concentrates the theme of contradiction in Concezione's character. In the scene with Calogero, the narrative's political aspect culminates with the above-discussed innuendos of a nascent militancy of the impoverished. But the film's stylistic operations do not reflect that theme in the direct manner of late-1960s Godard and the other political modernists who opposed mainstream cinema's principle of pleasure. Instead, *Sicily!* points to the repressive circumstances of the novel's publication through adopting the oblique politics of the literary work. As many other Straub and Huillet films, then, *Sicily!* historicizes through intertextuality, the history hinted at being that of Vittorini's novel. In this respect, too, *Sicily!* resembles the group of Straub and Huillet films based on unfinished artworks, which likewise invite the viewer to speculate on the alternatives to their present form: *Moses and Aaron*, *Death of Empedocles*, and *Class Relations* on their missing endings, and *Sicily!* on how the narrative and style of *Conversations in Sicily* would be influenced by a set of sociohistorical circumstances different from those of Italian Fascism.

Uncharacteristic of Straub and Huillet in general, the humor in *Sicily!* is unique in the context of their cinema. *Antigone* incites it by the use of actors of limited skills (for example, Werner Rehm, who has been described as "hammy" and "provincial" [Schmierenschauspieler]) (Winfried Günther, qtd. in Byg, *Landscapes* 222), while some other films produce humor by a peculiar combination of the performances and other stylistic elements (for example, the standing in silence of Klaus Traube, the captain in *Class Relations*, while the anthem of the United States of America is resounding from a source unidentified by the narrative). The humor of *Sicily!*, in contrast, results from the actors' physical appearance (the bulging eyes of Giovanni Interlandi, the Catanian in the novel and the mustached passenger in the film), as well as the comedic acting style that certain scenes employ (for instance, the broad gesturing of the actor playing the part of Calogero). In spite of these examples, the performances—like those in the montage-based Straub and Huillet films discussed previously—center predominantly on the aural, rather than visual, aspect of the screen adaptation. But whereas the delivery in early films is "cinematically small," such films as *Sicily!* and *Antigone* "theatrically heighten" it. In impressionistic terms, while the actors in *Machorka-Muff* and *History Lessons* are acting for the camera, in the later films they are performing for the imaginary spectator in the last row.

In terms of its visuals, *Sicily!* belongs to the group of black and white films Straub and Huillet have made since 1982 (together with *En Rachâchant* [1982], *Class Relations*, and *From Today Till Tomorrow*), after making eight consecutive films in color. The absence of color from *Sicily!*

provides additional emphasis to the placement of figures and objects within the frame. In terms of shot composition, *Sicily!* is redolent of the filmmakers' most ambitious work from the first phase, *Chronicle of Anna Magdalena Bach*. Certain shots in both films achieve a compositional balance by treating human figures (ordinarily privileged as a presumed center of the viewer's attention) as even with other, narratively inconsequential elements of the frame. The high-angle image of *Chronicle*'s title character at a window exemplifies this strategy: in terms of both its light value and relative size within the frame, the figure of Mrs. Bach is comparable to the window (see Figure 3.9). The parallel lines of the bottom line of the window frame, the top line of the armchair, and Mrs. Bach's neck and shoulder enhance the geometric similarity between the two surfaces, in addition to diagonally dividing the frame in two. The composition deviates from the norm of mainstream cinema whereby a character should be set off-center toward the direction opposite the one they are looking at offscreen, leading Ursula Böser to describe the composition as "emphatically decentred" (37).

Figure 3.9. Decentered composition in *Chronicle of Anna Magdalena Bach* (Jean-Marie Straub and Danièle Huillet, Franz Seitz / Neue Filmkunst Walter Kirchner / Hessicher Rundfunk, 1968). Digital frame enlargement.

Sicily! offers similar examples. Two consecutive shots from the film's middle part feature unemphasized but meticulous shot symmetry. The first shot is a medium-scale image of Silvestro, leaned against the table on his fist and occupying the frame's bottom left part (see Figure 3.10a). The diagonal of the upper line of the door frame in the background complements the opposite one of Silvestro's shoulder. Likewise, the diagonal lines of the table are complemented by the opposite ones of the cabinet in the bottom right part of the frame. The next shot, also in a medium scale, shows Concezione with one arm akimbo, looking offscreen toward the right side of the frame (see Figure 3.10b). The figure and the line where the walls behind it join form a vertical symmetry; the axis of symmetry falls right between the two. The diagonal symmetry is achieved through a predominantly black mantelpiece on the wall at the upper left edge of the frame and the black bottle at its bottom, close to the right corner. Concezione's black shirt, the visual dominant of the frame's central area, strengthens the effect.

The unorthodoxy of the described procedure is, like that concerning the film's editing patterns, subtle. As do many other Straub and Huillet films, *Sicily!* uses slow panoramic shots of landscapes devoid of human figures. The first two of these occur between the sequence of traveling scenes and the scene with Concezione. The camera pans right, across the hills with vineyards and a town in the far background, to a road with a living fence and white tombstones behind it. No sooner than the movement ends does the camera start panning again in the opposite direction, to finally stop in the middle phase of its trajectory, with the vineyards and the town occupying the frame. Next, the camera performs the same two movements with an unchanged speed, shot scale, angle, and—most importantly—subject. The only readily perceptible difference between the two consecutive shots concerns the lighting: its intensity and the shadows cast by the objects within the frame reveal the shot to have been photographed at an earlier time of the day than the previous one. Like the absence of sound from the traveling shot that precedes the described two, the described reverse of chronology is narratively unjustified. The two examples represent the film's rare metafilmic moves.

The film departs from the norms of continuity editing also in its use of black screen in the scene with Concezione, none of which exceeds a fraction of a second. The brevity of black screens in *Sicily!* makes them less conspicuous than those employed in earlier, montage-based Straub and Huillet films, such as *History Lessons* and *An Introduction*. Here, the black screens differ also in terms of function: they merely emphasize the pauses between the characters' exchanges (which average ten seconds in length), while in the earlier films they typically serve as a source of pauses. *Sicily!*, therefore, relies more heavily on the performances as

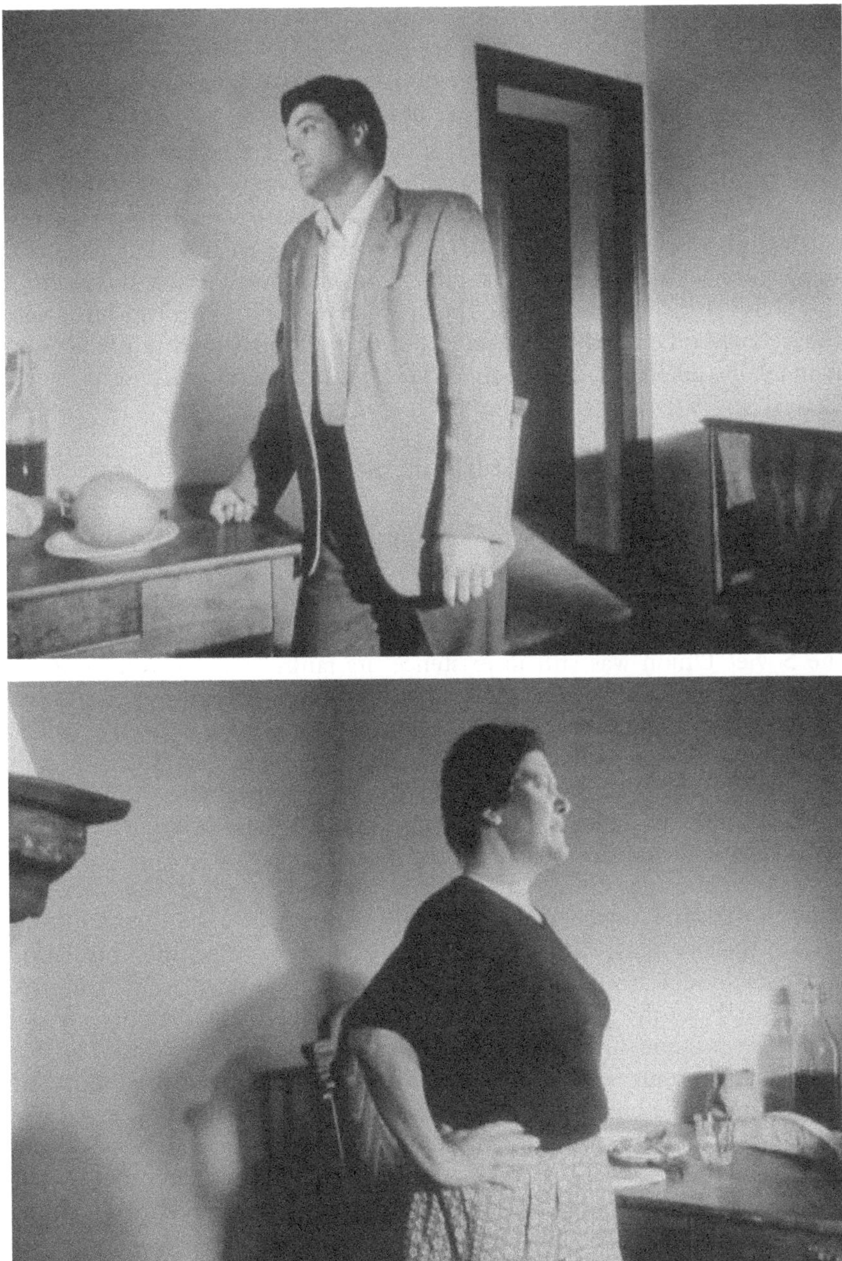

Figure 3.10a and b. Unemphasized frame symmetry in *Sicily!* (Jean-Marie Straub and Danièle Huillet, Straub-Huillet / Pierre Grise / CNC, 1999). Digital frame enlargement.

agents of the film's rhythm and tempo than Straub and Huillet's earlier works.

The Brechtian overtones of *Sicily!* are more delicate than those of the other three Straub and Huillet films analyzed earlier. Unlike *History Lessons* and *Machorka-Muff*, *Sicily!* is not based on a text of Brecht's, nor does it refer to him through the filmmakers' commentaries. Moreover, the film concerns itself with the theme of fascism—which informs much of Brecht's work—only indirectly: fascism appears to affect the character in a manner not unique to the regime. This may be precisely the point: if the obliqueness with which the theme was treated by Vittorini was a way to circumvent censorship, the relevance of the film's similarly roundabout manner lies in the gap between Western fascism until the end of World War II and that of today.

Cézanne: Self-Portrait in Absentia

If the 1980s saw a crisis of political modernism, the 1990s can be said to have marked the demise of the aesthetic trend. At the time when D. N. Rodowick was formulating the diagnosis for the leftist-oriented film practice and theory committed to alternative modes of representation, the Soviet Union was still in existence, its tanks placed throughout the Eastern Bloc. By 1990, the year when Straub and Huillet released their *Cézanne*, the country that for most of the century symbolized communism in the West had dissolved. To what extent does *Cézanne* and its later counterpart, *A Visit to the Louvre* (2003), resonate with the described cultural moment, and the contemporary work of film practitioners once associated with political modernism?

A laconic answer of "none at all" would be analytically useless, albeit not entirely inaccurate, as perhaps suggested by the thematic concern of the two films with an artist who spent most of his life in isolation and detachment from politics. But we must be immediately reminded of a fact that runs counter to the possible conclusion that Straub and Huillet's Cézanne films are less political than the other works by the filmmakers. Straub and Huillet never fit Rodowick's category as neatly as, for instance, Godard in the late 1960s and the following decade. While they tirelessly proclaimed their politics as radical in interviews and the intertextual references that pervade their cinema, they never represented the activities of partisan political groups as directly and timely as did Godard in such films as *La chinoise* (The Chinese Woman, 1967) or *Sympathy for the Devil* (1969) (focusing, respectively, on the Maoist movement in France and the Black Panther Party at the times when the international influence of the two entities was at its zenith). With a risk of oversimplification, the fact that Straub and Huillet have maintained a distance equally from the common model of cinematic representation and political activity in the usual meaning of the term can be singled out as a key difference between them and Godard as a paradigmatic political modernist.[22]

But the project that Godard was working on at the time of *Cézanne*'s production is comparable in key respects to Straub and Huillet's film: the first installments of the *Histoire(s) du cinéma* (Histories of Cinema, 1988–1998), a series of video essays that explore the relationship between film, political, and history of ideas. Using the unique capabilities of electronic editing such as the video mixer and processor, *Histoire(s)* predicate themselves on a wide array of visual and verbal quotes, anchored by Godard's voiceover and recurrent superimposed images of the filmmaker typing and leafing through books.

Histoire(s) are not the first of Godard's works that feature his image and voice. As early as 1963, he appeared as an assistant director in *Le mépris* (1963) and as his directorial self in a segment of the Chris Marker–produced documentary *Loin du Viêt-nam* (Far from Vietnam; S.L.O.N., 1967). Yet the frequency and nature of Godard's performances changed noticeably during the period in question. Both of the roles he assigned to himself in his two films released in 1987 (*Soigne ta droite* [Keep Your Right Up] and *King Lear*), for instance, are removed from his other capacities in the productions as the writer and director. He is a loopy "monsieur Godard" in the former film, while in *King Lear* he plays the role of a pseudo-Shakespearean fool. In both cases, his flamboyancy is in certain moments comparable to that of Marcello Mastroianni and Jean-Pierre Leaud as the occasional alter-egos of, respectively, Federico Fellini and François Truffaut.

In the works of the 1980s and 1990s, Godard was no longer depicted as merely the master of the cinematographic apparatus (as is the case in *Contempt* and *Far from Vietnam*, which associate him with it through such props as a slate and a movie camera), but as the owner of a worldview transferable to media other than film. Without implying an influence on Straub and Huillet of Godard's contemporary ventures into forms of film and videomaking roughly analogous to autobiographies, programmatic statements, and journals, *Cézanne* allows itself to be fruitfully read in a similar key: as a self-portrait of the filmmakers at the pinnacle of their creative development.

Postdating such eminently theatrical Straub and Huillet films as *The Death of Empedocles* and *Black Sin*, and relying on extremely heterogeneous material—and therefore on montage—*Cézanne* hardly supports this book's guiding thesis. But the film's intertextual links with the adaptations of Hölderlin's mourning play, and the voiceover's theatrical delivery (connecting it to a range of other Straub and Huillet titles, from *Othon* to recent shorts), make *Cézanne* illustrative of Brechtian cinema's trend toward stage-like stylization.

The dialogues on which the films are based derive from the "Ce qu'il m'a dit" ("What He Told Me") section of Joachim Gasquet's *Cézanne* (1921, 1926), which features the writer's three conversations with the painter, each of them focusing on subjects informed to a varying extent by the locale where the given dialogue took place: the countryside of Aix-en-Provence, the Louvre, and Cézanne's studio. In both films, Straub and Huillet read abbreviated versions of the text in voiceover: she, the lines of the painter, and Straub, those of his interlocutor. *Cézanne*'s imagery consists of shots of Aix-en-Provence and Mt. Sainte-Victoire as one of the artist's favorite motifs, a shot of the gate of his Parisian studio, exterior photographs of him at work on a canvas, a small selection of his paintings filmed in the museums in London, Paris, and Edinburgh, two unused segments of *The Death of Empedocles*, and a sequence from Jean Renoir's *Madame Bovary* (1934). The ambiguity of spatial relations among the profilmic events in Straub and Huillet's films and the ideational associations they promote have inspired a range of corresponding critical metaphors: from Straub's own description of *Not Reconciled* as lacunary (Roud 41)—later echoed by Gilberto Perez (324) and Gilles Deleuze (234)—to Maureen Turim's "oblique angles" ("Jean-Marie"); from Dominique Païni's "archipelago of images" (n.p.) to Claudia Pummer's "ruin-image." But no other title in Straub and Huillet's body of work exemplifies as well as *Cézanne* the fragmentary nature of their films.

Instead of extending the above list of metaphors and emphasizing how the film's elements complicate interpretation, the following few pages will focus on the procedure whereby *Cézanne's* elements narrow the horizon of possible interpretations, and contribute to the film's formal cohesion. They do so mainly through their intertextual cues, in a manner not unlike that of Godard's *Histoire(s)*. Whereas an in-depth investigation of the latter work's extraordinarily dense imagescapes and soundscapes would require the space of an entire volume, several paragraphs should suffice to identify the links between the seemingly disparate segments of Straub and Huillet's structurally uncomplicated film. Most of the following observations concern the first three quarters of the film, which include both groups of the material without a direct relation to the space and time that the painter inhabited: the *Empedocles* and *Bovary* clips.

A detailed description of the film's indicated segment appears in order. Like a number of other Straub and Huillet's films, *Cézanne* opens with a panoramic shot. At first showing a characteristically unassuming part of a space the viewer will later infer to belong to Aix-en-Provence—a road with mountaintops in the background—the camera swivels leftward to reveal a line of trees before stopping at an image that makes literal the boundary between nature and architecture. Behind a shadowy lawn, one sees buildings and parts of the road. The left-right pan in the next shot, photographed with a lens of smaller focal length, complements the first camera movement. The shot's end composition is reminiscent of many Cézanne's paintings, with the previously seen Mt. Sainte-Victoire in the background of the road, occupying the upper-left section of the frame.

The ambience noise recedes when the film cuts to a photograph of Cézanne looking off-frame as he stands before an easel. Like the paintings in both films concerning the artist, and the still images used elsewhere in Straub and Huillet's cinema, the photograph is not recomposed so as to fit the screen's horizontal dimensions. Neither is the background of the image neutral in terms of color. Instead, the shot uses a reddish hue similar to that one encounters in *Joachim Gatti* (Straub 2009). The transition triggers the voiceover, which roughly corresponds to the beginning of the first conversation in the book. The first lines that we hear are Cézanne's: "That's what you have to attain. If I go too high or too low, all is lost. There must not be even one loose stitch, a gap where emotion, light, and truth can escape" (Gasquet 110).

Nearly four minutes in duration, the shot precedes the approximately one-minute shot of Cézanne's *Vielle au chapelet* (Old Woman with a Rosary). The transition to the image of the painting is motivated by the artist's reference to the painting in relation to "a tone of Flaubert, an atmosphere, something indefinable, a bluish and russet color which emanated, it seemed to [him], from *Madame Bovary*" (Gasquet 112). The painter goes on to recount how his unconscious recollection of the novel's description of a servant in terms of the two colors influenced his perception of the model for *Vielle au chapelet*, whose face and clothes—as he came to retrospectively realize—actually had different hues.

Next, the film transitions to an approximately seven-minute sequence from Renoir's film, which includes the agricultural fair scene, the introduction of Emma and Rodolphe to each other (see Figure 3.11), and his first advancements toward her. The voiceover continues a few sentences after the point where it left off in the book, accompanied by a photographed image of Mt. Saint Victoire, now occupying a central position in the frame and a large part of its surface (see Figure 3.12). Cézanne is heard declaring that the liberated brain of the artist should be like a photographic plate, and rhetorically asking who will paint "the

Figure 3.11. Intertextual borrowing in *Cézanne* (Jean-Marie Straub and Danièle Huillet, Le Musée d'Orsay / La Sept / Diagonale, 1989). Digital frame enlargement.

accident of the sun's rays, the sun's movement, its penetration, . . . the incarnation of the sun across the world" and "the psychology of the earth," "the atmosphere in which we live our lives" (Gasquet 113).

The film then cuts to the deleted scene from *Empedocles*. Featuring the titular character and Pausanias, the approximately four-and-a-half-minute insert matches lines 369–423 of the play, which consist of Empedocles' monologue, interrupted only by a three-word Pausanias utterance. The monologue's speaker laments his imminent death and makes repeated references to the notions prominent in the conversation with Cézanne heard in the segment of the film immediately preceding this: life and living (ll. 412 and 415, respectively), nature (l. 409), mount (Olympus) and mountain heights (ll. 419 and 398, respectively), light (ll. 369, 381, and 416), color (l. 382), sky and heaven (ll. 369 and 380, respectively), and earth (ll. 385, 383, 394, 416).

The next transition brings the viewer back to the sight of the mountain, also mentioned in the voiceover, a direct continuation of the previous segment of the conversation with the painter. Among Cézanne's

Figure 3.12. Photographically representing the object of painterly representation: *Cézanne* (Jean-Marie Straub and Danièle Huillet, Le Musée d'Orsay / La sept, Diagonale, 1989). Digital frame enlargement.

other programmatic statements and poetic observations, we hear that "these boulders were made of fire" and "that there is still fire in them" (Gasquet 113). The textual affinity between the painter's words in this segment and those of Empedocles in the previous one stems mainly from the references in both to deities. The former, "For love expires as soon as gods have flown," is made conspicuous by being the last line heard in the segment (even though the monologue in the play does not end with it). Much of this part of the text, too, centers on the difference between one's visual perception of a shape and its actual physical properties. This time around, the focus falls on shapes rather than on colors: Cézanne relates that, before learning "how to see," he was under the impression that the mountain's shadows were concave, while they are in actuality convex.

A pan right to a line of trees similar in number and relative size to those seen previously concludes the four-minute shot, followed by three photographs of Cézanne with more of the painter's exchanges with Gasquet, spanning some six minutes. The first of those is a repeat of the one shown earlier, from which the third photograph barely differs in terms of camera angle. The middle one shows the painter posing for the lens in a somewhat different exterior setting and is dated "Aix 1904." This segment of the film features larger excisions of Gasquet's text, the general logic of which is commented upon below. As in the case of the previous transition to a scene from *Empedocles*, the painter's references to earth gain emphasis by being placed at the end of the sequence. "Stroke by stroke the earth comes alive again. Through my work, a beautiful landscape will grow in my field" (Gasquet 121) are the last words we hear before the film cuts to a long shot of birch trees beneath mountain tops in haze and clouds.

The film has thus established connections between all five groups of images it has employed by this point, the mountains of Sicily—where the play and the screen adaptations are set—figuring as a visual variant of the Mt. Saint Victoire. Delivered offscreen and corresponding to lines 1503–1581 of the play, the text is both structurally and lexically similar to that heard in the previously used, deleted scene from the screen adaptation. Empedocles speaks the entire text save for a short Pausanias exclamation, and "earth" and an array of words related to nature, gods, life versus death, and the four elements permeate the monologue. "Nature" is mentioned in lines 1510, 1531, and 1574; 1508 refers to "ancient gods," 1510 to "godliness," and 1581 to "the goodly gods"; 1516, 1529, 1544, 1554, and 1569 mention "life" and 1571 mentions "living beauty"; 1510 refers to "light of heaven"; 1519 "glisten[ing]," 1549 "glowing," 1552 "sun god," 1555 "rays," 1562 "morning light," 1511 "flame," and 1556 "splendid things," "The wind" is mentioned in 1515 and in 1559 "the ether." Different forms of water are referred to in 1520 ("seas"), 1546/1547 ("the fount will flow"), 1548 ("the stream"), and 1549 ("the father ocean"), the last one a variation of the phrase "father ether," heard in the previous *Empedocles* insert and found in line 418 of the play. This monologue adds vision to the range of the film's themes (the word "eyes" is used three times: lines 1510, 1522, and 1562), the significance of which is addressed below.

Consisting of long sequences and unconcerned with suggesting causal relationships between its events, *Cézanne* invites the viewer to construct a meaning for it by seeking ideational matches not only at the junctures of its individual segments—as does, for instance, the scene from *October* this book repeatedly uses as an example—but also across them, as well as among major facts about the historical figures and fictional characters on which the film focuses. This strategy merits Païni's use of the metaphor of the "archipelago" to describe the film's organizational pattern: the film consists of islands of visual and aural elements that simultaneously gravitate toward each other and assert their relative independence. Sally Shafto, in her reading of the film, delineates one example of Straub and Huillet's use of the described strategy: while the transition from the photograph of the artist to "Old Woman with a Rosary" coincides with the reference to the painting in the voiceover, more than five minutes of *Madame Bovary* separate the shot's end point from the appearance in Renoir's film of a visually similar character. To borrow the vocabulary of chemistry Cézanne himself figuratively uses in the book, the two elements form a weak, albeit indisputable, valence-bond.

But the strong resemblance between the woman portrayed on Cézanne's canvas and that in *Bovary* surely cannot be the sole reason the film includes the long sequence. Extratextual information about the novel and its screen adaptation can help illuminate the motivation for that structural choice. First, Cézanne and Flaubert—besides being compatriots and contemporaries—occupy a similar place in the history of art as precursors of modernism. The painter was claimed as an influence by different avant-garde movements, most notably cubism and fauvism. Similarly, an array of critics have noted in Flaubert stylistic elements that qualify his prose as proto-modernist. For example, in his seminal essay "Flaubert's Silences," Gérard Genette notes the novelist's refusal to subordinate the style of descriptions in *Bovary* to the logic of character subjectivity that is called for by verisimilitude as the genre's contemporary norm (187). Along the same lines, he observes the novel's suspension of narrative movement (193), resulting in equal parts from its use of "gratuitous and insignificant detail" (198) and the motif of silence that runs throughout the narrative, interrupting dialogue and action (195). All of these features of *Bovary* and other Flaubert fictional works, claims Genette, assert the writer's presence in the texts and his authorial voice. As a consequence, the novel is de-dramatized, a quality Genette sees as marking the beginning of modern literature (199). This conclusion has a particular resonance in the context of Straub and Huillet's cinema, where the narrative is often reduced to its barest minimum, the position of formal centrality held in its stead by the meticulously composed and illuminated imagery, the poetry of the text employed, and the music of its delivery. (The *Empedocles* film, as a drama of stasis whose verse is recited in an overarticulate manner, is no exception to the described tendency.)

While the mentioned commonality of Cézanne and Flaubert alone does not adequately recommend them as counterparts for the filmmakers themselves, the attitude toward modernity they all share does. Contrary to what one might expect from someone who helped inspire the rebellion against mimesis, verisimilitude, and realism that took place in the arts between the late 1900s and late 1920s, Cézanne explains his ultimate artistic goal in terms tantamount to the three mentioned ones. In the conversation with Gasquet upon which the film is based, the painter declares that he enjoys transposing colors on his canvas the way he sees them (117), proclaims copying to be "the only thing there is" (125, 126), and likens the canvas, the artist's brain, and himself with a photographic plate (111, 113, 115).

Equally ambiguous is Flaubert's attitude toward the narrative and stylistic unorthodoxies in his fiction, which made the *nouveau roman* authors identify themselves as the writer's descendants a whole century after the appearance of *Bovary*.[23] Genette reports how Flaubert complied with docility to the requests by Louis Brouilhet, the novel's editor, to eliminate "parasitical sentences" and "hors d'ouevre that slowed up the action" (Maxime du Camp, qtd. in Genette 193). One result of such interventions is the paring down to a single page of a description of a toy that originally spanned a tenfold space. Straub and Huillet were similarly reserved about their position as avant-gardists of political cinema: one of their aforementioned self-descriptions reads as an almost verbatim quote of Cézanne's reference to himself as "the primitive of [his] own way" (Gasquet 111). But while the filmmakers have aligned themselves stylistically with the practitioners working in the pioneering phases of both the medium's silent and sound periods, their scripts have drawn on an eclectic array of sources, including those by the writers as diverse as Stéphane Mallarmé (*Toute révolution est un coup de dés*; Every Revolution Is a Throw of the Dice, 1977) and Mahmoud Houssein (*Trop tot, trop tard*; Too Early, Too Late, 1981). A large percentage of those texts are of neoclassical variety: from *Othon* to two different versions of Hölderlin's *The Death of Empedocles* and his translation of *Antigone* as adapted by Brecht. Perhaps no other contemporary filmmakers have maintained a relationship with literary classicism as persistent, if also tenuous, as have Straub and Huillet. As demonstrated in the discussion of *Antigone*, this relationship manifests itself equally at the levels of narrative and style (even though the latter fact runs counter to the filmmakers' associating themselves with such practitioners as the Lumière brothers, who—producing films prior to the invention of "film language"—were not encumbered by its legacy).

While classicism and realism should by no means be conflated, the two notions have been understood as overlapping in the context of film studies. The status of Jean Renoir as a foremost representative of the strain of cinematic realism known as poetic may have directed the choice of his screen adaptation of *Bovary* as a source of the extended quotation over the other three that were available at the time of the production of *Cézanne*. A criterion perhaps more important in governing the decision to use the 1934 adaptation of Flaubert's novel is its status as a film marred by the producer and therefore partially lost. The original cut, as Dudley Andrew reports, was more than four hours long, and among the viewers who enthusiastically received it was none other than Brecht (*Mists* 283). The extant cut, more than two times shorter, is then comparable to the other artworks that Straub and Huillet's film draws on: Hölderlin completed neither of the versions of the *Empedocles* play that the filmmakers adapted for the screen; Flaubert deleted a great number of pages from *Bovary*; Cézanne left many of his paintings unfinished.

Cézanne, then, presents us with fragments, whose status as such is accentuated by the film's collage structure. The many hands that have contributed to the film's elements elaborate the question of the film's authorship, raised already by the collaborative nature of Straub and Huillet's work. If, for example, the novel *Madame Bovary* as we know it has resulted from the projection of its editor's vision onto the original text, and if the screen adaptation quoted by *Cézanne* is the result of the projection on the novel of Renoir's vision, then Straub and Huillet's film can be said to dispel the notion of the author as a singular creative force, which proliferated in the modernist epoch. Yet this does not make the filmmakers postmodern artists that Ihab Hassan would call selfless—the concept that, as we shall see, is crucial for Lars von Trier's understanding of authorship—but rather as premodern artisans, whose reluctance to refract the real through their individuality evidences itself also by Cézanne when he cites "[copying] exactly what [one] sees" (Gasquet 127) as an aspiration.

The realism that informs the quote constitutes, for Barton Byg, one side of the dichotomy that Straub and Huillet aim to reconcile. The other one is modernism, epitomized by the filmmakers' "calling attention to the artificial devices by which film constructs meaning" (*Landscapes* 27). Representation, of course, inevitably entails distortion: in the case of Cézanne, that of his unique sensory apparatus as it processes the visual stimuli and the "translation" of the thereby-obtained mental image of objects into brushstrokes on a two-dimensional surface. Significantly, a segment of the first conversation with Gasquet not included in the film has Cézanne complaining about his eyes: "I see planes overlapping. . . . Straight lines look like they are falling sometimes" (Gasquet 118). Is the statement to be interpreted as a proof of the painter's deteriorating sight, or a description of what Boris V. Rauschenbach calls perceptual perspective?[24] Significantly, this commentator uses Cézanne's landscapes as examples roughly illustrating the alternative to linear perspective. But whereas perceptual perspective has greater accuracy than the other kind, it is vulnerable to distortions, too.[25] *Cézanne* compounds those with the distortions inherent to photographic representation (by Henri Alekan, a "master" of visual expression in his own right), concerning the choice of intensity, direction, and color of the lights illuminating the paintings, the relative size of the paintings within the film frame, and the various properties of the stock. If Straub and Huillet's cinema explodes the unity of the author, as Byg claims (*Landscapes* 27), then *Cézanne* supremely exemplifies this effect, the multiple visions put forward by the film making the question of who owns the true, accurate one all the more acute. The status of "What He Told Me" as a major problem in Cézanne studies, because the text "[combines] the authentic with the speculative" (Doran 107), only further complicates this matter.

The notion of vision in a literal sense is central also for another key element of the film's intertextual nexus: the *Empedocles* inserts. The hero of the film and the play lived approximately between 490 and 430 B.C. in Agrigentum in Sicily and was a well-known poet, thinker, and statesman. Besides the aforementioned four elements (or "roots," as he called them), his main concepts were the binaries of love (*philia*) and strife (*neikos*) as the world's major powers that determine the dynamics of the elements: alternately, love brings them into union whereas strife separates them. But more important here is the fact that Empedocles authored the first exhaustive theory of light and vision. According to the theory, we see by virtue of light emanating from both the eyes and the object observed (Zemplén 34). The theory reads as a metaphor for the principles of representation by Straub and Huillet as described by Byg: a simultaneous foregrounding of the artifice and "invoking its immediate relations to the reality of the world" (*Landscapes* 27).

The hubris of Empedocles as portrayed by Hölderlin is the hero's equation of himself with gods, a deed paralleled by Gasquet's Cézanne himself. At a point in the film following the ones described above, the painter announces his wish to lose himself in nature, where "green would flow through [his] entire brain like the sap of the tree" (Gasquet 126). Having made a remark that resonates with the line "the earth's green will shine again for you" heard in the second *Empedocles* clip, Cézanne goes on to state the following: "There, before us, a great being of light and love, the flickering universe, the hesitation of things. I will be their Olympus, I will be their god" (Gasquet 126). The film, however, omits the latter two sentences, thereby avoiding the making of too strong a "valence bond" between the film's two neighboring segments and keeping the affinities among its various segments evenly distributed.

But upon a close extra-textual analysis, the deleted text confirms its importance as a conspicuous absence, as do the endings of the narratives about Empedocles and Emma. Examined together, they reveal an analogy: both characters have performed a moral transgression that is redeemable only by death. In light of this connection, Cézanne's words that conclude "What He Told Me"—"I want to die painting . . . to die painting" (Gasquet 160)—read as an expression of destiny too. When considered in relation to the theme of death, which connects all three of the film's sources, and to the filmmakers commonly associated with Brecht, this statement—which Straub and Huillet have often quoted in their interviews (Païni: n.p.)—brings to mind Brecht's parable "Üben den Flüss der Dinge" (On the Flow of Things). The text's opening lines are as follows: "And I saw also that nothing was quite dead, also not the thing that had died. The dead stones breathe. They change themselves and instigate changes. The moon itself, declared dead, moves. It casts light, even if it is alien, on the earth and determines the course of falling bodies and causes the ebb and flow of the ocean. And if it would only shock the one who sees it, yes if only one would see it, it would thus not be dead, but would live" (qtd. in Oesmann 30–31). Brecht's words read as a variation of "All that is solid melts into air" from *The Communist Manifesto*, and are indeed often used by commentators to metaphorically convey the idea of dialectical materialism in a manner similar to that of Marx and Engels (perhaps most notably by Fredric Jameson in *Brecht and Method*).

Straub and Huillet's dialectic resides in the intertextuality of their films (and particularly in *Cézanne*), as Dominique Païni notes (n.p.). In her own reading, the example of Hölderlin and Empedocles—the latter of whom famously added earth to the already existing triad of basic elements—represents an answer to the question Cézanne rhetorically asks in a conversation with Gasquet: who will paint "the psychology of the earth." By using Hölderlin and Empedocles as the answers to the questions asked by an artist from a different culture, and from an epoch that postdates his own, the film produces the impression of liberating history from the confines of space and time. *Cézanne*'s rejection of conventional audiovisual cinematic style, which imitates the logic of geographic space and time, promotes the same goal. The film thus functions as an alternative history, conceived in terms of polyvalent ideas whereby the gaps are collapsed that otherwise separate Brecht and Hölderlin, Hölderlin and Empedocles, Empedocles and Cézanne, Cézanne and Gasquet, Cézanne and Flaubert, Flaubert and Renoir, and Alekan as Renoir's cinematographer from Alekan as a cinematographer for Straub and Huillet. But it is not solely the power and will to create—as Empedocles' hubris that explains his pronouncement of himself as a god—that crucially connects the endeavors of the artists to which *Cézanne* refers, but also the impression the film creates of their reliance on each other to compensate for the parts missing from their respective works.

Conclusion

To one extent or another, all general characteristics of Straub and Huillet's cinema identified earlier in the chapter are related to the Brechtian notion of *Historisierung*. Serving as a reminder of the alterability of social phenomena, the process of *Historisierung* does not direct itself to the past as much as it constructs the present as a time in between, in constant flux. Deleuze's remark that the camera movements in Straub and Huillet "trace the abstract curve of what has happened" (234–35) applies also to other elements of the filmmakers' style. Their use of direct sound and, frequently, available natural lighting limits the possibilities of stylization through technology. The asceticism of Straub and Huillet's camera and sound recording equipment, along with the historical accuracy of their narratives, configures the profilmic event in their cinema as genuine. In a like fashion, the narratives construct their status as documents, as testimonies of the past, by being crucially shaped in terms of style during a single time span—that of the shoot. The acting style, subdued in earlier films (for example, those based on Böll fiction) and theatrically heightened in some later ones (especially in *Antigone* and *Sicily!*, initially produced as theater shows), performs the same distancing function. Byg is correct in identifying the interrelated elements of the use of language and work with the actors as Brecht's most significant influence on the filmmakers (*Landscapes* 24).

Seemingly paradoxically, Straub and Huillet's rejection of the possibilities of image and sound manipulation results in frequent autonomy of segments of their films, allowing—in rare but significant instances—for the use of the segments as Eisensteinian montage cells. For example, it is the sharp temporal fissure between the interview scenes in *History Lessons* and those of the young man's ride through Rome, and the absence of bridging audio such as voiceover or nondiegetic music, that facilitate the dialectical juxtaposition of the two kinds of material. And because Straub and Huillet's editing is overt, their films give the impression of stylistically operating within two separate time spans: that of photography and sound recording on the one hand, and that of editing on the other. On the meta-level of the filmmakers' works, a negotiation takes place of the relationship between the films' two "presents."

In relation to *Historisierung*, the filmmakers' fondness of setting dramatic scenes in landscapes can be accounted for in terms of a Rousseauian nature-society dichotomy: it is within this dichotomy where the true drama of Straub and Huillet's cinema often realizes itself. Just like the rejection of continuity editing functions as a reminder of the constructedness of their films, the natural settings the filmmakers use emphasize the man-made quality of social relationships and mechanisms, and therefore of their changeability.

4

Peter Watkins

Intuitive Brechtianism

THE EARLY WORK OF PETER WATKINS (b. 1935) is often associated with the dominant contemporary cinematic trends in Britain, the Free Cinema—which specialized in the documentary—and the British New Wave—which made fiction films only. With his trademark style of using the narrative and stylistic conventions of the documentary genre in feature films, Watkins falls somewhere between the two trends, rather than adhering to either of them specifically. That is where the comparisons end: Watkins does not share the Free Cinema's primary aim of capturing the lyrical quality of everyday life, nor the focus of the British New Wave filmmakers on working-class issues.[1] While he, like the members of the latter group, has consistently shown a flair for probing taboos, his choice of provocative topics distinguishes him from such figures as Tony Richardson and Karel Reisz, to mention two of the most celebrated filmmakers associated with both of the mentioned trends. The taboos touched upon by Reisz's *Saturday Night, Sunday Morning* (1960) and Richardson's *A Taste of Honey* (1961), which count amongst the most influential British New Wave films, are social: abortion, promiscuity, homosexuality. The controversial subject of Watkins's first film, *The Web* (1956)—as well as of most of the subsequent ones—has a more overt political dimension, centering upon the compassion of a French civilian for a fugitive Nazi soldier. The film was shot on 8 mm stock and funded by Watkins himself. The recognitions he received for this, and his subsequent amateur films (most notably *The Diary of an Unknown Soldier*, which centers on an English World War I soldier dying in a trench, and *The Forgotten Faces* [1961], on the Hungarian 1956 revolution) landed him an opportunity to produce for the BBC his first professional films, *Culloden* (1964) and *The War Game* (1965). After resigning from the company in protest of the internal ban on *The War Game*, Watkins went on to pursue an international career as a film practitioner and educator.

Commentators have pointed to the similarities between Watkins's and Brecht's projects (Lajtha; Wayne). Watkins replied to a *Cahiers du cinéma* interviewer's question about his relation to Brecht by stating that he was "still quite struck by his ideas about distance" (Méranger 82; translation mine). He acknowledges the elements of Brechtian stylistic procedures in *Edvard Munch*, but marks the 1980s—the years of preparation for, and production of, *The Journey*—as the period when he started to make true cinema of distantiation (ibid.). "For *La Commune*," he continues, "I looked for the alchemy of distance through different means, as I would never have liked to remake the same film" (ibid.; translation mine). In the same interview, Watkins obliquely suggests the usefulness of the concept of Brechtian distance in opposing the content and form of the MAVM (mass audiovisual media). A critique of the MAVM also constitutes the filmmaker's contribution to *Brecht Plus Minus Film* (2003), a collection of textual and visual documents from a conference, an exhibition and a series of screenings dedicated to the topic of Brecht's relation to photographic media, where Watkins was represented with a screening of *La Commune (Paris 1871)* (1999). In section eight of "The Media Statement" on his website ("Public-alternative Processes and Practices"), Watkins himself acknowledges Brecht's role in his project as a media practitioner and critic: "The principles underlying my attempts," he writes, "owe a lot to the work of Berthold [*sic*!] Brecht and others."

While not acknowledging Brecht, some of the ideas expressed elsewhere in the document read like paraphrases of "Notes to 'Mahagonny.' " In the segment entitled "Role of American MAVM, Hollywood and the Monoform," for instance, Watkins criticizes the "authoritarian basis" inherent to "the Aristotelian monolinear narrative structure" and describes it as "[desiring] nothing more of the spectator than his or her passive submission to a process of manipulated catharsis." The statement's shortest, ninth segment resonates with the above words. Entitled "Lena Israel and the Epic Cinema," it summarizes a chapter of the book by the identified Swedish cultural critic. Israel distinguishes "between two separate filmic processes—the Anglo-Saxon narrative, with its relationship to the Cartesian way of seeing the world, and the 'Epic-lyrical,' with its direct relationship to Hegel." In the view of Israel as interpreted by Watkins, Hegel aims to overcome the Cartesian dualism "by giving the individual an active role in the knowledge-creating process." Summarizing Israel's book chapter, Watkins comes close to equating the "Epic-lyrical" dramaturgical model with Hegelian dialectics, which crucially informs Brecht's dramatic theory, too. Importantly, however, "The Media Statement" does not highlight the kinship between the broader postulates of Watkins's critique of the MAVM and Brecht: the three examples provided all derive from the cited source. Often progressing through implications and suggestions rather than through unambiguous points precisely connected to one another and ranked on the basis of their contribution to a central argument, Watkins the essayist resembles Watkins the filmmaker: both his prose and his films oppose the linearity of discourse that he associates with Aristotle.

By way of further introduction, the following list briefly identifies recurring thematic and stylistic features of Watkins's films:

(1) They are often set in the past or in the hypothetical near future (for example, *Punishment Park* [1971] and *The Gladiators* [1969]).

(2) They frequently have for their main subject war or the threat of it (for example, *The Gladiators*, *The Diary of an Unknown Soldier* [1959], and *The Journey*).

(3) As mentioned, Watkins's films often push the boundary between documentary and drama.

(4) The feature films often include documentary material (such as historic images, objects, and music).

(5) The feature films usually use non-professional actors.

(6) Watkins's actors often acknowledge the camera.

(7) The feature films often use improvised dialogue.

(8) They typically rely on non-continuity editing.

(9) All films prior to *The Freethinker* (1994) use voiceover.

(10) In *Culloden* and *La commune*, Watkins's consciously uses anachronistic elements.

(11) The duration of Watkins's later films often exceeds the industry standard. (To give but the most radical example, *The Journey* is fourteen hours and thirty minutes long.)

A major part of Watkins's work are his essays on what he perceives as a crisis of mass audiovisual media. As a departure point for an investigation of his films most pertinent to this book's topic, *Punishment Park*, *Edvard Munch* (1973), *The Freethinker* (1994), and *La commune*, the next few pages summarize and critically comment upon these texts.

Watkins's Media Critique

Published in its entirety only on his website,[2] Watkins's "Media Statement" concerns itself mainly with what the author sees as the ongoing crisis of the MAVM. Watkins traces the crisis to the 1970s and sees it as responsible to a considerable extent for other major societal issues of today, such as those concerning globalization, imperialistic warfare, and environmental devastation. Early in the statement, Watkins asks: "Is the role of the MAVM to overtly entrap/offend the public with monoprogramming and lack of choice, and with the most simplistic and crude commercial programming possible? Is it to create violence in society? Is it to set aggressive, pro-government, pro-military, pro-consumer-society agendas? (As well as keeping all of its decisions and methods secret?)" ("Media Crisis"). Watkins's ensuing conclusion that "television reality, in global terms, has become the latter" (ibid.) confirms the rhetorical character of these questions.[3] In Watkins's view, the culprits for the current state of the MAVM are their formal operations: the universal clock, the Monoform, and the standard Aristotelian narrative. The last of the three terms (the only one not coined by Watkins) pertains to monolinear narratives with a beginning, middle, and (typically happy) end. The "universal clock" denotes the practice of standardizing the length of all TV programmers, so as to facilitate scheduling: in case of the appearance of an "unexpected empty 'slot,' there is no problem finding a replacement program, since all films are now precisely the same length—regardless of theme or subject matter" ("Media Statement"). The Monoform is the term Watkins uses in reference to the "language" of all films and TV programs (with the exclusion of some documentaries), based on "the standardized and rigid form which had its nascence in the Hollywood cinema" (ibid.). As Watkins sees it, the characteristics of this language are "spatial fragmentation, repetitive time rhythms, constantly moving camera, rapid staccato editing, dense bombardment of sound, and lack of silence or reflective space" (ibid.). To these can be added the purportedly disappearing MAVM indexicality (to borrow for a moment a term from Peirce's semiotics, even though Watkins does not use it) of the moving image in the contemporary MAVM.

Commenting upon the CNN representation of the air raid in Iraq, Watkins criticizes the use of digital effects, distorted video-phone images and ghostlike scenes filmed with green night-vision lenses, as they "lent coverage of the war a distinctly video-game appearance" ("American MAVM"). In discussing the increasingly rapid editing patterns of the MAVM, he acknowledges the historical significance of montages of Eisenstein and Pudovkin (remarking that "the juxtaposition of two seemingly disparate images to create a third image in one's mind was a startling break from the rigidity of the traditional narrative process at that time" [ibid.]) but cautions against their use today. Usually implying brevity, speed—when it is the central aspect of a language form—becomes, in Watkins's view, anti-process: instead of enabling a two-way communication with the audience, speed renders it impossible by establishing itself as a definite voice whose authority is not to be questioned. He visually represents the rhythmic structure of the Monoform by a combination of vertical lines and dashes, the former signifying editorial cuts:

|-|-|---|-|---|-|-|

Watkins observes that the MAVM apply and perpetuate the same structure regardless of the demands of "the living tissue of the story" (ibid.). The result is a uniform impact that he likens to uncontrollable reflex jerks that occur when a healthy individual's knee is tapped by a small hammer. He remarks that the notion that professional filmmaking should have the described kind of simultaneous effect on the audience needs to be challenged, as it bases itself on a hierarchical—and therefore undemocratic—relationship to the public. Accordingly, stylistic operations of the MAVM of today are for Watkins intrinsically linked to ideology, despite the long-time denials of Hollywood executives that their films have anything to do with politics or social situations. This same connection purportedly exists also with regard to the narratives of the MAVM, which—overtly or implicitly—perpetuate "imperialistic visions and stereotypes" (ibid.).

The consequences of the Monoform's dominance that Watkins identifies are diminished attention spans, "a lack of tolerance for sustained process or for any form of communication that takes longer than ten seconds" (ibid.) and growing ahistoricity and need for incessant change. In Watkins's view, these constitute a factor in society's increasing privatization, insecurity, and restlessness. He sees "competitive thinking, egotism, personal gain, and an indifference to violence and suffering [as] increasingly the 'norm' " of the society of the present, whereas "genuine plurality and community interaction are vanishing into the past" ("Media Crisis"). For Watkins, complicit in the state of affairs with the governments—of which the MAVM are but extended arms—is professional media training, which "systematically indoctrinates young media professionals in the practice of the Monoform" (ibid.). As a remedy for the situation, he proposes that community groups demand the implementation of a system of genuinely critical and holistic media education or the creation of ad hoc universities or schools in people's homes. Watkins also encourages the filmmakers working in the MAVM to address the question of length, space, structure, and rhythm in the form of their own work, and of pluralism in their relationship to the public, and consider the expansion of "our truncated and fragmented message" into "slower, longer, less aggressive and more complex rhythms which allow the public to 'enter' the material, to reflect, to form alternative and critical interpretations, etc." (ibid.).

"The Media Statement" concludes with a summary, quoted below in full, of factors and ideas Watkins considers "essential to keep in mind when forging a new relationship between the media and the public" ("Public"):

- That to *communicate* indicates a two-way process of sharing and dialogue between parties, and that this meaning should apply equally to the process known as 'mass communications.'
- That the *meaning* of what we show on film and video is shaped by the filmic language forms that we use.
- That time, space, rhythm, and process all play an essential role in determining whether ours is a democratic or a hierarchical relationship with the audiovisual material.
- That the executives who run TV and the commercial cinema, and the filmmakers and producers who supply them and the MAVM with material, have not been elected to their position.
- That the concept of *objectivity* does not, and should never claim to exist in the mass audiovisual media. All we can strive for is responsible subjectivity.
- That media violence is not only images portrayed on a screen—it also exists in the editing process, in the use (misuse) of space, time, rhythm, sound, etc.

- That history is our life-blood. It is what we choose to call the 'past,' 'present,' and 'future.' The way we perceive these phases in the affairs of mankind now depends almost entirely on the role of the MAVM.
- That ethics, morality and spirituality play a vital role in our development and very being, and thus need to have a place in the process of the MAVM.
- That teachers should have the right to teach alternative, critical media education, without hindrance or marginalization.
- That every man, woman and child has a basic right to alternative forms of non-violent, noncommercial, non-hierarchical mass or local audiovisual media. And should they so desire—to create such (ibid.).

Laudable for its precisely formulated and well-documented diagnosis of the current state of the MAVM, for the viability of its propositions with regard to it, and for the humanism and non-conformist courage that underlie it, Watkins's critique is vulnerable to three criticisms. First, Watkins identifies the 1970s as the time when the present media crisis began, and when he first realized the shortcomings of the Monoform. It is hardly a coincidence that the mentioned decade was the heyday of ideological film criticism, which model had been introduced to the field in the aftermath of the 1968 student protests. In this period, the attention of the contributors to such influential journals as *Cahiers du cinéma* shifted from the strictly aesthetic questions to those of politics. In their seminal 1968 essay "Cinema / Ideology / Criticism," Jean-Louis Comolli and Jean Narboni put forward the thesis that the style of mainstream cinema is inherently ideological, regardless of a given film's subject matter. The production circumstances too entered the equation of film analysis, leading to the famous call of Godard—a filmmaker whose work in the decade was substantially informed by current theoretical trends—"not for political films, but for films made politically."

The ideological film critics of the Commolian/Narbonian provenance and Watkins's "The Media Statement" converge in a few points, but the latter fails to address the former's strain of film criticism and its relation to the practitioners who inspired it. One would expect Watkins to hail Godard, whose films from the period consistently display anti-imperialist and pacifist ideas, as well as a concern for those suffering from various kinds of oppression, and who dedicated much of the decade to seeking alternatives to the existing model of the medium of television as Watkins's primary interest. But Watkins nearly dismisses Godard by referring in one interview to his radicalism as "chic" ("Fear" 229), and—in another—by stating that Godard has fallen into traps by believing that the problems of manipulating the profilmic event can be worked out within films (MacDonald, "Peter" 412). Interestingly for a filmmaker who has produced many films exclusively for television, nowhere does Watkins acknowledge Godard's important experimental work for that medium. The "Statement" fails to refer also to "The Threepenny Lawsuit," with which it shares several key points. To give but a few examples, Watkins's critique of the standard Aristotelian narrative as a formal element inherent to the MAVM echoes Brecht's discussion of the former (Silberman, *Brecht on Film* 170–75); the filmmaker's view that the MAVM maintains an undemocratic relationship to the public is reminiscent of the ideas put forward in the segment of "The Lawsuit" entitled "*A film must be the work of a collective*"; and the analysis in "The Statement" of the various aspects of production and distribution of the MAVM resonates with the segments of "The Lawsuit" that constitute the article's bulk.

In addition, neither Watkins's discussion of the Monoform nor his timeline with regard to his alleged abandonment of the "language" are devoid of confusions. He identifies vastly dissimilar elements of film syntax such as constant camera movements and the zoom as different attributes of the Monoform, but he fails to elucidate their position and role within the alleged formal model. A quick comparison of the two should exemplify the methodological error carried by this move. A basic camera movement, the pan (the pivoting of the camera around its vertical axis) can be considered an equivalent to a person's turning her head to either side to shift her center of attention. In contrast, the zoom shot—which entails changing the lens's focal length during the course of a shot—is not a process that the eye can perform. Watkins's classification of the two techniques within the same category obscures the vastly different implications of their use.

Watkins hints that the ever-growing speed of the Monoform should be regarded as its essential quality: he singles it out as a new required 'norm' of the MAVM, and points to its role in forging "an increasingly hierarchical relationship, in the past decades, between TV-makers and the public" ("American MAVM"). The latter remark appears informed by the experimentally provable inability for reflection on the part of the recipient of audiovisual content when exposed to a sensory overload. In order for complex ideas to be grasped, slow pace and sustained length are needed instead of aggressive speed (ibid.). This view is open to attack on two grounds. First, the relaxed pace of Watkins's late films and their non-standard length can be regarded as aggressive in its own way. While the 14 ½ hour *The Journey* is divided into several parts, allowing a viewing in the increments of approximately 45 minutes, *La Commune*—the duration of whose shorter version nearly equals that of a regular job shift—is designed to be seen in one sitting. The film's very length thus places a demand on the viewer that is not commensurate with the lifestyle that a typical modern economy imposes upon its participants. Second, while one cannot but concede the obvious point on the relation between an idea's complexity and the time required for its processing, Watkins's insistence on it raises the question of whether grasping a work of *La Commune*'s length upon a single viewing is advantageous over comprehending after multiple viewings a hypothetically shorter, but also faster and denser, work. An argument could easily be made that the latter model is more viewer-friendly. The question could be pushed even further, into the realm of medium specificity. If the complexity of ideas *La commune* presents necessitates its non-standard length, is the choice of television film as a form suitable for those ideas' realization?

That question, when considered in relation to Watkins's interest in restoring and realizing the potential of television to forge a democratic relationship to the public and begin to function again as a means of communication rather than one-directional impact, brings about that of the artist's choice to produce *La Commune* in the film format and not as a TV broadcast. Liveness, a defining characteristic of the latter form, would have endowed the work with an air of unpredictability, thereby sharpening its aesthetic and political edge.

The difference between the Monoform and the alternative to it Watkins adopted in a later phase of his career can be explored best by comparing examples from the two formal models. What complicates such an endeavor is that Watkins, while suggesting more than once in his "Media Statement" that the narrative and stylistic patterns of his films underwent a substantial change in the period between the mid-1970s and mid-1980s, does not delineate the essence of this event. Moreover, he tends to emphasize the continuities rather than discontinuities in his work, while simultaneously acknowledging his own former use of the Monoform. *La Commune*, being his latest work, appears a logical choice for an example of the alternative formal model. Because Watkins, in his discussion of the Monoform, dedicates more attention to the questions of style than those of narrative, and because no film of his exemplifies this formal model in both of its aspects, it seems apt to briefly compare *La Commune* and *The War Game* (Figure 4.1). In terms of its audiovisual style, *The War Game*—a dramatic enactment of a nuclear war on England—is closest to his description of the Monoform.[4]

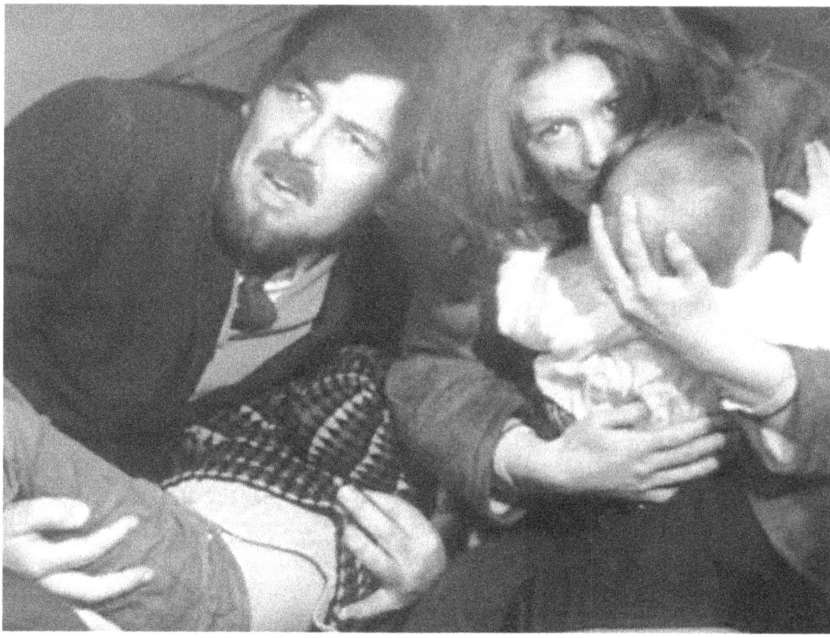

Figure 4.1. A nuclear family under a nuclear attack: *The War Game* (Peter Watkins, British Broadcasting Corporation, 1965). Digital frame enlargement.

(i) *The War Game* contains graphic scenes that aim for a controlled shock effect. An example of these is the fast-forward movement of the camera to a screaming face of a boy whose skin has burned as a result of the heat wave suddenly spread after a nuclear missile has airburst over the area. In contrast, *La Commune*—parts of which deal with extremely bloody historical events—signifies violent content via offscreen sounds or dialogue and intertitles.

(ii) Neither *The War Game* nor *La Commune* has a central character serving as a link between the various episodes of the films' respective narratives. In this vital respect, both films can be said to conform to the norms of Brechtian epic/dialectic dramaturgy. One can argue, however, that the relatively great length and slow pace of *La Commune* and the plurality of voices that characterizes it are correlated. As the film opposes the coherent cause-and-effect model, the narrative function of many characters becomes clear only after their repeated appearances. Thus the film's very length facilitates the narrative's collage structure.

(iii) *The War Game* ties together the multiplicity of its voices (the alleged experts on military affairs and the questions of nuclear radiation, representatives of various governmental agencies, the church, etc.) by the authoritative narration performed by Michael Aspel, the BBC television news reader, and Dick Graham, who lent his voice to many documentaries of the era. *La Commune* does not possess such a unifying element. It abandons what James Michael Welsh refers to as "the Watkins narrator"—the voiceover narration characteristic of earlier works by the filmmaker, both documentary and fictional.

(iv) The previous point already indicates the generally pluralistic principle that underlies *La Commune*'s narrative structure. The principle manifests itself further in the difference concerning the two films' respective scripting methods. With the exclusion of the interviews conducted with townspeople on the effects of Strontium 90 and about whether England should retaliate if Russia attacked it, all dialogues in *The War Game* were precisely scripted (including the pauses in the characters' lines) (Gomez 48). In contrast, the dialogues for *La Commune* were improvised from the rough indications prepared by Watkins and his collaborator.

(v) The shots of *The War Game* considerably vary in length. Thus, the duration of the film's first live-action shot, depicting a messenger's delivery of the government's communiqué regarding the ensuing evacuation of the London civilians to the nonmilitary region of Kent, is one minute and thirty seconds—approximately three percent of the film's entire length. In contrast, the average length shot for the fire storm sequence is about five seconds. *La Commune*, on the other hand, predicates itself entirely on long takes, the above-mentioned brief scene showing the journalist of the TV Versailles smiling at the camera being the sole exception.

(vi) *The War Game* uses lenses of various focal lengths, as exemplified by the two sequences discussed previously. The opening shot of the first of these employs a wide-angle lens, whereas the second of these sequences relies

> primarily on a zoom in the telephoto mode, occasionally closing out or in. *La Commune* does not show this kind of variety: it uses mostly a wide-angle lens for the scenes in the 11th arrondisement, and a normal lens for the TV Versailles news (complying in this with the actual stylistic norms of broadcasting). The relatively few zoom shots in *La Commune* are made inconspicuous by their small speed, which contrasts the other, rapid camera movements the film uses.

In conclusion, the elements of the respective narratives and styles of *The War Game* and *La Commune*—the former being an example of the Monoform as understood by Watkins, and the latter of an unnamed alternative to this formal model—differ more in degree to which they are utilized than in kind.

The Desert of Plenty: Punishment Park

Punishment Park (Figure 4.2) synthesizes Watkins's artistic experiences to that point, building narratively upon *The Gladiators* and stylistically

Figure 4.2. Political transgressors melting into a mirage in *Punishment Park* (Peter Watkins / Francoise Chartwell, 1970). Digital frame enlargement.

upon the docudramas. Photographed in the United States and concerned with the country's contemporary political actuality, the film was released when one of the era's defining events—the Vietnam War—seemed to be approaching its end: American troops were being withdrawn from the Southeast Asian country en masse, and the number of the U.S. Army's yearly war casualties was dramatically dropping: from 16,899 in 1968 to 2,414 in 1971.

But neither the deescalation of the fighting at the time when the initial circulation of Punishment Park was beginning, nor the gap that separates the film from such cinematic works on the subject as *Far from Vietnam* (S.L.O.N., 1967), *Hanoi, Martes 13* (Hanoi, Tuesday 13; Santiago Alvarez, 1968), and *In the Year of the Pig* (Emile de Antonio, 1968), takes away from the timeliness and originality of Watkins's film. Unlike its mentioned antecedents, *Punishment Park* is a fictional work that uses only formal conventions of documentaries. Unlike the three earlier films, it extends its thematic scope to encompass additional issues of pertinence to the United States at the turn of the sixth and the seventh decades of the twentieth century, most importantly the country's racial divisions and the ascent during the period of the hippie and black resistance movements. In spite of Watkins's aversion to all intellectual and artistic vogue, *Punishment Park* can be productively examined in connection to some of the then-trendy practices and discourses: on the one hand, anti-westerns, mondo films, and reality TV, and, on the other, the notion of the blurring boundary between the real and its simulations in our technology-driven era. The cited film and TV genres emerged or gained prominence in the 1960s and the following decade, the period that also saw a proliferation of postmodernist ideas, of which the mentioned one—advanced by Jean Baudrillard some years later—is an eminent example.

The film's title refers to a government-established institution in Southern California, where the individuals accused of subversive political activities are offered the opportunity to trek to the American flag located eighty-five kilometers away from the tribunal tent as an alternative to a severe prison sentence. Fulfilling this task is made nearly impossible by the constraints of time, nourishment, climate, and—most perniciously—the National Guardsmen and law enforcement officers pursuing the captives. *Punishment Park* intercuts throughout its duration between Group 638's hearings and Group 637's trajectory through the desert, configuring itself as a British television reportage with an offscreen Watkins in the role of the journalist. Considered alongside this foregrounded, metafilmic element, the film's locale—the home of Hollywood and the wealthiest American state—appears similarly significant. *Punishment Park* is an allegory of totalitarianism whose estranging power rests partly on its narrative's setting not in the Communist world—with which government control of civic life had been associated in the West since the Axis powers' demise—to California, the land of the "dream industry" and an epitome of the success of the American way. This formal choice is complemented by a mock-documentary style, which reformulates key features of mondo and reality TV to help produce the film's "reality effect."

The common characteristics of mockumentaries had not petrified into conventions by 1971, but the western—that most paradigmatically American of all film genres—had reached maturity decades before then, and was undergoing major transformations at the time of *Punishment Park*'s release. Such characters as the bearded, lean entrepreneur John McCabe (Warren Beatty) from *McCabe & Mrs. Miller* (Robert Altman, 1971) were refashioning the cinematic image of the western hero, memorably embodied during the genre's classical phase by the clean-shaven, stocky outlaw the Ringo Kid (John Wayne) of John Ford's *Stagecoach* (1939). The outer differences between the Ringo Kid and John McCabe were, of course, but a reflection of the more profound inner ones, just like the change of the way America was cinematically representing itself was merely a reflection of the distinctness between the country under Franklin Delano Roosevelt—during whose presidency John Ford's film was produced—and that of Richard Nixon, who presided over the country during *Punishment Park*'s production.

On account of the numerous violations of genre conventions by *McCabe & Mrs. Miller*, Altman described his film as an anti-western. A number of film practitioners and commentators accepted the term and applied it to a range of the period's other films, including *Little Big Man* (Arthur Penn, 1970) and *Pat Garrett and Billy the Kid* (Sam Peckinpah, 1973). As momentous as the western's changes during the period were, they left unchallenged the garden/desert antinomy that John Kitses (1969)—elaborating upon Henry Nash Smith in his *Virgin Land* (1950)—identifies as the western's basic structure. Western films play out the antinomy through the actions of their characters as much as through the setting, allowing further binaries to arise from that basic one: community/individual, East/West, and change/tradition, to mention but a few. Thomas Schatz uses the work of Claude Levi-Strauss to argue in his *Hollywood Genres* (1981) that westerns, like other generic films, provide the impression of resolving the antinomies that illustrate deeper cultural tensions. *Stagecoach*, for example, has nine characters contrasting with each other in terms of sex, age, class, level of education, and moral values—and therefore representative of society as a whole—who recognize their need to overcome their differences in the face of common adversity.

Whereas the film's setting and its emphasis on guns might qualify *Punishment Park* as a western, its failure to reconcile the conflicting politics of its characters aligns the film with cinematic works that define themselves against the genre. In a rare scholarly response to Watkins's film, Scott MacDonald's aptly notes that the reason *Punishment Park* consistently provokes emotional reactions paralleled by few other films he has seen concerns "the fact that [Americans] have not resolved [their] conflicts as to how [they] should function as citizens in [their] complex society" ("Punishment Park"). This lack of resolution reflects itself also in the film's structure. The ending is Senecan, with the entire Group 637 dead and a suggestion that the same fate is awaiting Group 638. By reversing the wilderness/civilization trajectory that defines the western and by positing the immediate future of the United States as one of a regression to violent barbarism, Watkins does not adjust the myth of the country for the contemporary circumstances—as innumerable westerns have done—but contributes to that myth's very subversion. The vitriol that American reviewers have directed at *Punishment Park*, made all the more striking in light of the odd positive reaction the film received domestically,[5] can be explained partly as an expression of patriotic fury against this rendition of the American Dream by a non-American as a game of survival that cannot be won.

The earlier of the other strains of film- and TV-making with which *Punishment Park* can be productively contrasted, mondo, has been described by Bill Nichols in his *Introduction to Documentary* as an "embarrassing fellow-traveler rather than a central element" of the documentary film tradition, and a "cabaret of curiosities" (87) that has descended from what Tom Gunning terms the "cinema of attractions" (86)—the early 1900s films that provided viewing pleasure through spectacle (Nichols 58) rather than through narrative operations. Nichols supports the connection between mondo, with its frequent focus on various forms of cultural exotica, and the "cinema of attractions," by referring to the 1904 St. Louis World Exhibition that recreated a Filipino village with real people (86)—an exhibit whose appeal, one suspects, lay in its ability to buttress the observers' sentiment of cultural superiority over the "primitives." Gunning's term was inspired by the vocabulary of the circus, as was Eisenstein's "montage of attractions." For the Soviet practitioner and theorist, however, the term refers equally to content and form of a theater show: its "attractiveness" stemmed as much from the arrangement of its units as it did from their individual qualities. In this respect, Eisenstein's "montage of attractions" bears comparison to mondo films, which often feature geographically and thematically diverse episodes connected through voiceover commentary. Thus, the early parts of *Mondo cane* (A Dog's World; Gualtiero Jacopetti, Paolo Cavara, and Franco Prosperi, 1962)—considered by many as the genre's founding film[6]—take the viewer to Castellaneta, the Italian village where a garish monument has been erected to Rudolph Valentino, across New York City, where the fans of the Rossano Brazzi rip the shirt off the Italian actor, to Kiriwina, the largest island of village of the Trobriand archipelago, where a group of women are pursuing a man for amorous purposes.

Another point of possible comparison between "montage of attractions" and mondo concerns the tension between "high art" and "popular culture" that resonates in Eisenstein and more ambitious mondo films such as *A Dog's World*. We have seen in chapter 1 that Eisenstein the stage director freely combined elements of both "high" and "popular art" so as to challenge the notion of the affluent and educated as the ideal theater audience. Cinema, whose development in such industrially crucial contexts as the United States was driven by its popularity with the working class population, scarcely shared theater's status as a bourgeois art from. In *A Dog's World* and the other films Jacopetti (co-)directed, one encounters a tendency opposite that of the young Eisenstein's theater productions: to provide the self-consciously tasteless subject matter with a veneer of finesse and make it palatable to the upper class.[7] In the film's opening credit, we read the following apologia: "All the scenes you will see in this film are true and are taken only from life. If often they are shocking, it is [*sic*!] because there are many shocking things in this world. Besides, the duty of the chronicler is not to sweeten the truth but to report it objectively." More substantially than the quoted reference to the documentarian's ethical mandate, such production values of early Jacopetti films as lush color photography and rich orchestral music provided early mondo films with an air of respectability enjoyed by Italian art films of the period (eminently exemplified by Federico Fellini's *La dolce vita* [Sweet Life, 1960] and Michelangelo Antonioni's *L'avventura* [The Adventure, 1960]). Jacopetti and Prosperi's debut film earned them prestigious accolades, including the nomination for the Cannes Film Festival's Palme d'Or in 1962 and the Italian Film Academy's David di Donatello prize for Best Production in the same year. Simultaneously, however, accusations of fabricating the events of their documentaries were leveled against the filmmakers throughout their career, a trend that culminated with the trial of Jacopetti for allegedly paying mercenary killers to conduct executions for the scenes of his and Prosperi's *Africa, addio* (Farewell, Africa, 1966). Even though Jacopetti was found not guilty, the scandal—combined with the steadily increasing graphic content of mondo—led to the ultimate critical dismissal of the genre as lurid and sensationalistic, an assessment echoed in the above Nichols quote.

Because the vast majority of Jacopetti and Prosperi's imitators were their compatriots,[8] mondo is sometimes seen as primarily an Italian phenomenon. Yet the genre possesses powerful ties also to the United States: many mondo films capitalize on the cultural otherness of America, including a few Jacopetti and Prosperi titles and Romano Vanderbes's notorious *This Is America* (1977) and *This Is America 2* (1980), which feature cocaine-sniffing Christians, children squeezing earthworms for juice, and an electrocution in a Midwestern prison. Moreover, a film that anticipates mondo in its collage structure and reliance on voiceover narration and orchestral music, Francois Reichenbach's *L'Amérique insolite* (America as Seen by a Frenchman, 1960), focuses on strange leisure and consumption habits of US citizens.

Another genre's characteristic relevant here is its common focus on violent cessation of life. From the self-immolating monk in *Mondo cane* to the *Faces of Death* series (an example of the latest phase of the genre's regression), forcible death can be seen in a myriad of mondo scenes. This subject can be regarded as at once eminently suitable and unsuitable for cinema. If the medium's destiny (to use a blatantly un-Brechtian term) is to represent phenomena perceptible by sight and hearing, then it is only logical that cinema will attempt to do so also with the final event in one's span of existence, whose prospect animates so many of our actions. The public's continuing fascination with cinematic portrayals of violence, and of death as its most drastic outcome, hardly needs to be proven: the innumerable fictional films that contain scenes of homicide confirm the act's everlasting visual attractiveness. But when bereft of violence that usually accompanies its onscreen representations, death isn't much to look at: corpses are devoid of expressiveness and their images leave unutilized cinema's pivotal capacity for representing motion. It is the experiential rather than the manifestational aspect of death that intrigues and mystifies most people, the aspect on which cinema is inevitably silent. This is the reason that death can serve as a marker of filmic representation's limits.

The four filmmakers on which this book focuses have taken conspicuously different stances on those limits. Straub and Huillet's films attenuate the spectacle through an array of recurrent stylistic choices and the use of non-images (for example, that of black screen), thereby proposing a restriction on and even a refusal of visual representation as viable strategies of cinematic expression. Lars von Trier's films, by contrast, frequently include taboo sights (for instance, the execution by hanging in *Dancer in the Dark* [2000], genital mutilation in *Antichrist* [2009], and unsimulated sex in *Nymphomaniac* [2013]), to a decorum-breaching effect comparable to works of cinematic avant-garde such as *Un chien andalou* (Luis Buñuel, 1929) to an array of mondo films.

In this respect, Watkins can be situated somewhere between Straub and Huillet and von Trier. *Punishment Park*, as a case in point, does not transgress through the manner in which it represents death (it includes a minimal amount of gore [Figure 4.3], and some of the killings are elided from the plot), but rather through the following interlocking narrative choices. The film configures the detainees as representative of all non-conformist groups in the United States, showing them dead or suggesting the imminence of their death by the end. These choices are combined with stylistic elements that function as codes of the film's realism: handheld camera, available lighting, non-scripted dialogue, and direct address of the camera.

Watkins appears well aware of the particular relevance of death and violence for the dichotomy between cinematic reality and actuality when he mentions the two motifs in a self-interview on *Punishment Park*. He charges the Monoform for "confusing and deadening our capacity to distinguish between the superficial and the serious, between (for example) actual death and staged violence" ("Peter Watkins Self-Interview"). At first visually manifesting itself in mere stillness, death is exceedingly easy to simulate, which seems the reason that representations of death in

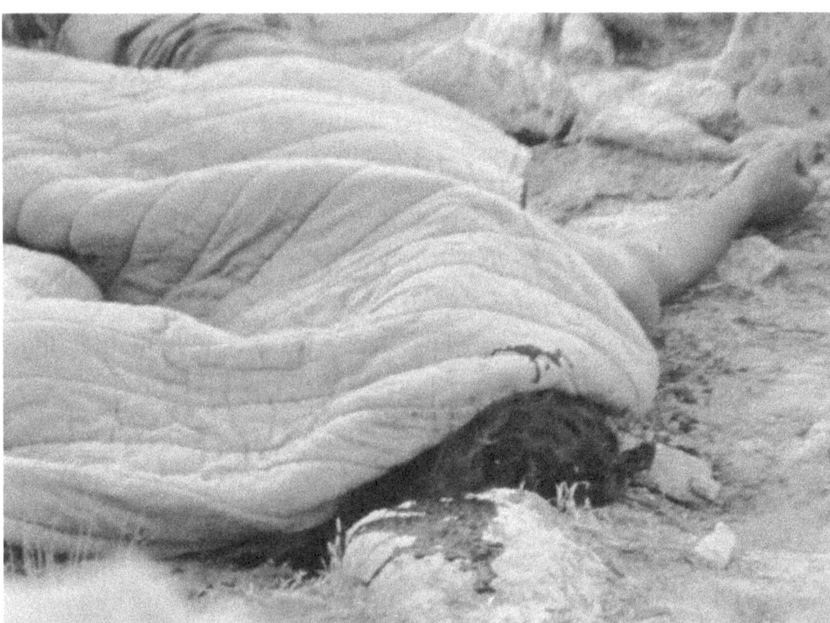

Figure 4.3. An image of death in *Punishment Park* (Peter Watkins, Chartwell Artists, 1970). Digital frame enlargement.

mondo often provoke the question of genuineness.[9] Yet the difference between the states of life and death is absolute and comparable to few other subjects commonly represented in cinema. A shot in a documentary film that depicts, say, a lion walking can only be successfully used as a platform from which to communicate via the voiceover or caption *inaccurate* information about the animal on condition that the image passes the viewer's test for accuracy (i.e., the lion looks and moves like the other examples of the species in the viewer's visual experience). Representations of human death invite the same procedure, but also frustrate its execution, as death in many cases lacks a distinctive visual appearance. Even so, mondo films treat death as a spectacle too, while the TV genre often quoted as its successor, the reality show,[10] often despectacularizes its material. For example, *The Osbournes* (2002–2005) depicts the rock singer Ozzy Osbourne and his family in mundane, everyday, and banal situations, which recommend themselves as worthy of the viewer's attention solely on account of the main protagonist's preexisting stardom.

Reality TV began before the letter with *An American Family* (1973), which comprises twelve one-hour episodes about seven months in the lives of the Louds, an upper-middle-class family from Santa Barbara. Jean Baudrillard uses the example of the show in his *Simulacra and Simulation* (1981) to illustrate the argument that the connection between the referent of the image and reality has been severed in the postmodernity of late capitalism. The image now "has no relation to any reality whatsoever," and is "its own simulacrum" (6)—"truth that hides the fact that there is none" (1). While Baudrillard's overall argument is questionable, his observation that *An American Family* abolishes the spectacular appears apt and relevant to invoke in connection to *Punishment Park*, as a film that constructs its realism along the lines of the TV show. A case in point is the lawn party sequence, which shows the hosts and their guests laughing, drinking, and exchanging muffled and incomprehensible words. Watching the cuts that mark the sequence's ellipses, one has difficulties imagining how the deleted images and sounds could be *less* engaging than the ones that made it to the cut. If this is TV *vérité*, as Baudrillard calls it, evoking the strain of documentary filmmaking that inspired the show, and if *An American Family*—contrary to Baudrillard's argument—can still successfully claim its ties to the real, then the real is disappointingly sparse. The impression the show leaves contrasts the fame of America—the totality of which the Louds may have represented for a foreign viewer like Baudrillard—as a land of plenty and abundance, rich in visual and aural stimuli.

If examples of the optical peculiarity of the United States—which inspired *America as Seen by a Frenchman* and subsequent mondo films about the country—are few and far in between in *An American Family*, they are even more rare in *Punishment Park*. The austerity of the latter film's setting links it to the US-themed films of the other filmmakers this book focuses on. Straub and Huillet's adaptation of Kafka's *Der Verschollene / Amerika* (The Missing One / America), *Klassenverhältnisse* (Class Relations, 1983), contains few shots filmed in the country where its narrative is set, the only one immediately recognizable as an image from the United States featuring the Statue of Liberty. Similarly, von Trier's *Dogville* (2003) and *Manderlay* (2005) were shot on a black soundstage with minimal setting, a selection of archival documentary stills being the sole variety of pictures of America employed by the two films.

The wasteland that makes the film's setting is another reason for introducing Baudrillard into the discussion, with "desert of the real" as its central metaphor. Baudrillard opens his book by evoking Jorge Luis Borges' fable on a map so detailed that it entirely covers the territory. As the country declines and falls into ruins, the map deteriorates, until eventually only shreds of it remain in the deserts. This fable, Baudrillard comments, does not apply to our time, in which

> simulation is no longer that of a territory, a referential being, or a substance. It is the generation by models of a real without origin or reality: a hyperreal. The territory no longer precedes the map, nor does it survive it. It is nevertheless the map that precedes the territory—precession of simulacra—that engenders the territory, and if one must return to the fable, today it is the territory whose shreds slowly rot across the extent of the map. It is the real, and not the map, whose vestiges persist here and there in the deserts that are no longer those of the Empire, but ours. The desert of the real itself. (1)

It seems doubtful that Brecht would accept the pessimism imbuing the above words, or approve of Baudrillard's diagnosis on the whole. But the persistence with which Brecht investigated the relation between the signifier and the signified of the photographic image in both this practice and theory, and his continuous efforts to reconcile the invention's inherent but deceptive realism with montage as a central concept in his thinking about art, suggests that he would find Baudrillard's ideas at least intriguing.

Punishment Park illustrates some of the earlier discussed points of convergence between Brecht's ideas on dialectical form and Watkins's own theorizing about moving-image media. Commenting on the film's formal procedures, Watkins emphasizes its use of improvisation as one element that is "straining the Monoform to its limits," and mentions the factors structured into the film's presentation that "create a critical dialectic which not only challenges its 'factual' appearance, but also throws light onto many of the standard practices of today's mass audiovisual media" ("Peter Watkins Self-Interview"). As the quote implies, *Punishment Park* calls for an alternative viewing procedure, a view previously put forward by Scott MacDonald in a review of the film reproduced on the filmmaker's website. MacDonald acknowledges audience's dissatisfaction with *Punishment Park*, and goes on to remark that the phenomenon is due to the situation in which the film is typically seen, with the viewers arriving for the screening and leaving immediately after the film ends. He elaborates his point thus: "As far as Watkins is concerned, *Punishment Park* is first and foremost an attempt to create an on-going discussion of the issues raised in the film. It is only when viewed in this context that *Punishment Park* can be recognized as the fine film it is, for when a screening is followed by a discussion, a fascinating thing frequently happens. Certain specific questions are usually asked, and a certain kind of interaction begins to take place as a result of the questions" ("Punishment Park"). MacDonald's and Watkins's words echo Brecht's proposal of techniques whereby a theater performance could "spill out" into the audience. This proposal is reminiscent of Brecht' s *The Good Person of Szechwan*, which concludes with one of its actors apologizing to the audience for leaving the play's issue open (*Werke* 6: 278), and especially of the *Lehrstück* theory, discussed later in this chapter in relation to *La commune*.

Watkins admits in the self-interview that *Punishment Park* deliberately erodes the Monoform through its use of improvised dialogue—a technique that allows for expression and comparison of contrasting viewpoints—but retains a connection to the mentioned audiovisual style through editing. By "holding" the audience, Watkins explains, the editing maintains a traditional, hierarchical relationship to it ("Peter Watkins Self Interview"). Another element of *Punishment Park* that could have countered the tendency displayed by the arrangement and pace of the film's images and sounds are its telephoto long shots, where the figures and objects appear to melt in the heat of El Mirage Dry Lake. If they were foregrounded, these images could supremely illustrate the boundaries of filmic and televisual representation—a topic that was gaining prominence at the time of the film's production in the apparatus theory, and which lies at the core of Watkins's later written media critique. But being few and without an immediate connection to the film's commentaries on how the TV crew affects the events it is supposed to report on objectively and without a bias, the referred images fall short of that possibility, instead seeming inconspicuous and incidental. Less in tune with the view Watkins subsequently developed of the MAVM is *Punishment Park*'s narrative conclusion, where the filmmaker is heard threatening the police and the military who have murdered the members of Group 637 that he will expose the truth about Punishment Park to the world. Such conclusion implies a faith in the power of TV, which is hardly reconcilable with the vision of America as a totalitarian place that most of the film puts forward. It would take Watkins's committed study of the contemporary media to develop his critique of the Monoform and a model alternative to it.

Between the Poles of Eisensteinian Aesthetics: Editing Patterns in Watkins's Biographical Films

Watkins's cinema has been compared with Brecht's aesthetic and political projects mostly in relation to *La commune*.[11] Like many of Brecht's plays and theater productions, the film emphasizes the individual's social rather than psychological traits, combines props that conform to the norms of realism with a minimalistically stylized setting, and points to itself as a construct through such techniques as the actors' acknowledgment of the camera. The critical attention received by the mentioned Brechtianisms came at the expense of those that do not reveal their debt to the German practitioner and theorist with equal readiness: the medium-specific ones concerning Watkins's editing. Since Brecht did not develop a distinctive film editing style in the two films he collaborated on as a film director, it is necessary to consult the work of another theorist and practitioner—Eisenstein—in order to elucidate the above-posited connection between Watkins and Brecht.

Within Eisenstein's voluminous theorizing on editing, two essential original concepts can be identified: that of a montage of attractions, and that of intellectual editing. The former notion, first formulated in 1923 in relation to theater, pertains to "any element that subjects the spectator to sensual or psychological impact, experimentally regulated and mathematically calculated to produce in him certain emotional shocks" ("Montage" 34). In contrast to the emphasis on the affective aspect of film image and sound in the montage of attractions, the historically subsequent concept of intellectual montage entails connoting abstract meanings through denotative images. The aim of the technique, then, is to render visible the truth beyond the apparent phenomena, to convey abstract ideas through select and tactically arranged segments of photographable reality.

Both montage of attractions and intellectual editing rely on aesthetic estrangement, a modernist concept that refers to the renewal of one's perception (as in *ostranenie*) or cognition (as in *Verfremdung*). Unlike many of their contemporaries, who employed montage primarily to affective ends (as in the case of humor and horror in Surrealism), Eisenstein and Brecht often used montage to thwart the perceiver's excessive emotional arousal, a strategy governed by the view of emotional excitement as a state unconducive to analytical thinking. In Eisenstein, this tendency is most evident in the middle phase of his filmmaking career, which culminated with *October* and the unproduced cinematic rendition of Marx's *The Capital*, the projects immediately preceding the Communist Party's imposition in the 1930s of the socialist realist representational model. Brecht, for whom the term is intrinsically linked to the notion of dialectics as a method of revealing societal contradictions and their changeability, utilized montage in the vast majority of his contributions to theater and film.

While the topic of *La Commune*—the 1871 Parisian socialist revolution and the short-lived government formed in its aftermath—corresponds more closely than other Watkins's films with the mandate of some of Eisenstein's and much of Brecht's art, the earlier *Fritänkaren* (The Freethinker, 1995) is a richer source of examples of intellectual montage as a medium-specific example of dialectics applied in film. The following comparison between the editing in this film and Watkins's biographical film that precedes it, *Edvard Munch*, will illuminate the convergences and divergences between the filmmaker, Brecht, and Eisenstein.

The two films mark both continuity and discontinuity with the filmmaker's other works. Like *Privilege* (1967), they center on artists with tumultuous careers and carry prominent autobiographical overtones.[12] Unlike *Culloden* (1964) and *La Commune*, for example—two films focusing on significant historical events—and *The War Game* (1965) and *The Journey*—which concentrate on vital political issues—*Edvard Munch* and *The Freethinker* have at the heart of their narratives significant individuals.[13] The following analysis of the two films' editing patterns illustrates the shift from the expressionistically affective mode of Watkins's earlier works to one based on cerebral associations.

Edvard Munch

Commenting on *The War Game* (1965), Joseph A. Gomez speculates that the key reason for the controversy around the film concerns its blurring the difference between the alleged "subjective" and "objective" approaches to documentary filmmaking (57).[14] Gomez's lack of hesitation in classifying the entirely enacted *The War Game* as a documentary speaks about the effectiveness of Watkins's use of nonfictional cinema conventions in his docudramas. Yet *Edvard Munch* stands out from this corpus of films: mostly rejecting the continuity editing "syntax," the film highlights its own "subjectivity." Manifesting itself most conspicuously in the film's shuffling of different timelines, this quality appears inspired by the style of Munch's diaries—on which the voiceover is loosely based—as well as on the narrative circumstance of memories haunting the protagonist.[15] Welsh rightly notes that the "psychological structuring" of *Edvard Munch* approximates the structuring process of the human mind (177), but fails to take into account the dynamic the film maintains throughout its duration between the "subjective" (or "first person") and "objective" (or "third person") modes of narration. The film's oscillations between the two modes can, again, be attributed to the style of Munch's diaries. (Significantly, the film opens with a voiceover communicating over an intertitle that "in the diaries which he is to write later in his life, Edvard Munch often refers to himself in the third person." An image of the young Munch tying his shirt while Sophie is making the bed in the background follows immediately.)

The complexity of the film's editing can best be gleaned from the relationships formed, and the connotative implications carried, by shots similar in terms of narrative action with the images and sounds that surround, or are simultaneous, with them. The film's first shot, the beginning of whose narrative action has been described, continues with Munch taking a seat in the armchair. After the two characters have discreetly glanced at each other, Sophie leans to whisper into his ear that he can meet her after dinner. This last major movement motivates the film's first cut—to a close-up of the two characters' heads. The transition follows the rule of invisible editing whereby approximately one-third of a movement motivating the cut is to take place in the first of the two shots that are being joined together. But the film disrupts the time-space immediately thereafter by juxtaposing the image of Sophie and Edvard (after the protagonist has looked into the lens, at once suggesting his identity to the viewer and announcing the film's other estranging effects) with that of Munch's mother coughing blood in bed while her relatives provide her assistance. The scene cuts to the intertitle with the words "Edvard Munch" at the point when the third figure blocks our view of the mother, the color of her dress matching the intertitle's background. In retrospect, it will turn out that the themes of the two brief scenes—which might broadly be designated Eros and Thanatos—are central for the film as a whole. Indeed, it is the tension between the two Freudian notions, and its influence on the central character's maturation as an artist, that informs the groupings of many other images and sounds in the film. Consider, for example, the following series of shots:

1. MEDIUM CLOSE-UP.

Over-the-shoulder shot. *The sound of coughing.* Munch puts his hand down on the self-portrait that he is holding. His fingers travel across the painted lips. *Voiceover*: "Hans Jaeger has told Munch that the human function of sex is the most important single process known to man. It is a source of . . ."

2. EXTREME CLOSE-UP.

The narrative action from the previous shot continues. The camera pans left, following Munch's hand. He is now touching his own lips. *Voiceover*: ". . . pleasure, a wave of sweetness and warmth through which man is elevated and made less lonely." A beat. *Munch's sister* (offscreen): "In her testament, Mamma asked us to be good . . ."

3. MEDIUM SHOT.

Munch's brother and sister are at a table, shown *en face*. He looks at her as she finishes the sentence that has begun in the previous shot. *Munch's sister* (offscreen): ". . . and to love Jesus."

4. AS # 2.

Munch touches his lips while looking at the offscreen self-portrait. *Munch's mother* (offscreen): "Sophie . . ."

5. CLOSE-UP.

Munch's mother, photographed in right profile and partially obscured by glistening objects out of focus (which will, later in the film, turn out to be Christmas tree ornaments). *Munch's mother*: ". . . shall we sing a Christmas carol?"

6. MEDIUM SHOT—CLOSE-UP.

Sophie is now standing by her mother's right side, a few candles twinkling in the foreground. (The cut violates the scene's spatio-temporal continuity.) *Sophie and Munch's mother sing a Christmas carol.* As Sophie turns away from the mother and starts singing, the camera zooms in to the child's face.

Her eyes meet the lens for a moment. When she looks away, the scene cuts.

7. CLOSE-UP.

Christmas carol continues. Sophie—now a couple of years older—is lying in bed, her face pale and her chin red from blood. The hands of a female figure, whose face remains unrevealed to the viewer for the whole duration of the brief shot, are adjusting the child's head on the pillow. Sophie glances at the camera (Figure 4.4).

8. AS # 6.

The camera pans right and stops on Munch as a boy, who appears to be sitting in his mother's lap. He is looking up into his mother's face (offscreen) as she caresses him.

Voiceover: "And suddenly something opened, and we could see far, far into heaven . . ."

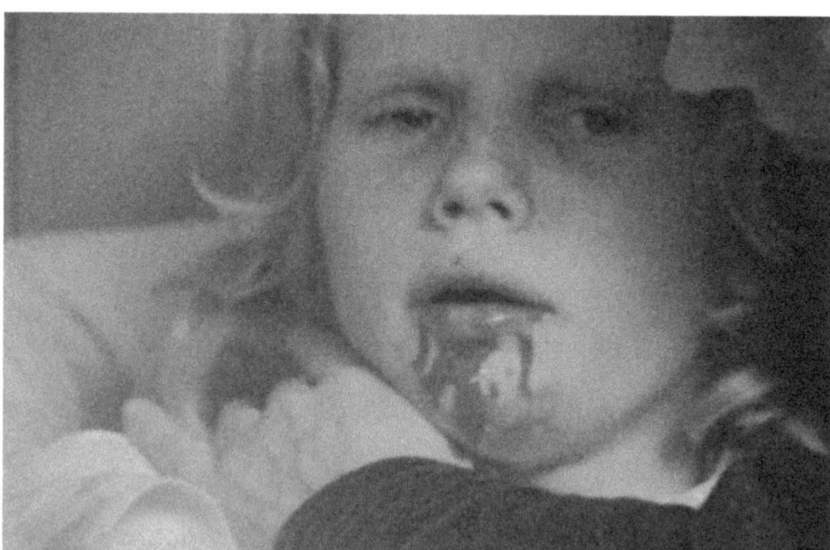

Figure 4.4. An actor acknowledging the camera in *Edvard Munch* (Peter Watkins, NRK / SVT, 1973). Digital frame enlargement.

9. MEDIUM CLOSE-UP.

> Munch as a young man, sitting in a chair and facing the camera, writes as Sophie is dusting a lamp in the background. She coughs as she travels the frame to exit it right. *Voiceover*: ". . . and so angels float, quietly smiling." Munch stops writing and looks at her askance, his expression and the jittering of his leg suggesting distress. Having continued to write, Munch coughs, and Sophie reappears for a moment, this time traveling the frame in the opposite direction. Her movement coincides with a zoom in to Munch's face.

The basic factors of the sequence's rhythm are the images of Munch's face from different phases of his life—the first one being his painted self-portrait, and the subsequent ones constituting photographic representations that purport to be unmediated. Functioning as the "frames" of the sequence are the voiceover (heard at the beginning and toward its end), as well as the theme of eroticism, put forward in the first shot, where Sophie whispers to Edward, and the last one, which features the same characters in a similar domestic scene.

Besides the principal, sexual undertone, the scene possesses an element that links it to the theme of illness: Edvard and Sophie's coughing, which aurally dominates the two preceding scenes. In addition to elaborating on the basic Eros-Thanatos dualism established already by the shots that precede the appearance of the film's title, the sequence complicates the dynamic of its themes by introducing an element that stresses a similarity between them. This new element is the realm of the spiritual, connoted through the theme of Christmas, and the line from Munch's diary with its reference to heaven and angels. In comparison to it, both sexuality and illness—to put the aforementioned principles in the concrete terms suggested by the sequence's imagery—are revealed to be but different aspects of corporeality. The shots of Munch observing the self-portrait, now touching the painted lips and now his own, assert themselves in this narrative context as illustrations of the paradox of art-making as an instance of concretization aimed at transcending the concrete. The associative logic that governs the sequence can be subjected to a finer analysis, to reveal the mechanisms that motivate the connections of images and sounds within it. The example of the last pair of shots described above should suffice. The Christmas carol sung by Sophie motivates the other component of the sound track, the voiceover starting in shot eight with its religious references. Deriving from Munch's diary, the voiceover in turn triggers the cut to the image of Munch writing.

The interpretative possibilities for the sequence become limited after the two related juxtapositions have unfolded. The first of these involves a shot of vermillion red paint cascading out of tube in an extreme close-up, and a shot of Munch as a boy coughing blood into a handkerchief. The second conjunction of shots consists of an image similar to the former in both style and content, and of Munch as an adult, lying in bed with closed eyes and motionless after freezing from an accidental winter fall into a pond. All these groups of images interweave the tropes of sexuality and mortality and point to the rootedness of Munch's art in both.

As another testimony to the sophistication of Watkins's editing, the three pairs of images involving a sick member of the Munch family exemplify the more complex among the editing techniques described by Eisenstein in "Methods of Montage" (1929)—metric, rhythmic, tonal, overtonal, and intellectual. The last among these, the transition from the image of the bloody-faced Sophie to that of her brother in his father's lap, exemplifies tonal editing—joining two shots similar in content and the atmosphere they exude. The middle pair of images, featuring a match between the red paint squeezed out of the tube and the blood Munch the boy coughs out, is an instance of overtonal editing. The transition employs as agents of unity all central visual elements of the shots joined—the shapes and their colors, positions and speeds of movement—and establishes a narrative link between the two actions only gradually, altering and interrogating it throughout the film's duration. The first couple of shots, showing Sophie as she sings a Christmas carol and coughs blood, represents intellectual montage, the contrast in terms of atmosphere that unites the two images being tempered by the resonance at an ideational level between the otherworldly imagery of Christmas carols and the image of Sophie presumably on her deathbed.[16] But the brevity of the last example, its rarity within *Munch* as a whole, and the possibility it affords to be interpreted as a glimpse into the protagonist's association process (and, therefore, as one of many examples of the film's "subjectivity") do not allow intellectual montage to assert itself as the work's dominant structural method.

In addition, while Watkins employs in *Munch* a variety of techniques that evoke Eisenstein, he hardly shares the Soviet practitioner and theorist's pseudo-scientific stance, which configures a film as an equation with definable variables. In Watkins's own account, the process of editing the film was based entirely on instinct, and not on theoretical principles of any kind. Working from a loose script, the filmmaker claims not to have known from one day to another how the next day's cutting would develop (Welsh 181). Even for the era still influenced by the paradigm of auteurism, marked by deliberate challenging of the norms of conventional film production, this mode of working and the resulting product—a film based entirely on associational editing—represent a transgression. This becomes evident in comparison of *Munch* with a film of the most internationally acclaimed Scandinavian filmmaker of the era, Ingmar Bergman. In such Bergman films as *Persona* (1966), associational editing usually connotes interiority, and is used to depict a given protagonist's dreams.

As stated previously, *Munch* fluctuates throughout its duration between the "objective" and "subjective" modes. The above-discussed sequence can serve as an example again. The scenes chronologically predating that with Munch at his self-portrait are configured as flashbacks, and are therefore equivalent to first-person narration in literature (flashbacks always representing a character's memory, always "belonging" to someone). The voiceover, however, challenges the status of these scenes as representations of Munch's recollections. The narrator's introductory note on Munch's diaries as a key source of material cues the viewer to assume that the sentence referring to angels and heaven is the painter's. Yet the quotation does not merely further the depiction of Munch's inner self that has begun with the first flashback, but also distances and objectifies it, its speaker being the same one who previously referred to Munch in the third person. In addition, the same voice (Watkins's) punctuates the entire biopic with information on the contemporaneous world events not directly related to the narrative. The other sequence also unfolds in a non-linear, meandering manner, evidenced by the shot segmentation below.

1. MEDIUM SHOT.

Munch the boy sits in his father's lap, his face buried in the man's shoulder. The aunt is standing in the background, eyeing the camera. *Voiceover*: "Illness, insanity and death were the black angels that kept watch over my cradle, and accompanied me all my life." The aunt goes frame left and reaches for something, as the father is saying to his son inaudible, but presumably comforting, words. The camera zooms to a close-up of the two; Edvard's face now revealed. *Father*: "We can sit by the fire before you go to bed." The boy looks at the camera.

2. CLOSE-UP.

Left profile of Mrs. Heiberg discreetly smiling in a dark interior, her features "softened" by what appears to be a veil of tobacco smoke. She turns her head to the camera, and—the smile now gone—resumes the previous position.

3. CLOSE-UP.

Sophie, shown *en face*, with an expression of guilt and sadness. She spends a few seconds with her eyes cast down (perhaps in prayer before a meal) before looking offscreen right. *Coughing.* Throughout the shot, a blurred segment of another character's head occupies a fraction of the screen's left side. (The first three shots suggest eyeline matches between the three characters) (Figure 4.5).

4. CLOSE-UP.

Edvard coughs into his shoulder (thus making the viewer perceive the shot as spatially and temporally connected to the preceding one) and looks screen right.

5. LONG SHOT—CLOSE-UP.

Edvard the boy, the camera behind his back, peeps through the ajar door where Sophie, her hair wet and her body barely covered with towels, is sitting in a chair, apparently unaware that she is being observed. *Splashing.* The camera rapidly zooms to the girl's crotch and tilts up to her face. *Karen* (offscreen): "My sister Sophie . . ."

6. MEDIUM CLOSE-UP.

Karen, photographed frontally and looking at the camera. *Karen*: ". . . also died from tuberculosis."

7. MEDIUM CLOSE-UP.

Karen is sitting in Sophie's lap. They are both looking just beside the camera, at the blurred, barely recognizable figure of the father. *Karen* (offscreen): "She was 15 years of age." *Father*: "And I saw the dead standing before the throne and

Figure 4.5a, b, and c. "Impossible" eyeline matches challenging the sense of filmic space in *Edvard Munch* (Peter Watkins, NRK / SVT, 1973). Digital frame enlargement.

books were opened." The camera pans right, to reveal Laura sitting in the lap of her aunt. *Father* (offscreen): "*The Book of Life* was opened and the dead were judged in accordance with their deeds and the sea gave up its dead . . ." *Karen* (offscreen): "My sister Laura was very talented. She learned languages and mathematics effortlessly." The camera starts zooming in.

8. MEDIUM SHOT—MEDIUM CLOSE-UP.

Karen, seen from the same angle as in shot # 6. *Karen*: "She got honors in Latin. But she was born with a nervous disposition so she could never . . ."

9. CLOSE-UP.

Laura, slightly frowning and shown in half-left profile, looks up to screen left. *Karen* (offscreen): ". . . make use of her education." Another character's shoulder, out of focus, is seen at the lower left side of the screen. *Father* (offscreen): "Edvard, I want to talk with you."

10. MEDIUM SHOT—MEDIUM CLOSE-UP.

Reacting to the father's words from the previous shot, Edvard the boy straightens up in bed, looking up and right at his father (offscreen), as the camera zooms in rapidly.

11. MEDIUM LONG SHOT—MEDIUM CLOSE-UP.

Sophie is sitting at a bed, looking screen up and right. *Father* (offscreen): "Your aunt says that a plate was broken." The camera pans left to Peter Andreas, who is being tucked in bed by the aunt. *Father* (offscreen): "Was it Peter Andreas?"

12. CLOSE-UP.

Edvard as a young man, veiled by smoke, his eyes cast down. *Peter Andreas* (off-creen): "No, it was Laura." *Karen and Laura* (offscreen): "No, it was Edvard." Munch looks up in reaction to the words of Hans Jaeger (offscreen). *Hans Jaeger* (offscreen): "The Bible says that you're punished. Onan was punished. It also says that man . . ." (At one point during the shot, Jaeger's gesturing hand enters the frame.)

13. AS # 2.

Mrs. Heiberg takes a puff of her cigarette. *Hans Jaeger* (offscreen): ". . . must replenish the earth. One doesn't do that by masturbating!" Mrs Heiberg, smiles coyly as she glances offscreen right, just beside the camera, presumably at Edvard. She looks down. *Munch's aunt* (offscreen): "That was nice and warm, wasn't it?"

Throughout the sequence (and the entire film) Watkins uses select continuity editing techniques to smooth the connections between the imagery drawn from the narrative's vastly disparate time-space continuums. The first eyeline match in the sequence, occurring between the ending and beginning—respectively—of shots 1 and 2, does not conform to verisimilitude: the Munch from the present of the scene, featuring Mrs. Heiberg, is over a decade older than the Munch whose glance the editing configures as being directed to the woman. The shots joined through the glance-object cut between the subsequent two shots appear to belong to the same scene: the identical lighting in shots 3 and 4, and the fact that the blurred head seen in the latter shot is male—which reveals itself only upon frame-by-frame viewing of the shot—support this conclusion. The scene, however, preserves a degree of ambiguity as to the spatial relations between the figures, as it refrains from using a master shot, in accord with the film's general avoidance of the conventions of "invisible style."

Occasionally, however, the film betrays this principle. The scenes central to the film's narrative concerns of Munch's sexual and artistic maturation abandon the dominant technique of montage for continuity editing. The first prolonged use of the latter stylistic system occurs in the brief series of scenes depicting the beginning of Munch's affair with Mrs. Heiberg, and the second in the scenes showing the preparation of the painter's first solo exhibition, and the public's denigrating reactions to it.[17] While films of conventional formal operations often emphasize a narrative moment by foregrounding its cinematography, sound, or editing, *Munch* achieves this effect by temporarily reverting to the syntax of mainstream cinema.

The film delicately alternates between the "third person" and "first person" modes of narration, from the beginning to the longest and most polyphonous montage sequence toward the end, whose status in terms of the categories of "objective" versus "subjective" narration is ambiguous.

The alternations are, however, less frequent in the film's segment where the narrative shifts from the protagonist's interiority to the artistic endeavors he undertook as an already established artist. These involve mostly the acquisition of various new painting techniques, the reports of which are given through the voiceover. In this segment of the film, the voiceover is formal and detached as it is in most educational documentaries. The voiceover thus parallels the shift in the imagery to an "objective" mode, predicated on the significantly fewer intrusions of flashbacks in the narrative's present. The effect of the pseudo-expressionist editing patterns in *Munch* is more visceral than intellectual. The patterns can be associated only vaguely with Brecht's method of structuring an artwork: they are dialectical insofar as they employ contradiction, but not necessarily in the sense of the term that refers to the "art of practice of logical discussion as employed in investigating the truth of a theory or opinion" ("Dialectic"), and invariably not in the sense of dialectics that pertains to the philosophical tradition of dialectical materialism.

The Freethinker

While *Munch* narratively justifies the use of montage by configuring it as a reflection on memory's nonlinearity and the protagonist's diary prose style, *The Freethinker* does not make a similar gesture. If, as Joseph A. Gomez suggests, *The War Game* fell victim to the doctrine in the 1960s British media against "subjective" documentary filmmaking (57), *The Freethinker* can be said to mark an unexpected Watkins's return to the "objective" mode, albeit in the sense of the word much different from that normally employed by TV producers. The film also does not use the voiceover, which in *Edvard Munch* and other Watkins's films of similarly kaleidoscopic structure acts as an agent of unity. It also entirely rejects continuity editing, the elements of which system are consistently used in *Munch* to alleviate the estranging effects of the film's dominant technique.

Two facts other than the respective thematic contents of *Munch* and *The Freethinker* should be accounted for when considering the tremendous difference between the two films' stylistic operations. First, *The Freethinker* was a collaborative project, which involved twenty-four students of the Nordens Folk High School in Biskops Arnö, who—using Watkins's late 1970s screenplay for the unproduced film *August Strindberg* as a basis—made the film under Watkins's creative supervision. Second, the film was realized after Watkins's had already taken a decisive stance against the Monoform, "the standardized and rigid form which had its nascence in the Hollywood cinema" ("Statement"), characterized by "spatial fragmentation, repetitive time rhythms, constantly moving camera, rapid staccato editing, dense bombardment of sound, and lack of silence or reflective space" (ibid.). As mentioned, Watkins acknowledges the historical significance of montages of Eisenstein and Pudovkin (he remarks that "the juxtaposition of two seemingly disparate images to create a third image in one's mind was a startling break from the rigidity of the traditional narrative process at that time") (ibid.) but cautions against the use of the technique today. *The Freethinker* is, then, Eisensteinian despite its maker, who questionably links intellectual editing to the accelerated editing pace of much of today's cinema and television.

The following shot-by-shot breakdown of a sequence from *The Freethinker* illustrates the editing style of the film as a whole.

1. INTERTITLE:

"November 5, 1882. Strindberg's drama *Sir Bengt's Wife* premieres in Stockholm's New Theatre. Siri is in the title role." *Ticking of a clock's pendulum.* (The sound continues until shot 16.)

2. INTERTITLE:

"The drama does not please the critics and Siri's performance is judged the only redeeming feature. Strindberg feels that Siri, succeeding where he has failed, has humiliated him."

3. MEDIUM LONG SHOT.

A historic photo of Strindberg as a middle-aged man, looking at the lens as he sits on a bench in front of a house with a hand buried in his coat (Figure 4.6a).

4. MEDIUM SHOT.

Strindberg as an old man hangs a framed photograph of his daughter on a wall. Having adjusted the position of the picture, he steps back, leaving the frame.

5. CLOSE-UP.

Strindberg's handwriting. An underline emphasizes the word "*beröringen*" (contacts) (Figure 4.6b).

Figure 4.6a, b, and c. Diverse visual materials combined in a montage sequence of *The Freethinker* (Peter Watkins, Nordens Folk High School / Biskops Arnö, 1994). Digital frame enlargement.

6. MEDIUM SHOT, slightly high angle.

Strindberg, shown from the back, leafs through a book on the desk at which he is sitting.

7. INTERTITLE:

"1904. Strindberg and Harriet Bosse divorce but continue their intimate relationship until January 1907."

8. INTERTITLE:

"May 1908. Harriet Bosse marries the actor Gunnar Wingård."

9. AS # 6.

Strindberg munches as he reads, a fork with a piece of cheese in his hand. *Strindberg's humming* (the sound continues until shot 13).

10. MEDIUM CLOSE-UP.

A straight-on shot of Harriet Bosse, Strindberg's second wife, looking into the lens (Figure 4.6c).

11. EXTREME CLOSE-UP.

A slow pan across the spines of books in different languages and on a variety of subjects. (One of the titles mentions the Tibetan language.) *Hariet Bosse*: "While I was pregnant with Ann-Marie, Strindberg was kind and thoughtful to me the whole time. He couldn't help stirring up the matter of women's rights occasionally. Strindberg's whiskers quivered. He walked away to a washstand in his room. He washed his hands a number of times, nervously and quickly, which he always did when he was upset." *Trickling of water* (the sound continues until shot 16). *Hariet Bosse*: "Then the storm was over."

12.–16. CLOSE-UPS.

Fragments of Strindberg's manuscripts on the subjects of the Chinese and Hebrew scripts. (The word "Tibet" dominates the middle shot.) *A military march* (the sound continues until the end of shot 29).

17. MEDIUM LONG SHOT.

Still image showing about a dozen members of a military orchestra, playing as they march down a street. *The music intensifies in volume.*

18. INTERTITLE:

"Around the turn of the century, the Swedish authorities erect elaborate triumphal arches to celebrate the arrival in Stockholm of Important Personages . . ."

19. INTERTITLE:

". . . such as Kaiser Wilhelm of Germany, President Fallières of France, King Frederik of Denmark, and the explorer Sven Hedin on his return from Tibet."

20. INTERTITLE:

"Some of the costly receptions are staged around the time of the Great Strike of 1909."

21.–29. CLOSE-UPS.

Historic still images of the above-mentioned festivities.

30. MEDIUM SHOT.

Strindberg as an old man at his desk, occasionally looking at the camera as he writes.

31. INTERTITLE:

"At the beginning of 1910, Strindberg engages in the last struggle of his life, 'The Strindberg Feud.' "

32. INTERTITLE:

"Strindberg is angered by the recognition given to his rivals the explorer Sven Hedin and the writer Verner von Heidenstam, and by their reactionary stand against the labor movement."

No live-action shot included in the sequence features more than a single character. Its "drama" is abstract, the conflicts within it Eisensteinian (or Brechtian) rather than Griffithian (or Aristotelian)—to use somewhat simplifying comparisons for the sake of brevity. The main contrast within the sequence is, broadly, that between Strindberg's private life and his public endeavors. The film's already mentioned focus on the continuities, rather than discontinuities, between the two domains allows for the sequence's dramaturgical development and climax. The information on Strindberg's professional jealousy toward Siri links with his infamous misogyny, also thematized elsewhere in the film and in *Munch*. However, the unfavorable picture of the writer the film paints gets complicated no sooner than it is made. The historic image of Strindberg that follows the first two intertitles appears chosen precisely because it is unrelated to his marriage and profession. Strindberg is looking at the camera in a contrived pose, as though actively trying to conceal his true self, with which the viewer has been acquainted through the intertitles. The next shot, though, disturbs the established relationship: the suggestion of the character's tenderness and affection for his daughter counteracts the earlier one of Strindberg's conceit. The shot of his manuscript segment with the underlined word "beröringen" furthers this move. If considered in the context of the entire narrative, however, the image can be said to carry the opposite suggestion. Namely, one can attribute Strindberg's loneliness to his earlier decision to leave the family in pursuit of alchemy experiments. Yet neither of the two possible interpretations has a greater claim of accuracy than the other: through its peculiar ordering of story material, the film maintains a degree of ambiguity. Frequently singled out by commentators as a key feature of European art cinema, *The Freethinker*'s ambiguity differs from Buñuel's, Resnais's, and Antonioni's, to mention some of the most celebrated representatives of the mentioned strain of filmmaking. In Watkins's film, ambiguity represents not a structural corollary of its characters' confusion, trauma, or some other peculiar mental state, nor a demonstration of the filmmaker's demiurgic powers (as is often the case in the films of the mentioned art cinema filmmakers), but a tacit acknowledgment of the limits of the filmmakers' knowledge of the story world, an expression of a refusal to totalize the narrative by subjecting its elements to the Hollywood logic of cause and effect. In addition, the story's lacunae function as a proof of its accuracy: in not providing definite answers to all questions it raises, *The Freethinker* can be regarded as true to the contingency and untidiness of life.

The protagonist's relatively redeeming quality suggested by the shot where he hangs his daughter's photo is subsequently brought into question through the series of shots that explain Strindberg's progressive social activism in terms of his professional jealousy. If the explorer Sven Hedin and the writer Verner von Heidenstam were not given the recognition Strindberg had vainly desired, one is led to conclude from the choice and order of the related information in the intertitles, then the protagonist would not have minded their reactionary stand against the labor movement. The sequence thus dialectically moves from the realm of public into that of private life, while stressing the connection between them. First, the sequence juxtaposes a demonstration of Strindberg's professional jealousy to that of his love for his daughter, and then creates an association between Strindberg's politics and his professional envy. There lies the sequence's understated symmetry, whereby its various elements cohere together.

As the sequence unfolds, certain images—in line with the film's dialectical orientation—acquire meanings that cancel the ones they had initially. The shots of Strindberg's manuscripts and their temporal position, for example, at first connect merely to the negative critical response to *Sir Bengt's Wife* to form a connection that can be literally represented thus: the protagonist finds consolation from his public failure in the solitary studying of languages and reminiscing about his daughter. But after the information is conveyed that one of the celebrations hosted by the Swedish authorities at a triumphal arch was in honor of the explorer Sven Hedin upon his return from Tibet, the word "Tibet"—which dominates shot 14—gains a relevance. Considered in retrospect, the image can be interpreted as evidence that Strindberg, too, explored Tibet, albeit in a different (and perhaps more substantial) manner. Understood this way, the shot complicates the question of Strindberg's jealousy, making his anger more humanly acceptable.

If we figuratively divide the principles according to which a film sequence organizes together images and sounds into the "outside" and "inside" ones—the former group concerning the filmmaker's intentions with the material, and the "inside" ones on the intrinsic narrative and stylistic properties of the "raw" video and audio recordings—it becomes apparent that the sequence under analysis owes something to both. This might be obvious to some, but stressing it helps establish a distinction between the editing pattern of *The Freethinker* and the concept of intellectual editing as theorized and practically applied by Eisenstein. While Eisenstein—in the world's deities sequence in *October*, for example—freely combines diegetic and nondiegetic shots whose salient graphic properties are hardly comparable, the above-outlined sequence and *The Freethinker* as a whole carry out the abstracting process only to an extent. Besides the already-cited contrasts within the sequence, there are also key similarities between its two elements: its structure predicates itself equally on both. For example, the film's editing together of the historic image of Strindberg and the character hanging his daughter's image does not operate merely on the principle of contrast between the writer's public image of a vitriolic polemicist—embodied in the historic photograph—and his mellow private side—connoted through the shot that follows it, but uses also the principle of similarity: the motif of the photograph appears in both shots. Beside the foregrounded discontinuity from the one shot to the next in terms of space, time, and action, the transition is motivated by an unemphasized continuity. Likewise, besides the obvious difference between the documentary material and the live-action shots, the two groups of imagery comprising the sequence feature a salient similarity: the actors' movements are restrained (most strikingly in the shot where Hariet Bosse poses for Watkins's video camera, much like the real Strindberg poses for the still camera of the unknown photographer in his historic portrait).

In conclusion, the most conspicuous feature of the sequence's style—in comparison with *Edvard Munch*—is the replacement of the voiceover narration with intertitles. In the earlier film, "the Watkins narrator" functions as a structuring anchor, supplementing the voice of the taciturn protagonist and conveying an array of other information on the narrative and its historical context. And while the detachment of the voiceover from the diegesis inherently carries the implication of objectivity, the fact remains that the technique entails a performance. As such, the voiceover cannot be emotionally neutral. One could easily make an argument that Watkins, whose voice is the film's central organizing device, is more probable a point of spectatorial identification than the protagonist himself. The filmmaker's repeated statements on Munch's autobiographical dimension serve this argument well: the viewer aware of it may identify with the painter by identifying with Watkins and vice versa. *The Freethinker*, with its reliance on intertitles instead of "the Watkins narrator"—a device that simultaneously serves and dominates the narrative—theoretically allows its characters to come closer to the fore, thereby enabling an easier Aristotelian identification. However, the film circumvents this possibility by the following means: (1) the disruption of the story's chronology and, consequently, a blurring of the causal connections amongst its elements; (2) the use of historic visual material, which works to emphasize the gap between the actors and the characters they portray; (3) the use of an acting style that entails the distancing acknowledgment of the camera; (4) the use of an editing style that counters the idea of organic character representation through separating its visual and aural aspects; and (5) the use of metafilmic excursions (the scenes of the actors' commenting on and debating their characters). The above-outlined sequence offers examples for all but the last of the four identified strategies (the second and the third of which directly correspond to Brechtian ideas of *Verfremdung*, *Historisierung*, and *Prinzip der Trennung*). And while all but the last strategy are employed also in *Edvard Munch*, their combination with the other most prominent narrative and stylistic features of the film—its disinterest in visual representation of character interiority and the rejection of continuity editing—is unique in the corpus of Watkins's feature films.

The Freethinker's last two salient characteristics are related. The former stems from the film's exploration of biographical facts on Strindberg and his time less in terms of their emotional than their intellectual implications. Even the writer's well-known psychological turbulences concern the film only inasmuch as they are reflected in his art, whose narrative and stylistic properties are, conversely, relevant to the film only to the extent to which they inform Strindberg's thought system, its contradictions and its evolution. *The Freethinker*'s emphasis on the protagonist's intellect (announced already by the film's title) is achieved largely through the editing pattern whereby images and sounds are organized around ideas rather than the characters' life trajectories. In this respect, *The Freethinker* departs from the conventions of the Hollywood subgenre of biopic. This departure is radicalized by the controlled oscillations throughout the film in the logic behind this basic organizational pattern, which configure Watkins's editorial reasoning not as monolithic and superior to that of his protagonist and the other characters, but as equally contradictory and prone to change. In rejecting the largely "first person mode" of *Munch*, *The Freethinker* does not adopt the "third person mode" of Hollywood cinema, which predicates itself on the use of continuity editing. If we accept Colin MacCabe's view that this syntax implies a singularity of perspective whose existence it simultaneously works to conceal (MacCabe), then it follows that Watkins's choice of Eisensteinian intellectual montage as a structuring technique for *The Freethinker* was intended to enable the film's dialectical maneuvering.

Considered alongside each other, the two films are illustrative of the trajectory that has led Watkins from Eisensteinian montage of attractions, used in conjunction with select genre conventions and elements of mainstream cinema syntax, to *The Freethinker* as an example of intellectual montage, comparable with the Soviet filmmaker's unproduced *Capital* as much as *Munch* can be likened with *Battleship Potemkin*. The strong affinities of that film's formal operations with those of Brecht's own works for the stage and screen are attributable broadly to *The Freethinker*'s refusal to subsume its stylistic unorthodoxies to the logic of psychological realism. In contradistinction, *Munch* espouses that strategy, using instead characterization as the primary among the film's narrative elements. This brings *Munch* close to the tradition of the organic work of art, which Brecht opposed throughout his theoretical and practical oeuvre, but which retained a positive connotation over the course of development of Eisenstein's aesthetics.[18]

Revolution as a Brechtian Lehrstück: *La commune* (Paris 1871)

Watkins's most recent film, *La commune (Paris 1871)*, is also the filmmaker's most ambitious docudrama to date, surpassing in both thematic scope and length all his previous works within the category.[19] While his early epic film *Culloden* focuses on a single historical event that transpired in a matter of days, *La Commune* spans the whole two-month history of the world's first socialist republic, referencing through its frequent metafilmic excursions also a number of topical events contemporary with the political entity or with the film's production. A viewer of *La Commune* whom Watkins quotes in his commentary of the work praises the film for "[containing] everything: emotion, a sense of struggle, poetry, psychodrama" ("La Commune"). The comparison with psychodrama, a technique developed in the early 1930s by the Austrian American psychosociologist Jacob L. Moreno, owes to Watkins's combining of historical reenactment with improvised dialogue. Yet the function of psychodrama is strictly therapeutic, while the result of the cast's work on *La Commune*—which one is led to conclude from the interviews with them that the film includes—is their enhanced understanding of the short-lived political entity, and its relation to the present of the film's production. Based on this, it would be more apt to compare *La Commune* and the Brechtian *Lehrstück*.

Bertolt Brecht's earliest use of the term *Lehrstück* was in reference to *Das Badener Lehrstück* (The Baden Learning Play), premiered in 1929 at the *Kammermusikfest* in the play's eponymous city, and he wrote most of the other plays within the category before 1939.[20] The first commentator to try systematizing Brecht's thought on the *Lehrstück* into a coherent theory, Rainer Steinweg, points to the misleading quality of the play type's name (literally rendered into English by Martin Esslin as the didactic play). Contrary to what might be intuited from its name, the *Lehrstück* is conceived as a means not of transmitting a lesson contained in the text to its players and observers, but of investigating an issue (which, in all six completed and a few unfinished *Lehrstücke*, concerns the relationship between the individual and society, the contradiction between social responsibility and a fulfilled private life [Vaßen 202 and Steinweg, as paraphrased in ibid.]). Aimed primarily for the player, the

Lehrstück challenges the principle of *Verfremdung* (in the sense of spectator distantiation), as developed in epic/dialectic theater. (Rainer Friedrich notes the paradox that Brecht, whose epic/dialectic theater project conforms to "the Benjaminian program of emancipating art from its parasitic dependence on ritual" ["Postmodernism" 52], returns with the *Lehrstück* to the ritual drama, as testified by his instructions on how the plays of this type should be performed: "spiritually, ceremonially, ritually") (Brecht, qtd. in ibid.; translation mine). To avoid the widespread associations of the *Lehrstück* with vulgar Marxism, Agitprop, and political indoctrination, Steinweg uses the term *Entdeckungsstück* (discovery play) to describe Brecht's intention for the play type (19), while Florian Vaßen considers the rendition of the term as learning play (and its reverse translation as *Lern-Spiel*) as more true to the spirit of the dramaturgical model (201).

Apart from its abolishment of the performer/spectator dichotomy, the *Lehrstück*'s defining characteristics are its use of the chorus and music, and of types instead of fleshed-out characters. For example, *The Measures Taken*—the *Lehrstück* Brecht singled out in a late interview as an exemplary play for the future (Hertoffer 214)—identifies its parts in terms of their respective social functions: the Young Comrade and Four Agitators.[21]

In disputing the dialectical nature of *Lehrstücke*, which other Brecht plays written after his discovery of Marxism in 1926 aimed for, Friedrich cites the enthusiastic reception the first performance of the play in Berlin in 1931 enjoyed by the Right ("Brecht and Postmodernism" 53–54).[22] Yet this view can be easily challenged: Brecht's handling of the narrative element of the play that Friedrich cites as the reason for its critical success with the Right—the Four Agitator's sacrifice of the Young Comrade to a Great Custom of which no rational account could be given (54)—can be said to successfully oppose ideological petrification, hence its ability to attract audiences from the part of the political spectrum opposite to the playwright's. Indeed, one can easily imagine the narrative of the play remolded as to fit a doctrine that surpasses the Left-Right dichotomy: for example, that of liberal capitalism. In such a version of the play's plot, the five protagonists could be turned into representatives of a soft drink company investigating the possibility of erecting a bottling plant in a country with cheap labor, and the Young Comrade could be replaced by an agent whose discovery of the unionizing issues underlying the enterprise gives her second thoughts about the political correctness of the company's policy.

But to return to Watkins's film: in what ways does it correspond to the *Lehrstück* as a theatrical *model*? One of these is thematic. Vaßen points to the prevalence of the topics of violence and bodily destruction in the

Lehrstücke, both of which marked the short-lived Parisian government of 1871 (Vaßen 204). True to the aesthetic principle suggested by his critique of the increasingly violent content in the MAVM expressed on his website, Watkins avoids graphic depictions of the violent acts perpetrated by both the Communards and the Versaillaise: an intertitle conveys that the archbishop Darboy has been executed, and offscreen sounds of rifle shots convey the mass executions of Parisians affiliated with the Commune. Save for the oft-reproduced photograph of the bodies of twelve Communards in lined-up coffins, none of the visual documents the film includes show a scene of death, despite the ample availability of such imagery: two of the relatively few illustrations in David A. Shafer's *The Paris Commune* (2005), for example, depict killed national guardsmen and children. Perhaps wary of the potentially melodramatic effect of graphic imagery, Watkins evading the events stylistically while insisting upon them narratively.

The film resembles a *Lehrstück* also in terms of its characterization, dialogue, and acting style. About 60 percent of the cast, comprising over 220 people, had no prior experience as performers. While the credits cite Peter Watkins and Agathe Bluysen as the script's writers, it was the actors who provided the dialogue, whose accuracy was ensured by the research they had been required to conduct on their own. To evoke the multiplicity of accents and dialects that had been spoken in the Paris Commune, Watkins and his casting crew also enlisted people from different regions of France. The political conviction is genuine of both the actors who perform the Commune's sympathizers and of those playing their opponents: through the conservative press in Versailles and Paris, the film's casting crew also engaged people of conservative politics.[23] Later in the pre-production process, the cast formed groups on the basis of their respective characters' occupation and social position to discuss the background of the people they were portraying, as well as the relevance of the Commune for the present sociohistorical conditions. The dialogue's pace was narratively controlled by the journalists of the Commune TV (Gérard Watkins and Aurélia Petit), and by Watkins's and Agathe Bluysen's editing.[24]

A majority of *La Commune*'s scenes are configured as footage recorded by the fictitious broadcast station's journalists and their cameraman. The potentially estranging effect of this anachronism represents another point of continuity with earlier films by Watkins, whose first feature, *Culloden*, uses the same technique. In his "Media Statement," Watkins explains this aesthetic choice for his debut feature as follows: "I employed the style used in Vietnam War news broadcasts in order to bring a sense of familiarity to scenes from an 18th century battle, in the hope that this anachronism would also function to subvert the authority of the very genre I was using" ("Introduction"). Similarly, the journalists in *La Commune* wander through the 11th arrondisement of Paris (one of the city's twenty administrative districts, populated mostly by the working class), interviewing people about the situation, often moving from one group to the next in the midst of a debate they have initiated. This strategy requires long takes, which are, again, enabled by the use of a mobile, handheld camera in combination with a unique lighting scheme and sound-recording technique. The former predicates itself on neon lights, regularly spaced on the ceiling of the improvised studio to give an even illumination, while the sound was recorded using a portable mixing system, which followed the actors through the set (ibid.).

As can be inferred from my description, the film mimics the style of documentary reportage. It rejects continuity editing and the various elements of its syntax in favor of more specifically televisual techniques, a strategy most conspicuously manifested in the film's reliance on close shots and its dramaturgy of numerous "low peaks" that goes against the Aristotelian three-part structure. But unlike Godard in his Marxist phase, for example, Watkins does not lay bare the arbitrariness of the mainstream style of filmmaking by deconstructing it, instead merely replacing it with the exaggerated conventions of a related medium.

La Commune compensates for its timidity in probing the medium's conventions by an effective use of the estranging devices that can best be described by the Czech structuralists' term *aktualizace* (topicalization). The use of the device is common in theater: examples include the allusions in Adrian Noble's 1984 Royal Shakespeare Company production of *Henry V* to the Falklands crisis, to the war in Bosnia in Mark Wing-Davey's 1995 staging of *Troilus and Cressida* at the Delacorte Theater in New York, and to the Iraq war in Deborah Warner's 2005 production of *Julius Caesar*. In cinema, whose capacity for mimeticism practitioners more readily embrace than interrogate, the use of *aktualizace* is less common. Examples include the frequent anachronisms in the cinema of Straub and Huillet—which work to draw the viewer's critical attention to the continuities and discontinuities between the present of a given film's narrative and that of its production and/or reception—and Lars von Trier's use in *Dogville* (2003) of documentary images of the American poor—some of which postdate the era in which the film's story is set—in conjunction with David Bowie's 1975 song "Young Americans."

Apart from the mentioned anachronistic presence of television in Peter Watkins's *Culloden* and *La Commune*, the latter film contains an example of a different kind of *aktualizace*. After the film has made numerous but indirect references to the present of the production through its commentaries on television, the relation of its narrative to the sociohistoric circumstances of today comes to the fore. This takes place approximately three hours into the film's duration, in the first of the improvised scenes with the performers out of their characters. A remark by a citizen on the media's producing the false understanding that "economic problems come before social ones," and the example of Japan's economic decline in the late 1980s, triggers an intertitle with statistics on the continually widening gap between the world's rich and poor since the days of the Commune. This is followed by a scene showing five *fédéres* and citizens of the 11th *arrondisement* sitting at a table in a wine pub. The actor playing a *fédére* says that "there are problems everywhere: outcasts, illegal aliens, destitute people who need help. Now's the time to open the phone book, call, do something." The narrative excursion owes its effectiveness to occurring relatively late in the film. The intertitles that compare the late nineteenth and late twentieth centuries and the conditions of the first and third world among others do not sufficiently prepare the viewer for the scene's complete merging of the two timelines (that of the Commune and that of the recent history of France and the rest of the world).

The film's dominant technique of pulling the dialogues forward, the interviews the Commune TV journalists conduct with people tied to the government, has both advantages and limitations. The interviews facilitate swift introduction of characters, the large number thereof reflecting the revolution's popular character. But even when the interviewers manage to incite a debate between the interviewees, the viewer is left with the impression that the presence of their microphones is thwarting the full development of the dramatic situation's potential. The performers often appear reluctant to express themselves with the intensity of which they seem capable, a fact that might be attributable to the predilection of the Commune TV to abandon their subjects in the midst of their improvising. The political thrust of the scenes where the performers comment not just on the Commune, but also on its global legacy and the world's current global sociopolitical landscape, surpass those that constitute the film's bulk. This assessment can be illustrated with an example from the scene whose beginning is described above. To the remark of the actor performing a *fédére* concerning the need to "open the phone book, call, do something,"[25] another actor in a *fédére* costume replies: "So you open the phone book, what page?" Following this, the first actor mentions the many NGOs in existence, thereby opening a genuine debate.

This aspect of Watkins's method evokes the narratologist André Jolles's term *casus* as used by Fredric Jameson in his reflection on Brecht.

Referring broadly to character's judgment making, and exemplified by the decision Shen Te makes in *The Good Person of Szechwan*, *casus* is linked to the broader project of Brechtian dialectics. ("Once a *casus* is settled and a judgment made," writes Jameson, "the 'case,' as it were, drops out of the form, and we have merely a simple empirical narrative. It is the contradiction which makes for the uniqueness of this simple form" [*Brecht* 121]). The debates in *La Commune* are dialectical insofar as they are open-ended, a quality that owes to the filmmaker's editorial interventions of balancing arguments and counter-arguments, of treating antagonistic views as if their weights are equal. The actors with conservative political views (performing the representatives of the Versailles government and its television station, as well as its troops) are conspicuously absent from the debates. A direct confrontation between the politically antagonistic groups of performers would, perhaps, result in a demonstration of either side's militancy, or a necessity for such stance for the achievement of a social upturn of the Commune's scope. But Watkins, who has consistently shown a pacifist agenda in most of his films from the amateur shorts to *The Journey*, would have problems reconciling such conclusions with his own politics.

Commentators on the Paris Commune from Engels onward have identified as key factors that contributed to the political entity's quick demise the failure of the revolutionaries to seize the Bank of France, to prevent the evacuation of Thiers and the members of his government to Versailles, as well as two military decisions. The first of these was to take no military action against Versailles (even though on the second day of the Commune's existence, when calls for such a move were first made, the National Guard numbered 200,000 soldiers in contrast to Versaille's 12,000 to 20,000 troops, dispirited from the loss of the war with Prussia) (Shafer 65). The second decision was not to occupy one of the forts surrounding the city—that of Mont-Valérien, described by Shafer as arguably the most strategic one (64). In accordance with the views of scientific socialism, according to which the liberation of the oppressed cannot occur without a violent revolution, Brecht echoes the above detailed criticisms of the Communards' strategy in *The Days of the Commune*. He highlights these criticisms by frequently ending a scene with a representation of their occurrence. Two examples should suffice. Scene 7c focuses on the negotiations of Beslay, a member of the Central Committee, with the governor of the Bank of France. The latter character, having dismissed Beslay after deflecting his threat to loot the bank if the sum of ten million francs is not redirected from Versailles to the Central Committee, opens the door to the room where a priest has been hiding and ends the scene with the following words:

"You may tell the Archbishop, the ten million francs will go by way of the usual route to Versailles" (61). Scene 11a, which shows a session of the Commune, follows a similar procedure. Toward the scene's end, Delescleuze gives a monologue against violence. "Let us continue peacefully to bring harmony into human relationships and to end man's exploitation of man," he says, convincing a majority of the Committee members to vote against reprisals. The stage direction "*Loud gun fire*" (75) follows Delescleuze's summing up the mentioned decision, whereas the character's "Let us continue with the matter in hand" (ibid.) constitutes the scene's last line.

Watkins's film, too, includes the facts considered to be the causes of the Commune's failure, but it does not give them the hierarchical position they hold in historical accounts or artistic representations of the short-lived government. A comparison of a scene from *La Commune* with the one from the discussed Brecht's play clearly evidences this assertion. Filmed in one long take in medium shot, with the camera occasionally panning to reveal the figures at the opposite sides of a table, the scene in question also shows a meeting of the Central Committee. An intertitle identifying the Committee members in attendance (Eugène Protot, Edouard Vaillant, Eugène Varlin, Augustin Avrial, Leo Frankel, Francis Jourde, and Augustin Verdure) sets up the scene, whose dialogue is as follows:[26]

> Concerning the artillery, there's no shortage of cannon, ammunition, even gunners. What's lacking is organization. We always come back to this. Instead of endless discussions and quarrels, the Commune should split into two groups. One would stay here, and the other would go and fight. That's our role and our duty. Enough discussion and waste! We must act!
>
> You might recall how enthusiastic I was about a month ago. Today I can't hide my despair. Being so close to the cause of women, I find, we've done nothing for them . . . even though they have such dire needs.
>
> Sorry to come back to this again. . . . We're talking about organization, wasted time, our failure toward women and education. But I believe that it's due to our lack of clarity regarding the central political question. We can tackle social progress with strong republican institutions, and a firmly established power and administration. Instead we tried to handle everything in one go.

> No. It's a question of time. You can't say that!
>
> We're assessing 40 days' work. We can't do everything!
>
> So we need an executive power.
>
> Yes. A strong executive power. Right now we have an assembly of 85 members. Everyone debates, no one obeys.
>
> We're often fewer than 85.
>
> True, and probably so much the better!
>
> What are our priorities? We can make long-term plans, but if the Versaillais arrive, it's finished.
>
> We've lost Fort Issy now! So let's not forget the urgency of the military situation.
>
> But wait a minute. I was the first to talk about priorities. The National Guard, feeding the people, keeping alive trust, etc. But we should not go against our own principles. We've been chosen to organize a government, a Commune, to be as democratic as possible. Circumstances are difficult.
>
> We know that. We did our best. If we don't succeed, it will serve as a lesson for others. And I'm not at all in favor of handing over power to a dictatorship, just because the situation is extreme.
>
> You prefer not to make the necessary means to save a revolution because of your principles? What other solutions do we have? None. People getting ruffled if it's called a Committee of Public Safety is of no importance compared to what will happen to us if we're not swift and efficient.

Both Brecht's and Watkins's scenes prompt the same conclusion of the necessity of the Parisians' mobilizing against the Versaillais. But while *The Days of the Commune* allows the viewer to infer the conclusion herself, *La Commune* makes it on her behalf. Hence the arguably weaker effect of the latter work in comparison with that of Brecht's scene.

As implied, the principal source of theatricality of *La Commune* is not the acting style, which evokes documentary reportages, but the setting and—as the corollaries of it—the props, the lighting and the figure placement. In his discussion of the film, Watkins explains that "the set was carefully designed to 'hover' between reality and theatricality, with careful and loving detail applied for example to the texture of the walls, but with the edges of the set always visible, and with the 'exteriors'—the Rue Popincourt and the central Place Voltaire—clearly seen for what they are—artificial elements within an interior space" ("La Commune"). The first half of the remark applies also, for instance, to the loaves of bread on a shelf the camera glimpses while traveling through the deserted set in the first sequence. These props are convincing from the standpoint of verisimilitude, but too few to meet the pertinent criterion of "surface realism," the style concerned with the effects—rather than causes—of various social phenomena. Similarly, the neon lighting often successfully disguises its artificiality in the interior scenes, only to reveal it blatantly in the exterior ones. In the same vein, the figure placement follows the criteria of verisimilitude in the interior scenes, which employ relatively small numbers of figures, but fails to do so in the exterior scenes, as a consequence of the theatrically simplified setting they employ.

The setting's interconnected spaces facilitate the use of the long take, which dictates a slow editing pace. Still, the descriptor "Bazinian" Welsh uses to describe the aesthetic of later Watkins films (341) is only partly valid. Like the Gregg Toland–photographed films that Bazin celebrates, *La Commune* relies for much of its duration on the wide angle lens of a video camera, with its considerable depth of field (Figure 4.7). But the editing scheme of Watkins's film does not conform to Bazin's anti-Eisensteinian view, which privileges the creation of meaning through juxtaposing elements within an image over its creation through montage. Although the cutting pace of *La Commune* is slower than that of any Eisenstein's film, it abounds with examples of associational editing, a technique akin to that which the Soviet film theorist designates as intellectual.

Offered below is an example of Watkins's organizing the material according to the principle of association rather than dramatic action. Toward the end of a debate scene with the actors out of character, a young woman testifies about her personal gain from the participation in the production. "I had that feeling of giving and receiving," she says. "Especially receiving, a lot and from everyone." Next, we see two consecutive intertitles with the following text: "The participation of the cast in the making of this film is precisely what the global media are afraid

Figure 4.7a, b, and c. Depth of field in three consecutive phases of the opening shot of *La commune* (Peter Watkins, 13 Production / La Sept Arte / Le Musée d'Orsay, 1999). Digital frame enlargement.

of, and probably one of the main reasons why the TV channels which were asked for support, refused to finance this film. What the media are particularly afraid of, is to see the man in the little rectangle, replaced by a multitude of people, by the public." The film then cuts to an image of a "man in the little rectangle," the TV Versailles news presenter, who announces that news has reached their teleprinters that a court-martial has been set up to rule on cases of insubordination among the National Guard officers. A moment of black screen follows, after which a scene opens where the officer Charles de Beaufort demeans the guardsmen by characterizing their fighting the Versaillais as "brave, but foolish," and describing them as "half-undressed, badly shaven, drunkards!" Next, we see an intertitle that describes the officer as an aristocrat sharing the political views of his cousin Edouard Moreau, whose dandyism and position as aide-de-camp arouse animosity.

The scene featuring the news presenter illustrates the intertitle's statement and establishes a new theme. The character's announcement also marks the beginning of a sequence that exemplifies a dominant structuring principle of *La Commune*: contrasting the TV reports on different Commune-related events with the images and sounds of the events coded as actual. As the above example demonstrates, *La Commune*'s shots often acquire additional meaning in conjunction with the preceding or subsequent ones, while functioning as self-sufficient sources of their respective primary meanings. This constitutes the greatest difference between the editing patterns of this film and Watkins's earlier works.[27]

Both the originality and the lack of it in *La Commune* appear to result from the work's disregard of the history and yet unexplored potentials of the medium for which it was initially intended, television, as well as of the medium whose stylistic conventions it uses, theater. Bringing up the trope of originality appears apt in light of Watkins's statement that the film was made in reaction to the postmodernist state of affairs, even though he associates the cultural trend with "eliminating humanistic and critical thinking in the education system" ("La Commune") and not conventionally, as a feeling that "everything has been done." Claims of novelty pervade Brecht's discussions of epic/dialectic theater and the *Lehrstück*, and evoking the playwright and theorist repeatedly in this analysis seemed appropriate considering the stylistic similarities between *La commune* and the *Lehrstücke*, and the narrative ones between Watkins's film and *The Days of Commune*. The film's progressive aspects such as its participatory, democratic nature and political radicalism bring it close to the *Lehrstücke*, while the narrowly imposed limits of these features make *La commune* comparable to *The Days of Commune*. This play—its meanings fixed and its apparent purpose of "artistically softening" the truth of the Commune as formulated by the classics of scientific socialism—well exemplifies a didactic, as opposed to a learning, play. With improvisation as its principal acting technique, the difference between *La Commune* the film and the work's hypothetical live telecast would be greater than that separating Delbert Mann's film *Marty* (1955) from the original, live TV version of Paddy Chayefsky's drama (1953). If the film stops short of the avant-gardism of the *Lehrstück*, it does so because it does not acknowledge the tradition and engage with it, but arrives at its techniques intuitively.

Conclusion

In its professional aspect, Peter Watkins's trajectory as a filmmaker bears comparison with that of Orson Welles: like the maker of *Citizen Kane* (1941), Watkins found himself at the pinnacle of career success with his first features (the controversy around *The War Game* notwithstanding), only to get slowly but steadily marginalized with his subsequent efforts.[28] In its artistic aspect, Watkins's trajectory has zigzagged from the films that predicate themselves on Eisensteinian montage of attractions (*The War Game*, *Culloden*) to *The Journey* and *The Freethinker*, whose editing scheme frequently corresponds to Eisenstein's concept of intellectual editing. All the while, the filmmaker's thematic preoccupations (war, nuclear armament, different forms of social oppression, and famous rebel artists) have remained constant. In Watkins's latest work, *La Commune*, the stylistic emphasis shifts to acting: the cinematography, sound, and editing seem to adjust to the mise-en-scène—with the improvising performers as its central elements—more than in the earlier films.

Such details from the pre-production histories of Watkins's films as the drastic diversion of the finished *The Journey* from its originally planned length of ninety minutes (Watkins, "Fear" 230) give rise to the thought that the figure of a misunderstood and martyred artist Watkins has configured himself to be is not simply a product of the repressive production and distribution media system—as he consistently suggests is the case—but partly a result also of a self-fulfilling prophecy. A feature that logically accompanies the position Watkins has been forced into (or chosen) is that of "the last Mohican" of modernism—as suggested by the filmmaker's critique of postmodernism ("La Commune"). While he is in general a highly innovative figure, his individual films and writings do not always meet the modernist imperative of originality. Both kinds of his creative output fall between rather than within the contemporary theoretical and practical currents in cinema. That Watkins is, as Paul Arthur observes, less prone to intertextual homage than any other major director whose career began in the 1960s (63) is not as much an expression of a radical departure from the medium's tradition as a disregard of it. This merits the same writer's note that Watkins "has never ventured far from his amateur roots" (59).

Like Brecht, Watkins is less convincing when he presents his admirable political stance overtly (*The War Game*, *The Gladiators*, *Punishment Park*) than when he does so "in passing," while focusing on a thematic area only tangentially related to politics (*Edvard Munch*, *The Freethinker*). The aspects of his work that link him to Brecht most strongly are documentariness in its various aspects (a feature that obliquely reminds one also of Piscator's legacy in Brecht), and the dialectical relationships forged among different formal elements of his films.

5

Lars von Trier

Brechtian Cinema in the Postmodern Era

BECAUSE OF THE LACK OF IDEATIONAL and aesthetic consistency in the cinema of Lars von Trier (b. 1956), it is difficult to determine with certainty the filmmaker's relationship with Brecht. The films of the *USA—Land of Opportunities* trilogy (*Dogville* [2003], *Manderlay* [2005], and the unproduced *Wasington* [*sic*!]) directly allude to Brecht through their narrative preoccupations and stylistic procedures. Seen through the prism of the trilogy's overt Brechtianisms, certain stylistic devices used by *Dancer in the Dark* (2000) and *Breaking the Waves* (1996) recall Brecht, too: for example, both films are divided into "chapters" and punctuate the narrative action by songs. One can also attribute obliquely Brechtian resonances to *The Idiots* (1998), von Trier's contribution to *Dogme 95*, an emphatically realist and implicitly "anti-bourgeois" film movement. The filmmaker's familiarity with Brecht's artistic practice and theoretical concepts—demonstrated in his interviews—further supports the view of certain von Trier films as Brechtian. Commenting upon *Dogville*, for instance, he uses the term *Verfremdung* to describe the desired impact of the film's unorthodox framing ("Commentary").

Some other titles in von Trier's filmography, however, diverge from all defining characteristics of Brecht's thought and art. To use the example of one of his recent releases, *Antichrist* (2009) narrows the realm of the social to the nuclear family, depicting the institution as seemingly resistant to the influence of outside factors. Stylistically, the film often operates by the principle of shock, whose effectiveness for activating the audience's awareness Brecht doubted.[1] Examples like this have caused other commentators to interrogate the nature and scope of Brecht's influence on von Trier. Thus Jan Simons, in line with his book's argument that von Trier's cinema is based in the new media culture of virtual realities and video games as its dominant manifestation—describes the minimalist mise-en-scène of *Dogville* as anti-Brechtian (157). Its function, Simons suggests, is not to alienate the viewer but to facilitate her engagement with the narrative world. Reprising this view and elaborating on it, Linda Badley applies to her discussion of *Dogville* von Trier's commentary on his planned production of Richard Wagner's *Ring of the Nibelungen*, according to which the filmmaker's aim with the visual design for the abandoned project was to frighten the spectator, thus releasing the kind of affect Brecht prohibited (104–5).[2]

Considering the common perception of von Trier as a postmodern artist and the importance for the cultural trend of Lacan's concept of decentered subject can help us understand the gap that separates the political escapism of *Antichrist*, *Melancholia* (2011), and *Nymphomaniac* (2013) from the political activism of *Dogville* and *Manderlay*. Developed in contrast to the notion of the Cartesian subject, which achieves and maintains unity through reasoning, the decentered subject is a Lacanian concept referring to dispersed subjectivity and polyvalent identity.[3] The deliberate thematic and stylistic variety of von Trier's cinema, the filmmaker's theoretical awareness, and the self-image of a mad genius he has constructed[4] all link him to Lacan's concept.[5] Before arguing that von Trier's distinctly modernist rhetoric in his *Dogme 95* manifesto and his reference to Brecht as an artist exemplary of late modernism are postmodernist strategies of paraphrase aimed at making postmodernism itself strange, we first need to identify formal commonalities of his cinema, of which there are four:

(1) The narratives of some of the most influential von Trier films center on the themes of religion (*Breaking the Waves*, *Dogville*) and the United States (*Dancer in the Dark* and the *USA—Land of Opportunities* trilogy). Unlike many European filmmakers' films about America (for example, Wim Wenders's *Alice in den Städten* [Alice in the Cities, 1973] and Werner Herzog's *Stroszek* [1977]), von Trier's "American" films do not concern themselves with the country's visual exotica, but focus instead on the abstract social forces shaping the culture.

(2) His films often depict rituals of various kinds: Svend Ali Hamann's hypnotizing a medium "into the film" in *Epidemic* (1987); the

initiation of Dr. Stig Helmer into the secret society Sons of the Kingdom Lodge in *Kingdom I* (1994); von Trier's prescription of formal rules that the director Jørgen Leth must satisfy in remaking a film of his in the essay film *The Five Obstructions* (2005).[6]

(3) The "high" visual style of Von Trier's films is frequently contrasted with pop culture elements: pop songs (*Epidemic*, *Europa*, *Breaking the Waves*, *Dancer in the Dark*, *Dogville* and *Manderlay*) and select genre conventions: of horror (*Epidemic*, *Kingdom I* and *II*, and *Antichrist*), of melodrama (*Breaking the Waves*), and of the musical (*Dancer in the Dark*).

(4) A stylistic dualism lies at heart of every title in von Trier's filmography. For instance, *Epidemic* uses static camera and fast, grainy, 16 mm stock for the film's (pseudo)documentary portions, whereas its film-within-the-film scenes use mobile framing and 35 mm stock. Similarly, *Breaking the Waves* combines the Cinemascope aspect ratio, a hand-held camera, a desaturated color scheme for the scenes that constitute the narrative proper, and an oversaturated palette and static camera for the shots that divide the film into "chapters."

From the examples of *Dogme 95* and *The Idiots* as von Trier's contribution to the movement, and the films of the unfinished *USA—Land of Opportunities* trilogy (*Dogville* and *Manderlay*), a conclusion similar to Simons's and Badley's can be drawn: the descriptor "Brechtian" does not unequivocally apply to von Trier's cinema. This chapter elaborates on that conclusion by positing that the primary aim of the filmmaker's use of Brechtian modernist strategies is to make strange the cultural trend that has replaced modernism in the West. In the current, postmodern context, those strategies become subsumed within the category of the pastiche as blank parody,[7] whereby their political dimension—crucial for Brecht and the art made in his spirit—becomes neutralized.

Feigning Radicalism: Dogme 95

March 20, 1995, saw the first-time presentation of the *Dogme 95* manifesto to the public. Following his contribution to the panel discussion on the future of cinema held that day at the Parisian Odéon Theatre, Lars von Trier asked for permission to digress from the panel's topic. He then read the manifesto aloud, threw copies of it into the audience, and departed the venue (Stevenson 102), leaving behind a trail of calculated mystery. The presentation's histrionic flair notwithstanding, no point of the manifesto—quoted below in full save for its introduction—evokes theater: central for each point are specifically filmic terms.

VOW OF CHASTITY

I swear to submit to the following set of rules drawn up and confirmed by DOGME 95:

Shooting must be done on location. Props and sets must not be brought in (if a particular prop is necessary for the story, a location must be chosen where the prop is to be found).

The sound must never be produced apart from the images or vice versa (music must not be used unless it occurs where the scene is being shot).

The camera must be hand-held. Any movement or immobility attainable in the hand is permitted (the film must not take place where the camera is standing; shooting must take place where the film takes place).

The film must be in colour. Special lighting is not acceptable (if there is too little light for exposure the scene must be cut or a single lamp attached to the front of the camera).

Optical work and filters are forbidden.

The film must not contain superficial action (murders, weapons etc. must not occur).

Temporal and geographical alienation are forbidden. (That is to say that the film takes place here and now.)

Genre movies are not acceptable.

The film format must be Academy 35mm.

The director must not be credited.

Furthermore, I swear as a director, to refrain from personal taste. I am no longer an artist, I swear to refrain from creating a 'work,' as I regard the instant as more important than the whole. My supreme goal is to force the truth out of my characters and settings. I swear to do so by all the means

> available and at the cost of my good taste and any aesthetic considerations. Thus, I make my VOW OF CHASTITY. (qtd. in Hjort and Mackenzie 199–200)

The manifesto, signed by von Trier and Thomas Vinterberg,[8] marked the beginning of an international film movement that yielded almost forty full-length feature films certified in compliance with the rules. Even though the board has ceased to issues certificates, *Dogme 95*-style films continue to be made.

Commentators on the *Dogme 95* manifesto have singled out the document's unstated yet consistently implied concern with realism.[9] It is in this aspect of the manifesto that Brechtian resonances show themselves most obviously. The notion of realism is central also in the earlier film movements frequently cited in discussions of *Dogme 95*: the *Nouvelle vague* and Italian neorealism. One can compare the latter two movements on two grounds: the similarly great influence they have had, and—predominantly—an allusion to the former in the manifesto's paragraphs that precede the "Vow of Chastity." These segments of the text reference François Truffaut's famous indictment of the aesthetic that dominated contemporary cinema of his country as formulated in the critic's 1954 essay "A Certain Tendency of French Cinema," as well as the year 1960, when a foremost representative of the country's cinematic New Wave was produced: Godard's *À bout de souffle*. Neils Weisberg, in his contribution to the *Dogme 95*-dedicated issue of *p.o.v.*, delineates similarities and distinctions between the Danish-conceived film movement on the one hand, and, on the other, the *Nouvelle vague* and Italian neorealism ("Great Cry and Little Wool"). The strongest similarities Weisberg draws amongst the three corpuses of films are the mutually linked ones that concern the rejection by all of studio shooting, as well as the insistence of the adherents of Italian neorealism on contemporary stories, or—as Weisberg would have it—"topical scripts inspired by concrete events" (ibid.).[10]

The absence from the "Vow of Chastity" of a claim to novelty limits its comparison with neorealism and *Nouvelle vague*. In contrast to the earlier movements, the perspective of *Dogme 95* can be described as backward. While its manifesto at first glance appears to urge two irreconcilable moves—a return to tradition and a break away from it—a closer reading reveals that the text's underlying sentiment is a yearning for the "goode olde dayes" of the past. The context of the predominantly secular Western world of today lends an estranging power to the religious and clerical associations evoked by the document. Those aspects of the "Vow of Chastity" rhetoric that allude to the historic avant-garde movements, and the text's genre, imbue the document with the same kind of energy. A majority of today's programmatic texts belong to the category of the personal statement, written after the artist has finished working "without rules in order to formulate the rules of what will have been done" (Lyotard 1984: 81). This, in combination with Hayden White's insight that the manifesto is an inherently radical genre, presupposing a time of crisis and—usually—a call for action (220), may suggest that *Dogme 95*'s use of the manifesto is itself intended as an estranging device. But this variety of estrangement should not be equaled with *Verfremdung*, with its prominent political dimension.

Vague and relativized by the manifesto's general "tongue in cheek" tone, the manifesto's accusation of "bourgeois cinema" reads as an articulation of nostalgia for political radicalism—the frequency of whose expressions in institutionalized art has waned—rather than a sincere political statement. To be sure, this, and the movement's other salutes to the spirit of revolution (for example, the emulation of early Soviet visual design by the poster for *The Idiots*), would resonate differently in a time when the specter of communism was still haunting the world. By 1995, however, the edge once possessed by the politics had been blunted, courtesy of the return to capitalism of a vast majority of former state socialist countries. Like the politics of most of its representatives, the avant-gardes experienced a failure: instead of destroying the very institution of art, their products are today collected in museums alongside the art they had rebelled against. In this regard, the *Dogme 95* manifesto demands to be understood as an expression of postmodernist referentiality, irony, and nostalgia.[11] Besides, the Cannes Film Festival, which has supported von Trier from the beginning of his career and cultivated him into the directorial star that he is today,[12] has proven unshakable by actions more politically subversive than *Dogme 95*.[13]

Von Trier's own acknowledgment that some of the manifesto's rules are impossible to follow (Knudsen 119) betrays the half-jesting spirit of the *Dogme 95* project as well. This broad paradox comprises a number of other ones, many of which have been identified by Achim Forst, the author of the first book-length study on von Trier in a major language (171–72). First, while the tenth rule forbids the director to credit herself (presumably with the idea of replacing her privileged status as an artist to that of a humble artisan), the *Dogme* filmmakers satisfy it only technically. Even though the credits of *The Celebration* do not include Thomas Vinterberg's name, no other attempt was made to conceal the filmmaker's identity, and he personally received the prize awarded to his film at the Cannes Film Festival. Second, while the ninth rule specifies the 35 mm format as the only acceptable one, a vast majority of *Dogme 95* films are shot on digital video (the fact enabled by the filmmakers' interpretation of the rule as pertinent to the *distribution* format). Third, while rule eight proclaims all film genres unacceptable, some Dogme films can be easily categorized in those terms (for example, Lone Scherfig's comedy *Italian for Beginners* [2001]).

The text's other problematic aspects include its tacit equating of a narrative's asceticism and the technological means needed to convey the quality cinematically, and especially its lack of interest in editing, the aspect of film style traditionally regarded as a territory for manipulation. There are two possible inferences one can make from the document's latter feature. The first is that its authors deem the "Vow of Chastity" rules capable of neutralizing the technique's power for deception. Envisioned from the perspective lent by such a conclusion, the cinema of *Dogme 95* appears to favor mise-en-scène, recommending it as a primary field of stylization. The restrictions concerning mise-en-scène are much narrower than those pertinent to sound and cinematography, making the former relatively easy to circumvent. The other inference that can be made from the manifesto's disregard of editing is that the signatories' view of the technique diverges from the popular one, presupposing the viewer of today to be capable of distinguishing between the "lies" that can be constructed through editing techniques and actuality. (After all, the term "invisible editing" has always been a bit of a misnomer: even a classical Hollywood film, which wants the splices to go unnoticed, does not want their *effects* to be missed.)

As *The Idiots* exemplifies, the practice of *Dogme 95* renders the second inference unviable. Namely, the film's editing style simultaneously disrupts and reconfigures the illusion of the spatio-temporal continuum within a given scene. The earliest example of this effect occurs in the scene where Karen visits a restaurant. As the waiter, offscreen, lists available gourmet additions to the salad that Karen has ordered, we see her in a close-up, looking up, screen left (Figure 5.1a). The film then cuts to a wider shot of the same character, whose eyeline indicates that the offscreen waiter now occupies a different position (Figure 5.1b).

Similarly, in the exterior scene where Katrine complains to Axel about being neglected by him, the camera maintains its position at the same side of the "invisible line," but the figures switch positions between the scene's cuts (Figure 5.2). This strategy is curiously unobtrusive: that the jarring effect of the described two scenes is not a result of violating the 180-degree rule, but of manipulating figure position, is easier to miss than to see. If considered alongside the manifesto's critique of both art and commercial cinemas,[14] the lack of the described technique's impact on the viewer's orientation in screen space can be seen as a hint at the obsolescence of the continuity principle.

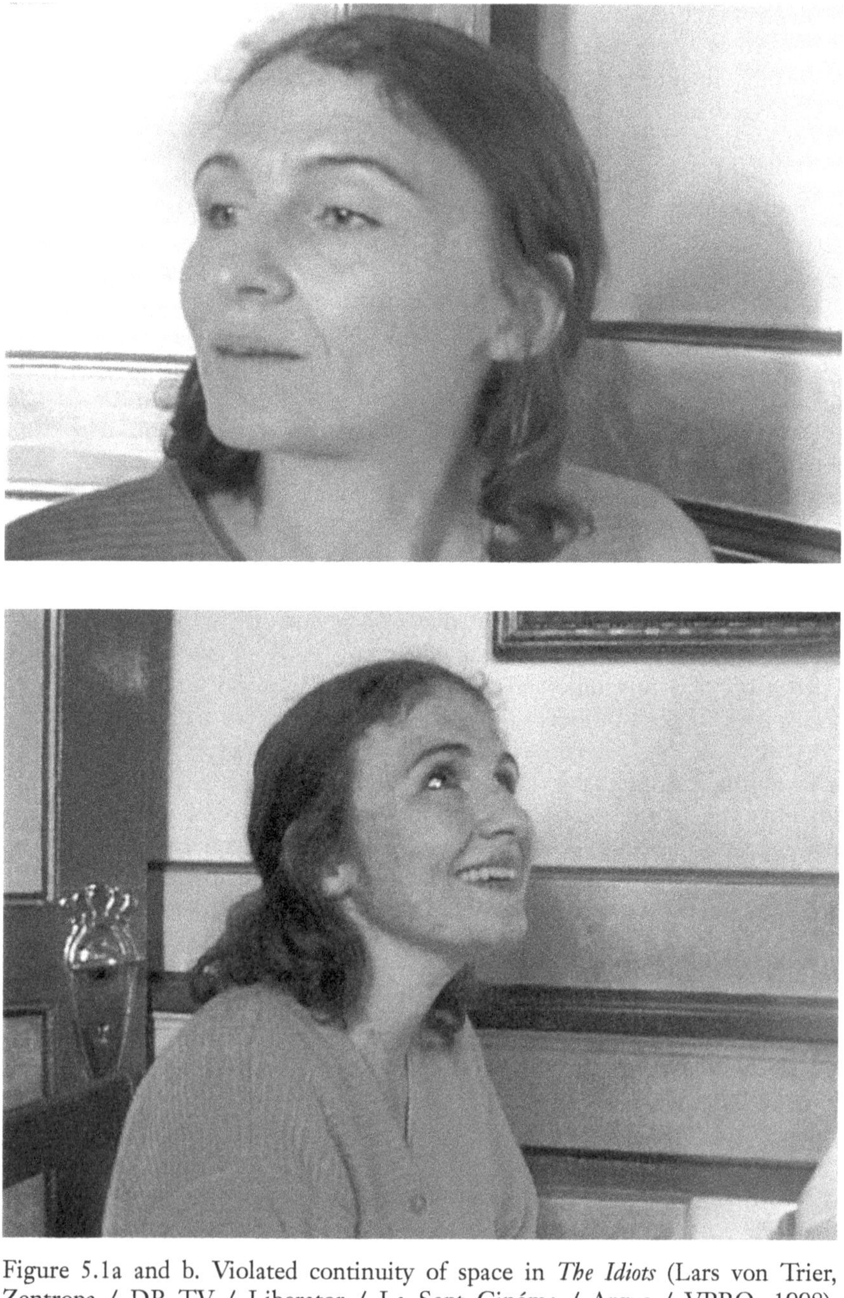

Figure 5.1a and b. Violated continuity of space in *The Idiots* (Lars von Trier, Zentropa / DR TV / Liberator / La Sept Cinéma / Argus / VPRO, 1998). Digital frame enlargement.

Figure 5.2a and b. An impression of shot-countershot created through figure placement in *The Idiots* (Lars von Trier, Zentropa, 1998). Digital frame enlargement.

The first of the possible two inferences from the manifesto's disregard of editing—that adhering to the other rules of the "Vow of Chastity" suffices to counteract and neutralize editing's power of deception—appears dubious in light of the predilection of the *Dogme 95* filmmakers for a technology that greatly facilitates image manipulation: digital video.[15] ("How can one trust what one sees" in our digital culture, asks Mark Williams in an essay on the contemporary crisis of indexicality of moving image media [172].) *The Idiots* illustrates the related contradiction between the manifesto and its practice. The fifth rule of the "Vow of Chastity" tends to limit the possibility of manipulating the profilmic event by forbidding optical work and filters. However, the erratic results of *The Idiots*' reliance on the automatically controlled camera divert the viewer's attention from the profilmic event to the technology, perhaps causing her to question the film's indexicality as she might that of a CGI-heavy Hollywood film.[16] To sum up, *The Idiots*—a film publicized through its relation to the manifesto as a work of rebellion against the falsity of the contemporary cinema—consistently "lies": about the spatial relations between the figures, about the identity of its actors (doubles were used for the shots of sexual penetration), and the accuracy of its representation of such aspects of mise-en-scène elements as colors and lighting. Thereby, the film points to the manifesto's inherent paradoxes.

Feigning Realism: The Idiots

It has been noted previously that the irony of the manifesto lends it to being understood as an expression of postmodernist irony. Further alignment of the movement's program with the postmodern can be found in the final point of the "Vow of Chastity," according to which *Dogme 95* entails a transcendence of personal taste and humbling oneself at the profilmic event. On the more obvious level, the statement calls for abandoning the view that informs much of film and other typically representational arts, according to which the artwork's goal is to show the observable real as refracted by the artist's personal vision, in favor of the related goals of objectivity and collectivism. Von Trier's theoretical awareness, as well as the characteristically postmodernist ideas and artistic devices his films employ, allows this point of the manifesto to be associated also with the aforementioned idea of the decentered subject or—in the terms of Ihab Hassan—the espousal of selflessness, an idea that resonates with the film's themes of performance and irrationalism. According to Rainer Friedrich, this idea is unique to postmodernism. The following few pages approach the film as a critique of this broad cultural trend using Friedrich's insights as a point of departure.

In "The Deconstructed Self in Artaud and Brecht: Negation of Subject and Antitotalitarianism," Rainer Friedrich builds on Gerald Graff's thesis that there is continuity rather than rupture between modernism and postmodernism (282). Friedrich notes that in the "definiens" of postmodernist practices offered by Ihab Hassan at the 1985 ICLA Congress in Paris (of which he cites as key "*fragmentation*, with its preference for montage, collage, pastiche and open form, *constructionism*; *decanonisation*; *irony*; *hybridisation of genres*; *ritual participation*; and *carnivalisation*, . . . roughly equivalent to Dionysianism"), one recognizes the central characteristics of modernism (ibid., emphasis mine). As has been already established, the only "definien" that pertains more readily to postmodernism than to modernism is the "espousal of selflessness," the tendency that "culminate[s] in the postmodernist negation of subjectivity and the deconstruction of the subject" (ibid.).

Friedrich uses two theatrical models he sees as conforming to the aforementioned tendency to illustrate the contradiction between postmodernism and its avowed antitotalitarianism. The first of these models is Artaud's theater of cruelty, celebrated by the adherents of postmodern thought for its re-creation of the ritualistic culture of tribal man, "the blissful regression to a pre-reflective and pre-rational age, before individuation, according to Nietzsche the *fons et origo* of all suffering, set in" (286). The second is the Brecht of *Baal*, with its celebration of "carnivalisation" and "polymorphous perversity," and particularly of the *Lehrstücke* (284–85).[17] The dissolution of the performer's and spectator's self in Artaud relates to the ancient religious and mythical traditions, with their practices aimed at the achievement of communal ecstasy and the feeling of Nietzschean *Einheit* (oneness), nostalgically delineated in his *Die Geburt der Tragödie* (The Birth of Tragedy, 1872). Brecht's "theater for the scientific age" seeks to sever all links with the identified traditions, replacing ecstasy (which Nietzsche sees as a precursor to Aristotelian catharsis) with individual enlightenment, a prerequisite for society's enlightenment and, concomitantly, betterment. Artaud upsets the hierarchy that the developed contemporary societies have established between *logos*—as a symbol of Western civilization, which his project was aimed at reforming—and *mythos*—as a symbol of the lost paradise of unity: with nature, with one another, and with themselves. The upset manifests itself already in the relatively inferior place that verbal language, with which *logos* is irrevocably connected, occupies in his theater. When one considers the effects of unsettling the boundary between the performer and the spectator in both theatrical models—which Friedrich highlights as a primary point of similarity between the theater of cruelty and Brecht's learning plays—another crucial difference between the two theorists and practitioners becomes evident: while Artaud's theater of cruelty seeks to abolish the spectator by transforming her into a participant whose experience of the performance will transcend the experience obtainable through the process of cognition, the aim of that transformation in Brecht is to enhance cognition. And the foregoing of self that Friedrich identifies as a defining feature of postmodernist art seems irreconcilable with it.

While it is disputable that the *Lehrstück* should be considered an example of a proto-postmodernist artistic model, and that it possesses the "totalitarian bent,"[18] the part of Friedrich's argument concerning Artaud—with a clearly drawn line between his "vision of an ecstatic liberation from the burden of reason" (287) and totalitarianism—is convincing. In support of the latter connection—and the possible implications of the postmodern, antihumanistic view of the tyranny of reason in general—Friedrich cites, on the one hand, Artaud's semitophobia, his genocidal fantasies about the necessity of exterminating seven to eight million human beings as useless parasites (288) and his dedication of a 1943 work to Adolf Hitler. On the other, Friedrich gives the example of the "antropophugal philosophy" of the contemporary German philosopher Ulrich Horstmann, who "advocates the instant nuclear destruction of mankind on the grounds that the present arsenal of nuclear weaponry in East and West provides the unique opportunity to return the planet to the 'beauty and freedom of the inorganic'" (ibid.).

To relate these ideas to *The Idiots*, the film's narrative can be regarded as antipostmodernist insofar as it critiques the dissolution of the subject (and its aggressive reassertion demonstrated in Stoffer's will to power [M. Smith 2003: 115])—a constituent of the film's central theme, and a defining feature of the broad postmodernist project. Because of its subject matter of feigning mental disabilities in public, *The Idiots* has been described in terms of therapeutic play (Müller 247), psychodrama (van Laak 312), Dadaism (M. Smith 2003: 119), Surrealism (ibid.), avant-garde performance art (Müller 247), a 1960s happening (Gaut 93), and Situationism (Walters 46–47). The film's politics have been variously reviled (for example, by *Artforum* critic Howard Hampton, whose review of *The Idiots* characterizes the film's principal characters as a "scraggly bunch of sadist-idealists" comparable to "slacker descendants of the Baader-Meinhof gang") (qtd. in Walters 49) and hailed (for example, by Tim Walters, whose reading emphasizes the self-reflexive aspect of the film,[19] and suggests that its themes are inextricable from the limitations of *Dogme 95*, the movement whose anti-bourgeois stance he sees as applicable also to the domain of politics in the term's narrow sense [43]).[20] The film's style has been likened to that of *cinéma vérité* (Gaut 92), presumably because of its use of interviews, a handheld camera, available lighting, and the frequent deviations from the patterns of continuity editing—stylistic characteristics commonly employed in the mentioned strain of documentary filmmaking. Simultaneously, commentators have stressed the film's emphasis on the performances (Chaudhuri 155; Laakso 203–14), whose "immediacy" (Chaudhuri) and "intimacy" (Laakso) have been attributed to the unobtrusive "prosumer" cameras used for its filming. While similar observations have been made in regard to *Dogme 95* films in general (see, for example, van Laak 310 and Lessard 103), *The Idiots* is unique in making performance its primary narrative concern.

As mentioned in this chapter's previous section, the notion of realism—although absent from the *Dogme 95* manifesto—has been central in the critical commentaries on the text. Since three full years separate the publication of the manifesto and the premiere of the first two certified *Dogme 95* films at Cannes in 1998, Vinterberg's *The Celebration* and von Trier's *The Idiots*, one can speculate that these commentaries have influenced the two works. They were presumably anticipated as litmus tests not only of the viability and validity of the "Vow of Chastity" rules, but also of the claim to enhanced realism at *Dogme 95*'s programmatic base. *The Idiots*, a work that explores the concept of realism at the levels of both narrative and style, supports this speculation particularly well.

The film focuses on a group of men and women from different walks of life, united by a common engagement in "spassing"— feigning mental disability in public for a vaguely explained reason of rebellion against the society whose incessant accumulation of wealth does not contribute to anyone's happiness. *The Idiots*' implicit theme of the espousal of selflessness interweaves with the film's theatricality, which corresponds to the first type in Jacques Gerstenkorn's classification cited in this book's introduction: the film references theatrical practice (Hamon-Sirejols et al.). Still, the correspondence is limited, as the "idiots" never invoke theater when talking about their public actions with each other or the offscreen interviewer (von Trier). In addition, the film repeatedly suggests that they do not spass for the benefit of the naïve "outsiders"—spectators—but for their own. (The nature of this benefit becomes increasingly unclear as the film progresses: such remarks as that concerning Axel's libidinal motives for joining the "idiots" will later weaken the link between the group's public actions and social rebellion, to which Stoffer points in the forest scene.) The group's *spiritus movens*, Stoffer, an arrogant choleric in the house of whose relative the spassers reside, cites the embracing of one's "inner idiot" as the goal of spassing, while Katrine—lamenting the group's disbanding in an interview scene—emphasizes the "thing" the members had amongst themselves, and not its potentially positive effect on the "outsiders." Most importantly, since the "outsiders" are unaware of the performative status of Stoffer and the others' behavior, their reactions to it are presumably identical to those they have to the manifestations of genuine mental disability. As such, they are not comparable to the perception of a theatrical performance (or, for that matter, of an artwork of any other kind).

Yet there are other grounds for regarding the spassing as theatrical. First, the existence of a witnessing "outsider" seems a fundamental condition for it. Stoffer sometimes assumes Susanne's usual function as a "minder" (for example, in the scenes where different visitors come to the group's residence). The group members, then, are not merely "losing themselves in the moment," as Josephine suggests happened to her at the factory. Unlike the participants in a ritual, they need to be watched by a non-participant for the action to be meaningful to them (although this last adjective hardly befits a discussion of the narrative action whose very point seems a rejection of sense).

As in all traditional acting methods, the spassers also perform the function of observers. In the scene following that of spassing at the factory, the group members discuss the performances we have previously witnessed, transforming the "Stanislavskian" identification into a "Brechtian" distantiation.[21] The spatial logic underlying their primary actions, too, connects the group's dynamics and theater. The house the group shares is the place where its members, like the ancient Greek actors in the space of the *skene*, are allowed to go out of their respective characters and be what they are: an employee in an advertising agency cheating on his wife (Axel), the employee's girlfriend, demanding that he abandon the family and devote himself entirely to her (Katrine), or an art history lecturer (Gabriel), about whose intimate life no substantial details are revealed to the viewer. In the instances when spassing occurs within the house, the described spatial configuration gets complicated by the former's subdivision: Karen, reluctant to join Stoffer and the others in group sex, leaves the room where the activity is taking place. Less hesitant to join the orgy, Susanne moves upon the event's beginning away from the naked group members, near a window (highlighted as a place for distancing reflection—but also emotional outbursts—by two scenes with Karen staged at the same element of the setting). Most importantly, the progressive blurring of the boundary between the group members' spassing and their normal behavior culminates in a small and intimate space of one of the house's small rooms, where the naked Jeppe and Josephine withdraw to make love while the others are engaged in group sex (Figure 5.3). Unlike that of the latter group of characters, the young man's and woman's lovemaking is devoid of irony and humor. Josephine's proclamation of love for Jeppe from a "place" between her persona as

Figure 5.3. Honest in the role: Jeppe and Josephine in *The Idiots* (Lars von Trier, Zentropa, 1998). Digital frame enlargement.

an "idiot" and her true self highlights the earnestness of their feelings: namely, the words "I love you" are the only ones we hear the young woman say while spassing. This scene, where the dichotomy between the "performance space" and the "auditorium" finally collapses, touches upon the inseparability of logos and language, the assumption of which—as it will be demonstrated later—underlies the film's key themes. Carried away by a mutual attraction of the kind evidently surpassing the merely physical, neither Jeppe nor Josephine functions as a "minder" here. Yet it is the latter character's embrace of language—an instrument of logos—that the narrative configures as a factor that enables the couple's love to be born.[22]

The group's dissolution can be said to occur as a result of its members' increased uncertainty between meaningfulness and purposefulness on the one hand and "something more" than that on the other; between rationality and irrationality, mental ability and mental disability, sanity and insanity. The film touches more than once upon the permeable boundary between these opposites. For instance, in a scene shortly preceding that of the sexual orgy, Stoffer—upon seeing the group prepare party decorations on the occasion of his birthday—notes that it is not his real birthday. Henrik replies: "Well, we're not real retards, are we?" After we learn that Josephine has a true psychological issue, Henrik's question acquires a different tenor. The broader dichotomy between the real and the appearance addressed by this scene ties in closely with the various commentaries on the realist mandate of the *Dogme 95* movement. Related to this, the process of the group's disbanding—which will reach its final stage with Josephine's departure—begins when the spassers experience a "reality check" during the visit by a group of Down syndrome sufferers, much earlier in the story (Figure 5.4). Josephine's strong reaction to the visitors (she withdraws into the house and, approached by Jeppe, asks to be left alone) in retrospect seems a hint of her mental problems, whereas Stoffer's rage at the curiosity that the other spassers show toward the guests underscores the scene's narrative importance. Without even trying, the Down syndrome sufferers thus manage to shake the status of the spassers' performances. Because they genuinely are mentally disabled, their presence amongst the "idiots" annuls the difference between the (potential) spectator and the (potential) performer necessary for this relation to be justifiably established. Ironically, it is the visitors' rendering spassing purposeless through their presence (purposeless, as the activity presumably would not provoke the reactions of repulsion that Stoffer and

Figure 5.4. The real spoiling the fiction: *The Idiots* (Lars von Trier, Zentropa, 1998). Digital frame enlargement.

the others look for) that bounces back amongst the group the idea of "purpose" and the unavoidability of it in relation to controlled behavior. The group's main mandate, as a group member suggests in an already mentioned interview scene, is to reject this idea. The sole realm to which the film connects the idea of purpose is that of political activism. As we shall see, it does so with the same vagueness that characterizes the references to the political of the "Vow of Chastity."

The equation that Gaut rightly establishes in his commentary on *Dogme* #1, *The Celebration*, whereby the bourgeois family on which the narrative centers parallels the bourgeois cinema (96), and whereby the class (and gender) revolt of the film's characters parallels the revolutionary impulse of the film movement's manifesto, does not apply to *The Idiots* neatly. The politics of the film under analysis here are more complex (but not ambivalent, as Müller describes them [253]). Indicative of the film's politics—and therefore good starting points for an analysis—are some of the lines Stoffer directs at Karen. In the forest scene, when Karen asks about the point of the group's spassing, he replies: "They're searching for their inner idiot, Karen. What's the idea of a society that gets richer and richer when it doesn't make anyone happier? In the stone age, right, all the idiots died. It doesn't have to be like that nowadays. Being an idiot . . . is a luxury, but it is also a step forward. Idiots are the people of the future." Gaut is right to observe that the reasons Stoffer cites—evoking the *Dogme 95* manifesto by his prophetic tone and the theories of Foucault and R. D. Laing by his unorthodox view of sanity and insanity—are "singularly unconvincing" (93). But a different explanation of spassing would be difficult to conceive of, if we accept John Roberts's view that the activity is motivated by "the infantilised pleasures of regression, loss of ego and lack of self-consciousness" (149), all of these implying a rejection of logos and, consequently, of language. Karen's critique of spassing, put in more narrowly economic-political terms, is met with an even clearer example of irrationality as a mode that underlies the group's principles of operation. In response to Karen's criticism of the group's spassing with outrageously expensive food items while "there are people starving," Stoffer replies: "There aren't any people starving. That's the whole thing." Stoffer's observation is not simply an escapist denial of a fact as constant as it is disturbing, but a vague rejection of the rational and—by extension—of the self.

As noted previously, Stoffer's rages occur at the narrative's climactic points. The first and the last of these (caused, respectively, by the arrival at the house of the Down syndrome sufferers, and by the group members' refusal to spass in front of those they know) have already been commented upon. The second of the character's fits of anger is the fiercest of the three the viewer witnesses, and is allocated the most screen time. The event that triggers the fit—the offer of a grant for the relocation of Stoffer's group made by the district council representative—distinguishes it from the other similar occurrences. Murray Smith's comment that the scene undermines the viewer's ability to distinguish authentic and fake derangement seems valid ("Lars" 117), but the relationship between the real and the appearance and the different above-identified derivatives of this dichotomy do not seem to be the scene's central thematic concerns. At issue here is the question of economic sustenance of a society within society, organized around the idea of protesting bourgeois rationality while indulging in cigars and caviar—paradigmatically bourgeois corporeal pleasures. In light of the multiple reminders the narrative offers of the group's dependence on money and the constant lack of it (to mention but one, their spassing at the restaurant is calculated to make the waiter ask the "idiots" to leave without charging them), Stoffer's furious protest against the city council representative's offer can be interpreted as a sign of understanding the impossibility of entirely breaking free from such social ties.

Chasing the district representative away, Stoffer takes off his clothes (symbolically rejecting his social self, and returning to the primordial one) and shouts curses, the recurrent among which is "Søllerød fascists!" Despite his likening of the district council's initiative with the ghettoization of minority ethnic groups in rightist dictatorships, it is Stoffer whom the narrative eventually configures as a regressive authoritarian figure. (The film repeatedly shows him controlling the group's dynamic, often at the cost of its members' embarrassment and humiliation, as exemplified by his insistence that the entire group engage in a sexual orgy.) Commenting on the film, von Trier singles Stoffer out as a culprit for the group's demise: "The idea has been corrupted by him, you could say, in the same way he tries to corrupt the other members of the group. You can draw parallels to politics or to people who, for various reasons, work in groups" (Björkman 205).

Two scenes that immediately precede the described one support its theme of performing. In the earlier of these (which roughly mirrors that with the Down syndrome sufferers), Stoffer lies to the potential buyers of the house where he and the others reside that there is a mental institution in the neighborhood. To prove this, Stoffer asks Susanne to "line up the retards," who ostensibly happen to be visiting. The scene's figure placement, with the "idiots" spatially marked off from the "minding" Stoffer and Susanne as well as the visitors, evokes the theatrical stage/auditorium separation, and configures the former group of characters as a spectacle. The spassers' attempt to break the invisible barrier that separates them from the potential buyers of the house results in awkwardness and the latter's hasty departure. The next scene is a "talking head" shot where Ped, the group's analyst, acknowledges the superiority of the "performances" by the Down syndrome sufferers: "They were highly credible," he admits almost grudgingly; "they were really good at it." The commentary relativizes the distinction between mental ability and mental disability, but also the distinction between the performer and the spectator, reminding us—in a manner reminiscent of Erving Goffman's *The Presentation of Self in Everyday Life* (1959)—that performance is inherently a two-way process. To elaborate on the association in regard to the narrative's narrow context, Ped's comment lends itself to being interpreted as a hint to the "idiocy" of social organization and its hierarchy—the notions central for Goffman's study.

The work's self-reflexivity, based on the subject matter of an activity that is, in certain aspects, comparable to artistic endeavors, as well as its status as one of the first two practical applications of the "Vow of Chastity" rules, led to the view of *The Idiots* as a film on the *Dogme 95* movement (Müller; Gaut; Walters) and of Stoffer as von Trier's double (Walters 49). If we combine the latter view with that of Mackenzie, according to which a filmmaker's willing subjection to the "Vow of Chastity" rules represents an instance of self-flagellation, then the narrative's critique of Stoffer's authoritarianism can be said to double this process, and—by doing so—critique the movement's theoretical foundation. In its implicit celebration of the rational, the film shows its modernist (and, more precisely, Brechtian) resonances, against the grain of Friedrich's view of the *Lehrstück*, but also of the broad postmodernist project.

The Techniques of Brechtian Theatre in Film: Dogville

If few critics noted the Brechtian dimensions of *Europa*,[23] many more noted Brecht's influence on *Dogville*: the elements of the work's narrative and style are compared with the theater of Brecht in—among others—the following texts: Bainbridge (2007), Elbeshlawy (2008), Fibiger (2003), Koutsourakis (2013), van Laak (2009), Penzendorfer (2010), Rissing and Rissing (2008), and Schepelern (2003). Von Trier himself acknowledges Brecht as a source of inspiration for the film (Björkman 243–44) and uses Brechtian terms to describe its formal operations ("Commentary"). Both the filmmaker's own and the others' commentaries variably emphasize the similarity between Brecht's theater and the film's narrative and style, a possibility granted by the eclectic nature of the cited influence.

In terms of its thematic preoccupations, the first major resemblance between the film and Brecht manifests itself in the narrative's geographical and historical coordinates. The film is set in the eponymous fictitious mountain town in the United States of America, the land where the narratives of some of Brecht's major plays are also situated: *In the Jungle of Cities*, *The Flight Across the Ocean*, *The Rise and Fall of the City of Mahagonny*, *The Resistible Rise of Arturo Ui*, and *Saint Joan of the Stockyards*. The commonality the five plays share is by no means accidental. Because the reasons that underlie Brecht's long-term interest in the country are relevant also for this reading of von Trier's film, a brief summary of its development—as delineated in Patty Lee Parmalee's study *Brecht's America* (1981)—seems in order.

Parmalee notes the existence of an Anglo-Saxon mythology and, more narrowly, a fascination with American culture ("jazz, Chaplin films, the Charleston, skyscrapers and neon lights, boxing, clothing styles" [9]) amongst the German artists of Brecht's generation in the years of and around World War I (11). From the evidence of this fascination on the one hand, and, on the other, Brecht's impression of Germany as a boring country dominated by "a degenerate peasant class" (6), the commentator develops an equation where, for the dramatist, "country = backwardness = Old World, and city = progress = America" (24). Brecht's interest in the New World had another side, marked by a realization of "the sharpening of the contradictions of [the country's] reality" (8), as exemplified in the side effects of "Fordism": the increased unemployment and exploitation of the workers (8). It is the economic nature of such issues that increasingly constitute the foci of Brecht's plays written after his discovery of Marxism in 1926 (220). Parmalee goes on to argue that Brecht turned away from his view of the United States as a healthy and productive reaction to the decadence of Europe in 1929. Fritz Sternberg, he notes, placed Brecht's dedication to the Party's cause in May of the cited year, when Brecht witnessed the police shoot twenty participants in a May Day demonstration (238). His commitment to communism was cemented a few months later as a result of the stock market crash and the world economic crisis caused by the event (225). From this point onward, it was socialism and the Soviet Union that became symbols of the new for Brecht, whereas capitalism came to symbolize the old (275). Consequently, Brecht was no longer interested in the American myth but only in America as an example of capitalism (265).

Von Trier's cinema shows a similarly consistent concern with the United States of America: it represents the setting not only for the first two installments of the *USA—Land of Opportunities* trilogy, but also of *Dancer in the Dark*. With this acknowledged, the differences between the choice of themes and the manner of their handling in the two artists' respective "American" works are vast. First, while von Trier's films often contain explicit or implicit references to the United States, they suggest not an enthusiasm about it comparable to that expressed by the young Brecht, but rather a hostility toward it. To give the example of but one film, *Epidemic* refers to the United States through an episode where Niels Vørsel, appearing as himself, sarcastically comments on the audio letter sent to him by his American teenage pen pal, as the letter is playing in the background. Considered alongside the scathing critiques of the United States implied by von Trier's "American" films, the example of the girl—whom the correspondence from Vørsel has led the girl to believe they are of similar age—calls to be interpreted as a synecdochal mockery of the alleged Americans' naïveté. Understood this way, the episode seems underwritten by a reversal of Parmalee's formula that illustrates Brecht's view of the cultural superiority of the United States over Europe. Second, von Trier's interest in the contradictions of the United States—unlike Brecht's—goes beyond the domain of the economic: *Dancer in the Dark*, for example, explores the interactions of the country's economic principles with its health and law systems, whereas *Manderlay* places its narrative focus on the racial relationships in the South.

While the setting's immense poverty and the narrative's temporal coordinates (the New Deal era) have considerable thematic implications, *Dogville* concerns itself primarily with an issue of a different, ethical order, framed in a religious context.[24] In the view of different commentators,[25] the Old Testament moral code of "an eye for an eye, a tooth for a tooth" (Exodus 21:24) informs the narrative's motif of revenge (taken from the "Pirate Jenny" song in *The Threepenny Opera* [Björkman 243–44]). Bo Fibiger formulates this observation in a more elaborate manner, singling out as the film's main point (60) the dialectic between the Old and the New Testament, with the Gospel of Matthew's replacement of the above dictum with "whosoever smite thee on thy right cheek, turn him the other also" (5:39). Ahmed F. Elbeshlawy further develops this idea by noting that "the film seems to communicate to the viewer that the idea of the ultimate sacrifice, the core of Christian thought and the constituent of its sublation, or its (anti)thetical departure from Judaism, seems to be alien to itself due to its incompatibility with [religious] eschatology" (n.p.). The film demonstrates the incompatibility in question, Elbeshlawy goes on to argue, through the discourse of Grace's father (James Caan), which suggests that "God sacrificing himself, or part of himself, purposefully for alleviating the sin of humanity, i.e. to make humanity sinless or innocent, seems to be a sacrifice of himself for himself" (ibid.).

In von Trier's "American" films, the formal strategy evident already in *The Element of Crime*, *Epidemic*, *Breaking the Waves*, and *Kingdom I* and

II becomes more apparent. To various degrees, all those films assimilate different genre and stylistic conventions associated with other forms (the novel and Brechtian theater) for the aesthetic effect of betraying what Hans Robert Jauss, in the context of his reception theory of literary criticism, calls the horizon of expectations. Broadly, the term refers to the set of loosely defined cultural norms and circumstances that inform the manner in which one perceives and evaluates a literary text. Defining the concept more narrowly, Jauss mentions *Don Quixote* (1605–1615), Diderot's *Jacques le Fataliste* (1773), and Gerard de Nerval's *Les Chimères* (1853)—the works that, as Robert C. Holub summarizes, "evoke the reader's horizon of expectations, formed by a convention of genre, style, or form, only in order to destroy it step by step" (60). The observation applies also to a range of other von Trier films, including *Dancer in the Dark*, the films of the *USA—Land of Opportunities* trilogy, and the entire *Depression Trilogy*. If it were described entirely in terms of its narrative, the first of these films would bring to mind Ken Loach's social dramas (it centers on an earnest immigrant single mother who falls victim to the legal system of her adopted homeland). In von Trier's hands, the story receives an unorthodox stylistic treatment, borrowing extensively from the genres of melodrama and particularly the musical. *Dogville* and *Manderlay*, conversely, betray the horizon of expectations formed by what Jauss refers to as conventions of form: the films reject the style of mainstream cinema, with which their star-saturated casts are associated, in favor of a Brechtian theatricality and baroque narration evocative of the nineteenth-century novel.

Von Trier's *Breaking the Waves*, *Dancer in the Dark*, and *Dogville* have been widely read in terms of Judeo-Christian theism, the keywords of those readings being "mercy" (Sandler), "righteousness" (ibid.), "grace" (Orth; Martig; Rissing and Rissing), "sacrifice" (Heath "God"; Mandolfo; Keffer and Linafelt), "scapegoating" (Mercadante), and "redemption" (Mandolfo; Solano). Superficially considered, those themes seem irreconcilable with Brecht in light of the common view of Brecht as an atheist. But Brecht was not being simply ironic when he cited the Bible as the strongest influence on his work (Esslin *Brecht: Man* 106). References and allusions are omnipresent throughout Brecht's body of literary work, as G. Ronald Murphy, S.J., painstakingly demonstrates in *Brecht and the Bible*. Murphy questions the perception of Brecht as an atheist by pointing out that the mystery of God is a constant presence in Brecht's works (90) and elaborates on the observation as follows:

> The God whose existence [Brecht] denies is the God of explanations, the God who is supposedly behind conventional moral conduct and against progress, the God of Job's friends.

> There is indeed no God for the people and the founders of Mahagonny—but is there a God to receive the dying weak, a God of the innocent, the God of the dying Baal, Paul Ackermann, Kattrin, and Jesus Christ? That is the question from which he can never seem to separate himself even though he is never able to give a definite "yes" answer to it. (ibid.)

Using *Die Bibel* (The Bible, 1913), *Baal*, *Mahagonny*, and *Mother Courage* as case studies, Murphy persuasively modifies the common view, originally put forward by Reinhold Grimm, "that Brecht's use of the Bible is a device of *Verfremdung*, an attempt to revive a cliché by the shock of seeing it either 'slightly' altered or in an entirely different situation from its original context" (7). Murphy allows that this holds for a majority of Brecht's plays, but demonstrates that those he analyzes in detail—the plays "characterised by the use of some variation of the 'city' or 'besieged city' motif" (11), with "the hero and heroine ultimately confronted with abandonment and death in a way that evokes the Crucifixion" (ibid.)—constitute exceptions. Murphy observes that the Old Testament sources Brecht most frequently uses in the selected plays are Ecclesiastes, Job, and Psalms—books commensurable with the writer's general worldview in "[operating] under the assumption that there is no real afterlife . . . for man, and have a dominating awareness of death and abandonment, unrelieved by their belief in God and His immortality" (11). As to the New Testament, Murphy notes that Brecht's empathetic use of the source in the four plays limits itself almost entirely to the events of the Passion and Death accounts, and St. Matthew's Passion in particular (ibid.). Significantly, the death of Jesus is, as Murphy concludes in his analysis of *Mahagonny*, for Brecht "a sacred event, an archetype . . . of the mystery of the death of the good man."

The third group of narrative elements of *Dogville* bearing association with Brecht consists of what Ahmed F. Elbeshlawy sees as direct allusions to and borrowings from Brecht's plays (n.p.). Beside the play containing the song acknowledged by von Trier as an inspiration for the film (alongside sources as diverse as the Winnie the Pooh tales and poems and a TV version of the Royal Shakespeare Company adaptation of Dickens's *Nicholas Nickleby*) (Björkman 245), the most important of these is *The Resistible Rise of Arturo Ui*. Elbeshlawy points to the semantic kinship between the name of the play's character Dogsborough and Dogville, as well as to the similarity between the morals of the town inhabitants and the Brechtian character, who is " 'reputed to be honest' " but "whose morals go overboard in times of crisis" (n.p.). Whether this is a coincidence or not seems impossible to determine, as von Trier alternates in his commentaries on the film between emphasizing and deemphasizing the scope of Brecht's influence on the film: a case in point is the remark that he experienced Brecht's dramas at a fairly young age and has never returned to him or his work, and that they exist in his memory mostly as feelings and atmospheres (Björkman 244).

Similarities between *Dogville* and Brecht's theater are numerous also at the level of style. Most broadly, the work's fusing of the conventions of different arts—as von Trier describes the film's stylistic operations (241)—corresponds to Brecht's *Prinzip der Trennung*. The most prominent among the non-filmic conventions that the work adopts are theatrical ones, and the Brechtian filmmakers' theatricalization of cinema is—according to Maia Turovskaiia—a tendency concomitant with cinematization of theater, characteristic of an array of influential theater practitioners of Brecht's artistic generation, including himself, Meyerhold, and Eisenstein (170–87; 210–44). The other art von Trier identifies as fused within the work (Björkman 241) is literature: the prose of the film's voiceover narration, more evocative of nineteenth-century fiction than of the major American representatives of the generation of writers termed "lost" by Gertrude Stein (Hemingway iv), the generation that, beside herself, includes Ernest Hemingway, William Faulkner, and John Dos Passos. Besides exhibiting great differences, the styles of these writers are all informed by one or another novel and dominant cultural phenomenon of their time: the American immigrants' speech idiom (Stein); jazz improvisations (William Faulkner); newspaper-style prose (Ernest Hemingway); mass media and particularly film (John Dos Passos). In its deliberate dissimilarity from these modernist examples, *Dogville* additionally removes its voiceover narration, with its air of old-fashionedness (which aligns it that much more with *Verfremdung*), from the cultural and temporal contexts of the film's narrative. While the American "lost generation" writers sought alternatives to the "literariness" of pre-modernist fiction, von Trier re-creates that quality in a manner conforming to Brecht's *Literarisierung*.[26]

The theatricality of *Dogville* manifests itself mainly in the interacting domains of characterization and the set and lighting design. Both show a minimalist reduction uncharacteristic of mainstream cinema (in which category *Dogville* can claim to have a place on account of its mainly Hollywood cast, as well as its modes of production and distribution). First, the entire town's population is represented by a mere couple dozen characters. The allocation of narrative significance to most of them adds to the film's "epic" quality. *Dogville* does not have a heroine in the conventional sense: Grace (Nicole Kidman) is too passive for the portion of the film preceding the final "chapter's" massacre for the descriptor to fit her. Rather than advancing the narrative herself, for most of the film's duration Grace merely catalyzes the others. Second, the significance of some of the characters' names is unusually great for a work that belongs to the broad category of mainstream cinema, where "surface realism" continues to prevail. When film is used as a photographic medium, it stylizes through subtraction as much as through addition. More concretely, a film practitioner designs the shot by removing from her frame and the microphone's range the elements whose visual or aural presence conflicts with the shot's intended function, as much as by bringing into the frame the objects whose visual or aural presence performs that function.

On the other hand, theater—in the typical cases when it uses a prebuilt venue generally based on the ancient Greek model of the sharply divided performance and audience spaces—operates exclusively through addition: for something to "speak" to the spectator, for a visual or aural element to become a sign, it needs to be added to the preexisting space and recognized by the spectator as an addition. For this latter process to occur, the element in question needs to be removed from the context of the venue: in other words, a sign will go unnoticed unless its constructedness is highlighted to one degree or another, by one means or another. Even the most credible performance of a "slice of life" play constantly reminds the spectator of the work's artifice, through the (perhaps involuntary) comparisons between the sights and sounds of the on-stage spectacle and those of the other audience members.

Film escapes theater's imperative to not show life "simply as it is" by virtue of two of its properties. First, it is first and foremost an image, too dissimilar from the three-dimensional, real world of the spectator for a comparison between the two to be feasible.[27] Second, unlike a theater narrative, a film narrative cannot claim to occur simultaneously with the audience's reception of it: an experienced film viewer knows that she is going to see a document of a profilmic event that has already transpired, upon entering the movie theater or pressing a button on her viewing device. The reception of a theater performance, in contrast, occurs simultaneously with its production. So essential is the category of liveness to this medium that some commentators (see, for example, Phelan) single it out as the foremost theatrical notion.

This lengthy diversion was necessary to set up the observation that character naming, which in mainstream cinema tends to conform to the norms of verisimilitude, is often used in theater as a space for stylization, for meaning creation. One finds examples of this throughout the history of Western theater: from Sophocles' Oedipus (swollen foot) to a range of Shakespearean characters, such as Caliban (an anagram of "cannibal") and the hard-drinking tandem of Sir Toby Belch (whose last name does not require an explanation) and Sir Andrew Aguecheek (the first part of whose last name denotes strong fever); from Calderón's Segismundo (a victorious protector) to Beckett's Godot (the diminutive form of God). In the context of mainstream cinema, such strategies are comparatively so rare that a concrete one comes to mind easily: the names in Hitchcock (perhaps most overtly, *Psycho*, with the names of the protagonists, Marion and Norman, being anagrammatic forms of each other). To finally return to characters' names in *Dogville*, that of "Thomas Edison Jr.," for instance, is a clear allusion to the American inventor, whose long list of patents includes some of the earliest devices for filming and projecting motion pictures, while Grace's name connotes a range of related but distinct meanings, of which "mercy; clemency; pardon" ("Grace" 826) is most overtly ironic.

Another domain through which *Dogville* achieves its theatricality is the set design. The town is represented by a large map, its significatory quality emphasized through the inclusion of the names of streets, significant structures, and the owners of households (Figure 5.6a). The map and the captions on it are written in white, and the alternating colors black (denoting night time) and white (denoting day time) dominate the floor and its entire surrounding. The film abandons the tonal schema only in the penultimate scene, showing the aftermath of the massacre. The dominant lighting here is top, hard, and of color temperatures different from sunlight and gas light (two primary diegetic sources of light in the film), readily revealing its artificiality. The figures' movements and sound effects indicate many of the town's walls and doors: an off-screen knocking on wood and the squeaking of a door can be heard when a character mimes the actions. Similarly, the film denotes Moses the dog through naturalistic barking and a combination of linguistic and visual signs (Figure 5.5). Along with the identified minimalist elements, the mise-en-scène uses naturalistic costumes and props, a combination that evokes the photographs from the model books (*Modellbücher*) of the Berliner Ensemble productions: a reduced color palette, authentic and well-worn props and setting elements, and pitiless white lighting.

While the visual design is reminiscent of theater and, specifically, Brecht's productions for the medium,[28] the size of the map that constitutes the setting's base exceeds that of the largest conventional stage, and the placement of the figures does not presuppose a fixed spectatorial vantage point. These two features counteract the theatricality suggested by the setting's other aspects.[29] The film's "stage," then, is purposely unfeasible, producing the same effect identified by Rosalind Galt in her discussion of von Trier's *Europa*: the film "brackets the mise-en-scène as a spectacle that refuses authenticity" (9).

Figure 5.5. Different types of signs combined in a single frame from *Dogville* (Lars von Trier, Zentropa, 2003). Digital frame enlargement.

The use of the 360-degree space, characteristic also of a number of earlier von Trier films from *Kingdom I* onward, here seems an extension of the setting's architecture, with two rows of houses separated by Main Street being at the core of its scheme. For a vast majority of its shots, the film uses a handheld and calculatedly negligent camera: in the audio commentary of the film's DVD edition, von Trier describes the allegedly estranging effect of shots that are "pointed" as opposed to "composed," referring to it as *Verfremdung*. As in the case of *The Idiots*, von Trier operates the camera in an "amateurish" manner that configures the cinematography as being of secondary importance in relation to the profilmic event.[30]

There are a few notable exceptions to the described cinematographic style: the aerial shots of the town (which create an impression of flatness and emphasize its similarity to a geographic map), and of Grace hidden in Ben's cart of apples. The former group of shots serves a twofold function. First, they enable a comprehensive view of the societal structure that constitutes the film's setting (Figure 5.6a), emphasizing—in a manner that brings to mind the "doll house" setting of the emblematically Brechtian *Tout va bien* (Figure 5.6b)—the narrative focus on the entire town rather than on a single character. Second, they resonate also with the film's biblical overtones, lending themselves to be interpreted as God's perspective. Relevant to this, the sole instance of acknowledging the camera in the film occurs in the shot immediately preceding the montage sequence, where the drawing of the dog with the weighty name

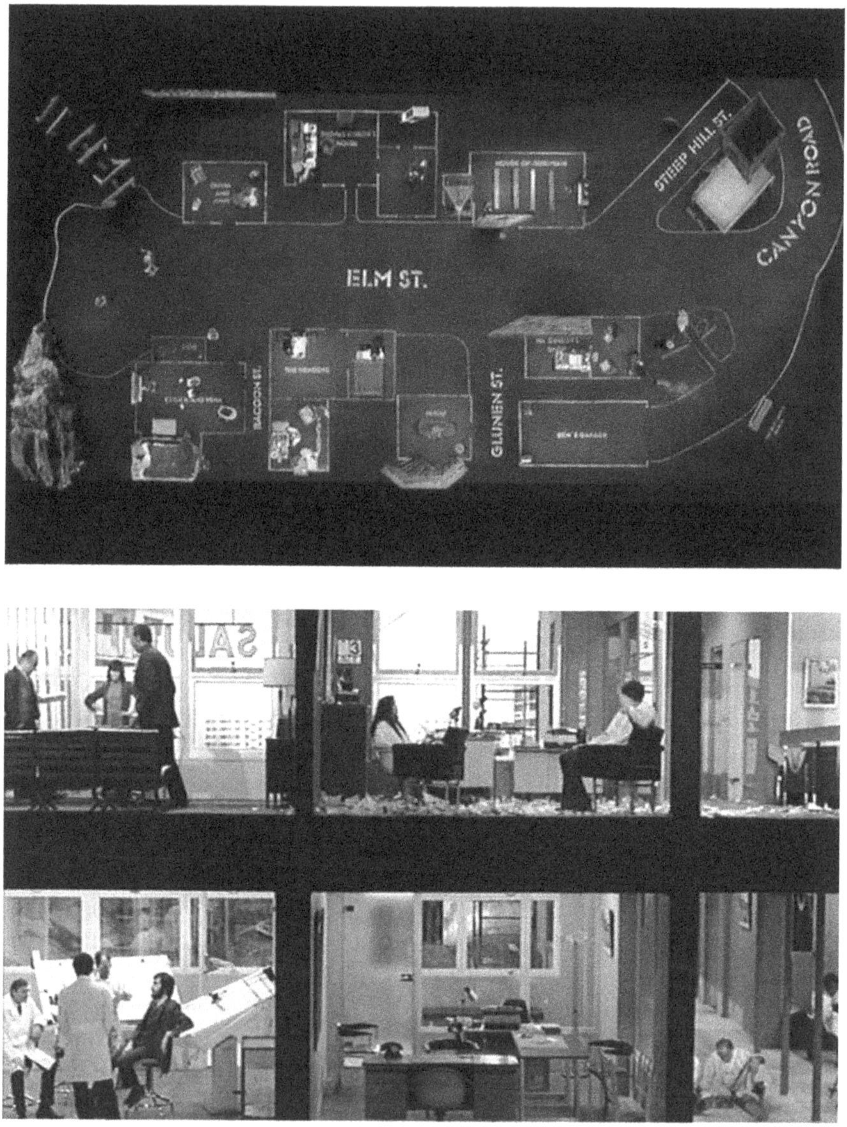

Figure 5.6a and b. "Mapping" the society in *Dogville* (Lars von Trier, Zentropa, 2003) and in *Tout va bien* (Jean-Luc Godard and Jean-Pierre Gorin, Anouchka / Empire / Vieco, 1972). Digital frame enlargement.

of Moses (hitherto "animated" solely through offscreen barking) being transformed into a real pit bull. Moses stands up and bares its teeth at the camera, connoting its divine quality and literalizing the metaphor from the announcing caption that summarizes the action of the film's "chapter six" ("Dogville bares its teeth"). The symmetry of the camera movements occurring in this and in the opening shot suggests the film's overall dialectical move from a sociopolitical analysis to a religious-ethical meditation.

The montage sequence, drawing on images from the Farm Security Administration—commissioned photographs by Dorothea Lange, Russell Lee, Jack Collier, Arthur Siegel, Ben Shahn, Carl Mydens, John Vachon, and Arthur Rothstein, and from Jacob Holdt's *American Pictures* (Römers n.p.), reverses this move. The two groups of images, different in terms of visual properties and the eras from which they derive (the former black-and-white images derive from the era in which the narrative is set, while the latter color photographs were taken in the 1970s), are thematically connected: they all show the destitution, squalor, and alcoholism of anonymous inhabitants of the United States. Michael O'Sullivan holds a view of the sequence as an allegorical version of America and its citizens (qtd. in ibid.) at once typical and questionable. A filmmaker of von Trier's intelligence and subtlety would hardly impose a blanket accusation on the entire nation of the United States, which O'Sullivan holds the sequence to be. Juxtaposed with the rest of the narrative, the sequence appears in line with Brecht's "first grub, then ethics," as W. H. Auden translates the famous line from *The Threepenny Opera*. The depravity and social injustices of the "land of plenty" leads to moral aberrations, its combination suggests, despite the vulnerability to criticism of this simplistic conjecture.

The final segment of the film is accompanied by David Bowie's song "Young Americans." Deriving from the 1970s and characteristic of the decade in its arrangement, the song constitutes an instance of *aktualizace*.[31] The sequence is irritating, as Römers describes it, not simply because it recontextualizes "one of the most famous bodies of work in the history of photography . . . within a surrealistic pandemonium of rape and massacre" (ibid.), but also because it constitutes an estranging stylistic shift from a theatrical representation to the documentary mode. The elements of the sequence do not contrast with one another, but suggest a similarly narrow range of themes and moods. However, the sequence's relation to the greater, preceding part of the film can be described as dialectical: the film's two parts concern themselves with the respective and related, albeit irreconcilable, themes.

The formal operations of this sequence and their relationship to the rest of *Dogville*'s narrative and style bear comparison with *Kuhle Wampe*. Embedded in the blue-collar milieu of contemporary Berlin, the film deals with a range of topical issues, including the rights to work, abortion, and political organizing. *Kuhle Wampe* uses montage as a key narrative and stylistic principle, its interrelated episodes being separated by montage sequences that show Berlin's buildings and natural surroundings. Like Brecht and Dudow's film throughout its entirety, *Dogville*'s montage sequence employs nonfictional imagery. Like the lyrics of Brecht and Hanns Eisler's songs heard over the montage sequences in Brecht and Dudow's film, much of the lyrics of "Young Americans" resonate with *Dogville*'s narrative, touching upon such neuralgic points of American society as its racial divisions, and referring to one of the least popular presidents in the country's history, Richard Nixon.[32] The irony that imbues the song, however, distinguishes "Young Americans" in *Dogville* from Eisler and Brecht's songs in *Kuhle Wampe*, with their stern earnestness and leftist militancy.

The second installment of the *USA—Land of Opportunities* trilogy, *Manderlay*, continues the story of Grace, here found on a southern plantation whose owners are keeping secret the abolition of slavery from their black workers. The film exactly replicates the audiovisual style of the trilogy's first part, down to the ending's montage sequence (which this time around encapsulates the history of the American Blacks, emphasizing their continuing social deprivation) and its musical accompaniment, "Young Americans." The comparatively small critical reception the film has had can be attributed to the film's problematic strategy of repeating a preexisting style, as a result of which *Manderlay* falls short of its Brechtian aim. As Brecht himself repeatedly points out in his writings, habit diminishes the power of an estranging device to fulfill its intended function. The only major stylistic change the film introduces, the replacement of Nicole Kidman with Bryce Dallas Howard, further contributes to the undesired effect. *Dogville* drew much of its power to astonish from its casting of an actress from Hollywood's A-list, whose fame considerably surpasses Howard's, in the role of a multiply raped woman turned multiple avenging killer.

One can speculate that the reason for the trilogy's being paused at the time of this writing (the release of its last part, *Wasington*, was originally announced on the Internet Movie Database for 2007, but the title has since been removed from von Trier's filmography on the website) has to do with the mentioned lack of aesthetic and political efficacy of *Manderlay*. The choice von Trier may be facing with *Wasington* is whether to relinquish the trilogy's stylistic unity, or to increase the risk—unsuccessfully borne by *Manderlay*—of its being seen as a series of mannerist exercises.

More recent von Trier films such as *Antichrist*, with its rejection of the realm of the political (at least in the term's vernacular sense) in favor of the mythical and archetypal, retrospectively cast doubt about the earnestness of the filmmaker's Brechtianism. In light of the postmodernist playfulness that characterizes the narrative and stylistic operations of this and the previous two von Trier films (*The Boss of It All* and *The Five Obstructions*), the filmmaker's embrace *in toto* of Brechtian theatrical techniques in *Dogville* and *Manderlay* appears ambiguous. Could it be that what informs the strategy is a twisted logic according to which following Brecht to the letter is estranging precisely because his aesthetic and political views are now obsolete? Yes, if we accept Heiner Müller's view that to use Brecht without criticizing him is to betray him; no, if we consider that *Dogville*'s appropriation of another artist's style can be considered Brechtian not only in terms of what is obvious (and superficial), but also in terms of what is hidden (and essential).

Coda: Von Trier after Brecht

After the project for the last installment of the (pseudo-) Brechtian *USA—Land of Opportunities* trilogy had been put to a halt, von Trier made a detour from the long series of films aimed at the international market with *The Boss of It All* (Direktøren for det hele, 2006). Unlike all of his previous and subsequent feature films, he did not premiere *The Boss of It All* at Cannes—a decision indicative of the modesty of the film's ambition. The Danish-language comedy is less memorable for its humor than its use of Automavision—a Zentropa-devised process that allows the computer to randomly modify the shot's visual parameters, resulting in unbalanced compositions and shifting illumination. Yet another result of von Trier's choice to relinquish the strict creative control that characterized his work prior to *Breaking the Waves*, Automavision links to the narrative of *The Boss of It All* in a manner that foregrounds the film's metafilmic aspect and allows for it to be productively read as a meditation on the character of authorship in collaborative filmmaking, comparable to the earlier, highly innovative *The Five Obstructions* (Lars von Trier and Jørgen Leth, 2003).

In *The Five Obstructions*, we witness the creative process of Leth's remaking his own short *The Perfect Human* (1967) five times, in each instance observing such formal limitations imposed by von Trier as the choice of a locale and the length of each shot. Combining the documentary and experimental film modes, *The Five Obstructions* explores the perpetual question of where the "essence" of an artwork resides: in its content (the term here pertaining to the film's narrative) or in its form (the term that, in the case of *The Five Obstructions*, refers to the work's visual and aural operations). Trier and Leth's film is lent an added complexity by the relation it establishes between the identified question on the one hand and, on the other, that of creative ownership of *The Five Obstructions* and the films whose making it documents. As the film progresses, a crypto-Oedipal contest between von Trier and Leth—under whom the former studied his craft—gains a narrative prominence. Its resolution, a decided blurring of the boundaries that separate the two men's creative identities, parallels the impossibility of practically separating *The Perfect Human*'s form and content. *The Five Obstructions* thus challenges the viability of a remake, in the sense of reproducing the aesthetic effect achieved by a preexisting film.

While its form strongly distinguishes itself from that of *The Five Obstructions*, *The Boss of It All* bears similarities with the former film in terms of how its narrative and style converge to foreground the theme of control. The narrative features an IT company whose owner (Peter Gantzler) attributes his unpopular decisions to a non-existing CEO. When he decides to sell, the owner hires an actor (Jens Albinus) to communicate the unpleasant news to the employees. The story of mixed identity is mirrored by the film's stylistic procedures, which involve a competition between von Trier—who asserts his authorial force by appearing in the film to comment on its narrative turns—and by Automavision, which subjects the products of von Trier's authorial force to revision based on the principle of chance.

Considered together, the two films read like essays on cinema and its industry by a filmmaker whose string of high-profile films produced up to then earned him the status of a master, and who is taking a respite from creating major works. *The Five Obstructions* and *The Boss of It All* also mark a departure from von Trier's overtly (if also problematically) political films that include all the titles from *Europa* to *Manderlay* to the *Depression Trilogy*, comprising *Antichrist*, *Melancholia*, and *Nymphomaniac*. Perhaps the most unique commonality of the latter three films, somewhat eclipsed by their dissimilar stories and formal procedures, is what can be termed a shift from the conception of man as a social animal to that of man as a natural being. While the narratives of earlier von Trier films, such as those of the *Europa* trilogy, are innately tied to their respective settings, transferring the narrative of the recent *Antichrist* from Seattle to Glasgow, or that of *Nymphomaniac* from Glasgow to Seattle, would leave intact the two stories' mechanisms. It is archetypal fears and needs—sexuality and extinction in ratios varying from one film to the next—rather than socially and historically constructed ones that represent the three films' thematic foci. *Europa*, set in Germany immediately after World War II and released a year after the reunification of Germany, was self-consciously timely. That it was also subversive in its suggestions of the threat of fascism as undying becomes evident in comparison with another film from the period that commented on the next development of monumental significance for the continent, the formation of the European Union: Krzysztof Kieslowski's *Three Colors: Blue* (1990). Chronicling a woman's coping with the unexpected loss of her child and husband—the composer of an unfinished piece dedicated to the idea of European unity—the film associates the then nascent political system with catharsis of emotional pain caused by a fortuitous event (the protagonist's family dies in a car accident). The film's uncritical celebration of the European Union combines with an array of melodramatic devices to create an effect of political kitsch.

Kieslowski in *Blue* is an orderly conformist, and von Trier is a mischievous troublemaker throughout his oeuvre. But while those amongst von Trier's film preceding *The Antichrist* invariably use broader social organizations as platforms for their provocations (the church in *Breaking the Waves* and Dogville and Manderlay in their titular films, to name but a few examples), this is not the case with the films of the *Depression Trilogy*. All of them focus on the family and depict the institution as autonomous from the other ones. The threats to it are depicted as either internal (*The Antichrist*, a horror whose monster figure is epitomized by the irrationally evil She [Charlotte Gainsbourg]) or external to mankind's influence (*Melancholia*, a science fiction disaster film that has Earth colliding with the titular renegade planet).

Like *Dogville* and *The Antichrist*, *Nymphomaniac* evokes de Sade's *Justine* (1791) in being structured as a series of the protagonist's confessions on her sexual experiences. Unlike the novel and de Sade's other works, however, the film fails to explore the relation between sex and politics in the manner that lent infamy to "the divine marquis." The fact that Jerome (Shia LaBeouf)—a steady lover of the film's protagonist, Joe (Charlotte Gainsbourg)—is a biker-cum-clerk seems as irrelevant for our understanding of the narrative as the clerical affiliation of Justine's abusers is crucial for how we interpret the novel.

Nymphomaniac complicates the principle of stylistic duality one encounters in all of von Trier's films. *The Antichrist* and *Melancholia* both combine gritty handheld cinematography and jump cuts with elaborate shots employing slow motion and composite imagery, the contrast between the two groups of images reminiscent of that between the scenes of *Breaking the Waves* that constitute the film's bulk, and the static, high resolution images of landscapes interspersed between them. *Nymphomaniac*, in contradistinction, uses fictional and nonfictional imagery as two basic groups of contrasting elements. Soligman's (Stellan Skarsgård) references to fishing motivate cuts to images of the activity from outside of the diegetic space, executed in a style evocative of mainstream documentaries. In a like fashion, the comparison that Joe makes between one of her lovers and a cat prompts a transition to a close-up of a tabby glaring at the camera. The technique is well known from such "lowest common denominator" TV shows as *TMZ on TV* (Time Warner, 2007), which follows celebrity-related rumors. The show visually dynamizes its scenes by the use of inserts showing the people and objects that the reporters reference, resulting in an inversion of montage as "denotation through connotations"—thus defined by Hans-Joachim Schlegel in the formulation cited previously (qtd. in Bogdal 263).

The technique evokes both the strategies of some of von Trier's earlier films and those by the other filmmakers this book focuses on. As discussed earlier, the faithfulness with which Straub adapts Böll's short story for the screen in *Machorka-Muff* works to expose the fissure that separates the logics of verbal and photographic signs, thereby buttressing the film's theme of uncertain historical knowledge and the unrecognized repetitions of the past. To a result at once similar and different from the described one, Watkins in *Culloden* identifies via the voiceover a round shot and its effect as an image unfolds of a cannon being loaded and fired, and *Dogville*'s map includes both a drawing of a dog and the species' name. The intentional semiotic redundancy helps dispel the shroud of the viewer's presumed notions, and sentiments about the profilmic events, the reduction of those events to their constituents—their analysis—produces conditions for a synthesis of them.

The Brechtian nature of the described strategies are clear. But what can one make of the nondiegetic inserts in *Nymphomaniac*, except that they break the visual monotony of the scenes featuring the barely mobile Joe and Soligman in conversation? If their supplementary function is to liken the banality of sound-image relationship in contemporary mainstream media with that of the sexual act as represented in pornographic films—of which *Nymphomaniac* is one—that function is amply fulfilled. But the film's flamboyant style must have been conceived with an eye to a larger goal. A consideration of this group of nondiegetic elements in the film alongside the other ones, which consist of superimposed captions and diagrams that illustrate an array of concepts from Fibonacci's numbers to Bach's polyphony, enables a pertinent inference. The "low-culture," pornographic aspect of Joe's flashbacks and the "high-culture" aspect of the scenes featuring her and Soligman form a contrasting binary that has characterized art in both modernity and postmodernity. But von Trier, who has configured himself as a trendsetter rather than a trend follower, surely aimed with *Nymphomaniac* for more than contributing to the vast and long-existing corpus of artworks that blur the boundaries between "popular" and "elite" culture. That aim can be gleaned more from the conditions of *Nymphomaniac*'s production and distribution that the film itself.

The film was vaguely announced as early as 2011, at the Cannes Film Festival press conference for *Melancholia*, where von Trier added to his notoriety by expressing empathy with Hitler and an antipathy for Israel almost in one breath. These remarks were followed by the filmmaker's admission, in a moment of feigned rhetorical defeat, that he was a Nazi. The festival reacted by proclaiming the filmmaker an unwelcome person, and von Trier followed up by declaring that he had realized that he does not possess the skills to express himself unequivocally and had therefore decided to refrain from making public statements and interviews (Shoard). However, neither party stayed true to their respective promises. The festival director Thierry Fremaux later announced that von Trier is welcome back to the Croisette (Bhushan), while the filmmaker has made numerous apologetic statements about the event while continuing to capitalize on the "scandal." He appeared at the Berlin premiere of *Nymphomaniac* in a shirt reading "persona non grata" under the Cannes Film Festival logo, and in the publicity photographs for the film with duct tape across his mouth.

These instances of a filmmaker's use of her own fame as a film's selling point are crucially different from those exemplified by, say, Hitchcock, who was shown pointing at his watch on the posters that advertised the "no late admission" policy enforced for *Psycho*. Namely, the policy and the image associated with its public announcements synecdochally stood for Hitchcock's auteurial control. In contradistinction, the version of *Nymphomaniac* the public has seen by the time of this writing opens with the caveat that it is released with von Trier's permission but without his involvement. The "real" *Nymphomaniac*, the five-and-a-half-hour director's cut, has yet to appear.

Nymphomaniac thus forms an incongruity between the publicizing campaign's emphasis on von Trier as a directorial star and his disavowal of the film. More intriguingly, it creates a discrepancy between the superfluity of its images (whereby the pornographic principle of transgressing the public decorum is applied also in the segments of the film devoid of sexual content) and the configuration of itself as an artwork that cannot be accessed, as its own conspicuous absence. Given the abundance of graphic imagery in the shorter version, one is led to speculate—and hope—that the longer one will include also sights and sounds of non-pornographic nature, that will redeem the seemingly uninspired film. The apotheosis of this characteristic can be found in the scene where Soligman interjects a reference to the Prusik knot at the moment when Joe refers to the knots on the rope that Mr. K (Jamie Bell) used to whip her. In the narrative world populated by mouthpieces for the director, Joe's assessment of Soligman's commentary as his weakest digression to that point—correct from my point of view—seems indicative of what is truly perverse about the film: not the pleasure its heroine derives from being inflicted with pain, but that it maintains its structural flaws despite acknowledging them as such.

Presumably conceived with the idea of transgressing through its subject matter of non-normative sexual behavior as much as through its pornographic treatment of it, *Nymphomaniac* seems bound to be regarded as part of a broader trend in contemporary European cinema, of which Abdellatif Kechiche's *La Vie d'Adèle Chapitres 1 & 2* (Blue Is the Warmest Color, 2013) and François Ozon's *Jeune & jolie* (2013) represent other notable examples. This restricts the subversive potential of *Nymphomaniac*, while the failure of all three films to render their subject matter in terms of partisan politics appears reflective of the current political standstill of the West, in most of which fierce liberalism is today the norm.

Conclusion

Like the other filmmakers on which this book focuses, von Trier has a unique relation to Brecht and the film criticism that Brecht's theoretical texts inspired. Straub and Huillet's most influential films and the latter corpus of texts were produced contemporaneously and appear to have influenced each other. Watkins, on the other hand, who prolifically produced films during the heyday of the Brecht-inspired film criticism in the 1970s, does not engage with it at all, and even confesses to having discovered Brecht only late in his career. Von Trier's films, for their part, make gestures that can be interpreted to implicitly emphasize the split between Brecht's dramatic theory and the mentioned interpretations of it. On the other hand, the films of *The USA—Land of Opportunities* trilogy apply many of Brecht's theatrical techniques directly, largely disregarding the uniqueness of film as a medium, thereby hinting at both Brecht's position on the characteristically modernist notion of medium-specificity and the rejection of it, widely associated with postmodernist artistic practices.

Von Trier's subsequent films represent a departure from the political impulse and effect of *The Idiots* and the films of *The USA—Land of Opportunities* trilogy, and a return to a distinctly postmodernist poetics.

This latter fact supports the impression that even the seemingly Brechtian von Trier films are, in fact, parodies thereof, pastiches (Fredric Jameson describes the pastiche as "parody that has lost its sense of humor" [*Brecht* 195]). To an auteurist-inclined viewer, interested in the continuity of a filmmaker's thematic and stylistic preoccupations from one film to the next, von Trier poses a deliberate challenge. A politically minded viewer in our era of growing global inequality and continuing political oppression will find troubling the possibility that the expressions of the political in the *Dogme 95* manifesto, *The Idiots*, *Dogville*, and *Manderlay* are, in fact, but a tacit mockery of Brecht and the cause he stands for. After seeing von Trier change aesthetic directions so many times during his career, one has difficulties resisting the feeling that whatever the filmmaker has "up his sleeve" will turn out to be but a trick. This diminishes the political efficacy of von Trier's Brechtianism.

6

Whither Brecht?

HAS THEATRICALITY DISLODGED montage as the principle source of *Verfremdung* it formerly was in Brechtian cinema? A final summary of how the two techniques are deployed in the films of Brecht and other filmmakers on whom this book has focused will, it is hoped, suggest an affirmative answer to this question with additional force.[1]

Most examples of montage in *Kuhle Wampe*, the only film where Brecht makes consistent use of the technique in the term's medium-specific sense, can be situated somewhere between the traditions of Vertov and Eisenstein. Like Vertov's, some of Brecht and Dudow's montage sequences are realized in the nonfictional mode, and serve as narratively—albeit not ideationally—neutral dividers between the film's three episodes. The Eisensteinian aspect of the film's editing evidences itself in the interior scene following the job hunt sequence, where a previously seen shot of the pedaling workers is recontextualized to suggest not a character's memory of the event (the function the described stylistic procedure would serve in a mainstream film), but to problematize the conceptual relationships among them. Still, Eisenstein's use of individual images as "montage cells," whose juxtaposition fundamentally alters their original meaning, is not compatible with Brecht's many aesthetic principles and techniques centred on and derived from his work with the performer. (To illustrate the pertinent distinction between the two practitioners, some of the famous *Gesten* in Brecht's theater were created in rehearsals as a result of trial and error; in contrast, Eisenstein cast his actors on the basis of physical features rather than acting abilities.)

More conspicuously than in *Kuhle Wampe*, the centrality of the actor for Brecht's film aesthetics—with theatricality as its concomitant—

manifests itself in such post–World War II projects as the screen adaptation of *Mother Courage*. Brecht's notes about the film's visual design suggest a dominance of cinematographic (Daguerreotype) effect as an intended source of *Verfremdung*. It seems a safe guess that this stylistic choice was also intended to secure an easy transfer onto celluloid of the many ideas developed for the play's earlier stage incarnations that Brecht had directed. To the viewer familiar with those works, the film's theatricality would appear as the stage productions' shadow, an instance of adaptation from one medium to another that has not run its complete course. As such, it must not be confused with the theatricality shown by the films of Straub and Huillet, Watkins, and von Trier this book has discussed. The latter films allude to theater directly, through their narratives (*The Idiots*) or style (for example, *Antigone*), foregrounding what would only incidentally characterize the screen adaptation of *Mother Courage* made in accordance with Brecht's ideas for it.

Straub and Huillet use montage in a series of earlier fictional films (to mention but a few, *Machorka-Muff*; *The Bridegroom, Comedienne, and the Pimp*; and *History Lessons*) and in the nonfictional *Cézanne*. In their later output, they use a version of continuity editing. Courtesy of the filmmakers' radical modifications of the style, continuity editing in Straub and Huillet functions as an arena for self-reflexive commentaries. *Antigone*, for instance, implies the parallel between the immobile camera and the theater spectator, while simultaneously questioning it through stylistic operations that deviate from our visual perception (the use of lenses dissimilar from that in the human eye, and of the cut as a device of transition between two points of interest). *Sicily!* "lays bare the device" of mainstream cinema whereby time passage is portrayed through select aspects of space (the film's two consecutive shots showing pans across a landscape in two different times of the day). Finally, *Machorka-Muff* interrogates continuity editing by inviting comparisons between the language of the medium and that of the short story upon which the film is based, revealing the arbitrariness of both. As far as theatricality is concerned, Straub and Huillet use it in most of their films, typically in conjunction with other estranging techniques: the compression of the full-length Ferdinand Buckner play into approximately ten minutes in one of the segments of *Bridegroom*, the use of the jump-cut in *Othon*, and of a single camera setup in *Antigone*.

Peter Watkins's films show a steady chronological growth of their editing patterns' variety and complexity, culminating in *The Freethinker*, a work predicated largely on what Eisenstein designates respectively as associational and intellectual editing. The long-take aesthetic of Watkins's most recent film, *La Commune*, diminishes further the role of editing in the filmmaker's overall stylistic system: the importance for meaning creation of the relationships among the film's shots there recedes behind the importance of the dialogue. The relationship in Watkins's cinema among the average shot length, editing style, and theatricality can be elucidated through the following example: if the acting style in the anachronistic interview scenes in *Culloden*, an earlier Watkins film, is less theatrically heightened than their equivalents in *La Commune*, it is so at least partly because the former film uses as the basic structural unit not the scene (in the sense the word has in Aristotelian theater and cinema) but thematically (meaning not necessarily spatially and temporally) related clusters of shots. This principle, which can be found at work in much of documentary film practice, does not facilitate lengthy dialogue improvisations that constitute *La Commune*'s stylistic core.

As is the case with Watkins, Brecht's influence on von Trier shows itself unambiguously only in the filmmaker's later works. Like Watkins, von Trier uses an array of principles and techniques today associated with Brecht even in the films that predate the overtly Brechtian *Dogville* and *Manderlay*. Examples include the frequent acknowledgment of the camera by the protagonist of *Breaking the Waves* (as the supposed filmic equivalent to Brecht's technique of "breaking the fourth wall") and the film's division into "chapters" (which corresponds to Brecht's techniques of *Literarisierung* and montage in the term's dramaturgical sense). The films of the *USA—Land of Opportunity* trilogy reject most medium-specific Brechtianisms in favor of historical techniques for which the former were an inspiration (albeit with a twist: the Brechtian stages of *Dogville* and *Manderlay* are not feasibly theatrical, since their respective architectures and sizes preclude the possibility of the viewer's visually absorbing them in their entirety from a single vantage point).

While the theatricality of Straub and Huillet's films illuminates the often disregarded affinities between Brechtian and Aristotelian theater, and whereas the theatricality of *La Commune* sheds light on the relationship among epic/dialectic theater, the *Lehrstück*, and psychodrama, von Trier's *Dogville* and *Manderlay* follow historical Brechtian techniques to the letter. The implications are open to different interpretations of von Trier's use of Brecht, a paradigmatic representative of late modernism, as a source of material for works that radicalize the postmodernist genre of pastiche. The positive one is obvious: von Trier renews the relevance of Brecht. The negative one is that *Dogville* and *Manderlay* are mere exercises in cultural archaeology, which blunt the political edge of Brecht's art by uncritically recycling its style.

Aside from the narrative and stylistic differences among Straub and Huillet, Watkins, and von Trier briefly reiterated above, these filmmakers—as well as others that deserve the descriptor Brechtian as this book defines it—share crucial similarities in terms of broader narrative preoccupations and formal principles. As for the former, the themes along the lines of resistance and rebellion pervade the films of the four filmmakers this book focuses on, as well as Brechtian cinema in general. In Straub and Huillet, these are sometimes overt (as in the case of *Antigone*), while their relevance for a given film can sometimes be understood only through exploration of pertinent extratextual material (for example, the significance for *Sicily!* of the publication history of the novel on which the film is based). Watkins's *Edvard Munch* and *The Freethinker* share the theme of rebellion against societal norms, which in such films as *Punishment Park* and *La Commune* receives an overt political dimension. Finally, von Trier's *The Idiots* and the films of his *USA—Land of Opportunities* trilogy have for protagonists individuals who have deliberately placed themselves outside the mainstream of society.

In terms of style, all films of the four filmmakers make evident the rootedness of *Verfremdung*—as the broadest aesthetic notion of Brecht's theory—in dialectics. Brechtian films tend to contrast and compare the elements of their visual and audio material abstractly (that is, ideationally) as much as concretely (that is, narratively). To reiterate some of the examples given in the preceding chapters: the relation between the narrative of *Dogville* and the photographs of the American poor from the film's final sequence; the relation between the events of the Paris Commune and the sociopolitical state of affairs in France at the end of the twentieth century, established in one of *La Commune*'s debate scenes; and, most abstractly, the exploration by Straub and Huillet's films between sound and image, story and plot, and filmic and geographical space/time. One can best realize the peculiarity of the described formal principle by comparing a Brechtian film with one whose politics are compatible with Brecht's but which follows the norms of Hollywood classicism. The illustration of a similar point that the journal *Screen* used was Costa Gavras's *Z* (1969); a relatively recent one that qualifies is Steven Soderbergh's *Che* (2008).

Before concluding, indicating two avenues for further research appears in order. The first is the application of Brechtian dramatic theory in nonfictional films, the mode this book has avoided because it uses the actor only atypically, and therefore has little relevance to theatricality, of which the actor is a principal source. But since non-Brechtian documentaries often employ the techniques that are, in the context of fictional cinema, commonly associated with Brecht (to mention but one, organizing the material according to the ideational, as opposed to spatiotemporal, connections among its constituents), film studies would benefit from a systematic exploration of the ways in which documentary filmmakers who align themselves with Brecht's artistic and political project seek alternative ways to produce *Verfremdung*.

The other avenue is the relationship between the theatricalization of Brechtian cinema and the growing reliance on technology of certain theater traditions. Challenging the common view of the actor as the central element of a theater production, which has also informed the present study, this trend may profoundly change the way we think about the medium. When the politically and aesthetically revolutionary Stephen Heath was proposing theatricality as another technique of Brechtian cinema beside montage, he presumably had in mind the period's most prominent avant-garde practices, many of which shared the aim of despectacularizing the medium and back-to-the-basics aesthetics (for example, the Living Theatre, with its nods to Brecht and Artaud, and Jerzy Grotowski, the ritualistic dimension of whose theater derives from the latter of the two practitioners). As a point of contrast, *Stifters Dinge* (Stifter's Things, 2007) by Heiner Goebbels, a foremost German stage director, uses no performers but only a combination of visual and audio effects produced by technicians offstage. Productions like this challenge the actor's preeminence in theater—which underlies also this book's methodology—and destabilize the meaning of "theatricality" as a set of fixed stylistic traits.

To risk stating the obvious: as change in relation to the dominant sociopolitical trends is Brechtian cinema's defining imperative, the phase of its development described in this book is not final. After many pages of discussing the past and present of Brechtian cinema, a speculation about its future seems justified. If the growing popularity of various portable media players prompts Brechtian filmmakers to start making films specifically for the small screen with which these devices are typically equipped, the current aesthetic trend may decline. Namely, the small screen is better suited for the close-up than for the long shot, which—being comparable to the perspective of the theater spectator—facilitates or even conditions the use of theatricality. In what formal procedures exactly would Brechtian filmmakers seek alternatives to theatricality, with montage long having been rendered aesthetically and politically inefficacious by mainstream media's appropriation of it, cannot be predicted. What seems certain, however, is that the direct causality between the use of a single stylistic technique and *Verfremdung* as its result—posited by the Brechtian film theorists of the 1970s and the following decade—has been abandoned (hence the appropriateness of the plural form "cinemas" in this book's title).

After acknowledging the problems of the coexistence of theatricality and montage, its possibility needs to be emphasized as a final proposition. To paraphrase Brecht's footnote to the dramatic versus epic theater schema, what this book has discussed concerns a shift in emphasis rather than in substance.

Notes

Chapter 1

1. For an early and comprehensive example on Godard and Brecht, see Lesage 1975.

2. For example, Jan Simmons (2007) puts forward the argument that von Trier's cinema can be more profitably regarded in relation to (postmodern) game theory than to Brecht's (modern) epic/dialectic theater theory, while Angelos Koutsourakis's recent study (2013) reincorporates von Trier into the context of Brechtian cinema.

3. It should be noted that cinematic theatricality by no means necessarily implies Brechtianism. The former quality is found, for instance, in the films of Peter Greenaway (*The Cook, The Thief, His Wife & Her Lover* [1989], *The Baby of Macon* [1993]) and Baz Luhrmann (*Moulin Rouge* [2001], *The Great Gatsby* [2013]), which scarcely conform to Brecht's worldview.

4. Josette Féral, in her 2002 article "Theatricality: The Specificity of Theatrical Language," states that the texts she has been able to assemble dealing with the notion date back only ten years (95).

5. The investigations of the history of anti-theatricality carry the insinuation that the antagonism toward the medium has been proving, and thereby reinforcing, theater's social relevance and potential for subversion. It is for that reason that, as Jonas Barish observes, hostility toward the stage erupts when the theater is flourishing and contributing to the community in vital ways (qtd. in Tassi 35).

6. Rozik here refers to Charles Sanders Peirce's typology of signs: the icon (which physically resembles its signified), the index (which directly correlates to its referent), and the symbol (which bears a strictly conventional, and therefore arbitrary, relation with its object). For a clear and succinct analysis of Peirce's sign model, see Merrell.

7. A further factor in the 1930s decline of montage-based cinema resulted from a correlation between technology and aesthetics. The global standardization of sound film between 1927 and the mid-1930s limited the use of montage, because of the perceptual difference between image and sound. An experienced

viewer can read a single frame's content, but it takes significantly longer than a twenty-fourth of a second for a sound to establish itself in the viewer's mind. In addition, the objects we perceive as unique for their aural qualities are fewer than those perceived unique for their appearance. Whereas the introduction of sound made it more difficult to oppose the linearity of Hollywood-style narration through juxtaposing visual signs as a film unfolds, it opened the possibilities for juxtaposing video and audio channels, as noted by Eisenstein, Pudovkin, and Alexandrov in their "Statement on Sound" (1928).

8. For more on the distinction as appropriated by film narratology, see Bordwell (*Narration* 49–56).

9. In his later theoretical writings, Brecht refers to a somewhat evolved version of his theatrical model presented in "Notes" as dialectical. To highlight the focus of its inquiry on the continuity between the concept's different articulations, this book refers to it with both terms.

10. Brecht's anti-Kantian stance, investigated by Jan Bruck in relation to the concept of realism in "Brecht's and Kluge's Aesthetic of Realism" (1988), manifests itself also in the antagonism Brecht shows toward Kant's dictum in his *Critique of Aesthetic Judgment*, that "the finality in the product of fine art, intentional though it be, must not have the appearance of being intentional, i.e., fine art must be capable of being viewed as nature, is by the presence of perfect exactness in the agreement with rules prescribing how alone the product can be what it is intended to be, but with an absence of laboured effect . . . i.e., without a trace of the artist having always had the rule presented to him and of its having fettered his mental powers" (qtd. in Friedrich, "On Brecht" 156). Robert E. Wood, in his discussion of the idea of art's imitating nature's modes of production, traces the idea back to Plotinus (308).

11. Some of the confusions surrounding *Verfremdung* seem due to the theorist's own changing understanding of the concept, and to his interchangeable use of the terms *Entfremdung* and *Verfremdung* until 1936.

12. This applies to an even greater extent to the theater of the absurd. While the pre–World War II avant-garde movements invariably aligned themselves with one political option or another (the frequent fissures between these and the theorists and practitioners of the movements notwithstanding), the most celebrated absurdist playwrights—Beckett and Ionesco—famously maintained decidedly apolitical stances. As a consequence, "the '*Verfremdung*' of the absurdist theater remains at the '*Entfremdung*': 'understanding—not understanding (as alienation)" (Knopf 1980, 401; translation mine). Significantly, Brecht wrote an (unfinished) rewrite of *Waiting for Godot*, in which the protagonists are depicted in terms of their class positions: Pozzo receives an aristocratic "*von*" and is described as a landowner, Lucky is "a donkey or a policeman," Estragon is a "prole," and Vladimir is an "intellectual" (ibid., 371).

13. This interpretation of *ostranenie* bases itself on the view that the concept's adjustment to the doctrine of socialist realism, whereby it acquired an overtly political dimension, constitutes a forced betrayal of its original, 1917 formulation.

14. Understood in this sense, *Historisierung* is echoed by the third in the triad of twentieth-century terms denoting estrangement in the arts, the Czech

structuralists' *aktualizace*. Interchangeably translated to English as foregrounding and topicalization, the first meaning of *aktualizace* concerns the upturning of the conventional hierarchy of artistic signs within an artwork, whereas the second meaning pertains to making the subject of an artistic presentation topical and contemporary.

15. Importantly for the main topic of this book, Brecht frequently uses cinematic tropes and examples when discussing *Gestus*. Writing in "Die Straßenszene" ("The Street Scene," 1938) about how the witness of a traffic accident should go about explaining the behavior of the driver and victim to a group of bystanders who missed the accident, he remarks that the demonstrator achieves the *Verfremdungseffekt* by "executing his motions carefully, probably in slow motion" (Brecht, *Brecht on Theatre* 126). Similarly, in the account of his collaboration with Lorre on the 1931 production of *Man Equals Man*, Brecht mentions a short silent film they made of the performance, and claims that the actor conveyed the basic meaning of each line of the play through miming (55).

16. The first to identify the former formula was Tzvetan Todorov. In his "Structural Analysis of Narrative," he writes: "The minimal complete plot can be seen as the shift from one equilibrium to another. . . . The two moments of equilibrium are separated by a period of imbalance, which is composed of a process of degeneration and a process of improvement" (75).

17. Problematically, Wollen's discussion of the two terms contrasts the effects of identification ("empathy [and] emotional involvement with a character") and the devices Godard uses to create the opposite effect ("direct address, multiple and divided characters, commentary") ("Godard" 500).

18. The terms Brecht contrasts in the earlier dramatic/epic theater schema correspond to Wollen's in many ways. As the most obvious connections, consider the following pairs (whose respective places within the schemas are indicated by the numbers): Brecht 1–Wollen 1,3,4,5; Brecht 2–Wollen 2; Brecht 3–Wollen 2; Brecht 4–Wollen 2,7; Brecht 5–Wollen 2,7; Brecht 6–Wollen 2,7; Brecht 7–Wollen 1. The link between the last two binaries becomes apparent when one considers Wollen's discussion of the rhetorical, rather than narrative, constructive principle of *Vent d'est*, whereby an argument is disposed ("Godard" 500).

19. Heath's definition of ideology as "a set of practical norms which govern the attitude and the practical stance adopted from men with regard to the real objects and the real problems of their social and individual existence, and of their history" ("Lessons" 113–14) differs from Brecht's, who defines the notion in terms of the break of ties between thinking and its material basis, as well as of nondialectical thinking.

20. The Aristotelian sense of *catharsis* is not to be confused with that in Freud: the process of discharging an affect that was "strangulated"—diverted from the normal paths that lead to consciousness and movement, thereby causing psychical traumas, which again manifest themselves in hysterical symptoms. Freud maintains that the uncovering of the symptom's meaning leads to their elimination (Freud 108–9).

21. For an illuminating discussion of the correlation between cybernetics and cognitive science, see Dupuy.

22. Smith follows Carroll in treating "illusion" as synonymous with deception in such writings as the latter's "Anti-Illusionism in Modern and Postmodern Art." But there is a crucial difference between the kind of illusion of which an example has been provided and perceptual realism in art on the one hand (both of which are pertinent to Brecht's argument), and, on the other, the illusion of the three-shell game, for instance. The game's "message" to the observer can be formulated as follows: "Your eyes can't be lying; the pea *is* under this shell."

23. Gunning's article is of further pertinence for the topic at hand. Building upon Barthes, Gunning notes the impossibility of reducing the photograph's reference to a signification, a result of the medium's automatic capture of overwhelming, excessive detail, and identifies the "noise" thereby produced as a source of the medium's realism ("What's" 45–46). Gunning's words bring to mind the internal drama of Eisenstein at work on a screen version of *Capital*, seemingly propelled in equal measures by a Dickensian (realist) impulse and a Joycean (modernist) one, attracted both to the "noise" offered by cinema as a photography-based medium, and the possibility for images and sounds to be rid of that "noise" and achieve the significatory economy of words. His commentary evokes also Godard's late 1960s films, where excessive elements survive all the attempts to be subsumed within a chain of signification: despite the use in *Joy of Learning* (1969), for example, of a monotonal background and hard illumination—stylistic choices that highlight the film's artificiality and the status of its images as images—the actors' hair continues to look "accurate" just as it would in a film that purports to have a strong and unmediated connection to the real as we perceive it.

Chapter 2

1. For more examples of Brecht's references to the painter, see *Werke* 22.1: 270–73. Besides the article from which the quotation corresponding with this footnote derives, for more on this consult Schöttker 244–52.

2. I thank Stefan Soldovieri for this translation.

3. In the category of parables, Fradkin classifies *Man Equals Man*, *Aufstieg und Fall der Stadt Mahagonny* (The Rise and Fall of the City of Mahagonny, 1929), *Saint Joan of the Stockyards*, all *Lehrstücke*, *Die Rundkopfe und die Spitzkopfe* (Roundheads and Pointedheads, 1934), *Das Verhor des Lukullus* (The Trial of Lucullus, 1939), *Der gute Mensch von Sezuan* (The Good Person of Szechwan, 1942), *Der aufhaltsame Aufstieg des Arturo Ui* (The Resistible Rise of Arturo Ui, 1941), *The Caucasian Chalk Circle*, *Turandot oder Der Kongres der Weiswascher* (Turandot or the Whitewasher's Congress, 1954), as well as, "with a certain justification," some other plays and play fragments, of which *Untergang des Egoisten Johann Fatzer* (The Downfall of the Egoist Johann Fatzer, 1930) is perhaps best known (Fradkin 364).

4. Note that if the variables *a* and *b* are broadened to apply not only to characters, but also to objects and abstractions, the simple formula becomes applicable to the dramaturgy of all mainstream cinema.

5. See, for example, Silberman "Brecht and Film."

6. See, for example, Hinck 71.

7. Brecht's directorial involvement in both films has been disputed. Although the credits identify Brecht as co-director, Marc Silberman, for example, cites Engel as the sole director of *Mysteries* ("Brecht and Film" 201). In the case of *Kuhle Wampe*, the disagreement over the authorship of the film seems to stem largely from the discrepancy between the credits on the one hand—which list Dudow as director—and, on the other hand, the censorship card, which lists Brecht as director and Dudow as assistant. In the heyday of Brecht-inspired film criticism in the 1970s (which the re-release of *Kuhle Wampe* in East Germany in 1958 helped initiate), the direction of the film was often attributed solely to Brecht.

8. See Knopf 2001, 431.

9. In his article "*Tonfilm 'Kuhle Wampe' oder Wem gehört die Welt?*" (The Sound Film *Kuhle Wampe* or Who Owns the World?," 1932), Brecht mentions the film's four parts, the last one consisting of the S-Bahn sequence. This division appears problematic, as the penultimate song featured in the film—which precedes what Brecht implies to be the film's final part—belongs to the story world, unlike the first two. For this reason, the structural functions of the three songs should not be considered identical. The literature on the film typically identifies three and not four parts of the film (Gersch; Happel; Turovskaia).

10. For Eisenstein's own explication of the concept, see Eisenstein "Vertical."

11. Pettifer uses Willett's rendition of the term as gest.

12. Still, the destabilization of the signifiers/signifieds relationship in the film never proceeds as far as it does in, say, Eisenstein's intellectual montages. The shots of groceries, for example, are unmistakably coded as belonging to the same timeframe as the Bönike family's activities and the space of their immediate environment. Brecht's moderate divergence from the dominant stylistic practices, of which the above is but one example, has led Peter Wollen to situate Brecht between what are—to him—polar views of cinema's ultimate aim as a medium. André Bazin, who envisions a cinema "in which there would be an 'effacement' and 'transparency' of technique" (as in technologically perfected 3D or holographic cinema), wherein "content would re-assert its primacy over form" (Wollen, "'Ontology'" 190), represents one pole. Materialist filmmakers and theorists who stress "the materiality of the filmic support" (193), thereby shifting the emphasis on subject matter shared by all narrative cinema to that of the medium itself, represent the other pole.

13. All quotations in this section are based on Marc Silberman's translation of the scene segmentation of the film, prepared by Wolfgang Gersch and Werner Hecht, and included in the Silberman-edited *Brecht on Film and Radio* (2000).

14. Brecht's practical dealings with cinema did not end with *Kuhle Wampe*. Besides a number of unproduced film adaptations of his plays as well as original scripts, he went on to co-write Fritz Lang's anti-Nazi epic *Hangmen Also Die* (1942). Brecht's Hollywood and East German film projects are, however, left outside of this investigation, as I see them as either deeply compromised by the production circumstances or not illustrative of a further development of Brecht's film aesthetic.

15. For more details on the film project, see Lang 228–34.

Chapter 3

1. Huillet was creatively involved in all of Straub's films after *Machorka Muff*, but she only received directorial credits for *Les yeux ne veulent en tout temps se fermer, ou Peut-être qu'un jour Rome se permettra de choisir à son tour ou Othon* (Eyes Do Not Want to Close at All Times, or Perhaps One Day Rome Will Permit Herself to Choose in Her Turn or Othon, 1969) and the films produced between 1975 and 2006 (her death). For simplicity's sake, the book follows the editors of the Editions Montparnasse DVD edition of the filmmakers' selected works—the only release of its kind so far—who attribute the authorship to all films on which Straub and Huillet collaborated to both filmmakers.

2. Recent scholarship has challenged the view of Bresson as a transcendental filmmaker, arguing instead that his films, in fact, exemplify a materialist perspective. For examples, see Le Dantec; Prédal; Quandt; Reader; and Rosenbaum.

3. The filmmaker's reservations about the quality of novum in the arts is redolent of Brecht, who—discussing in *The Messingkauf Dialogues* the theatrical traditions resemblant of his own project within the medium—more readily acknowledges the practitioners from the past historical eras (such as Shakespeare) than his immediate antecedents (such as Piscator.)

4. See, for example, Brady; Elsaesser "From"; and Byg "Brecht."

5. James Franklin, commenting on *Chronicle of Anna Magdalena Bach*, notes that Straub and Huillet insist upon accuracy of those details that could be verified (among the ones he mentions are the wigs and costumes, musical instruments and methods of playing them), while disregarding the details that could not be verified as historically correct (85–86). Straub and Huillet also ensure that the historical exactness of their period films avoids the pitfalls of illusionism. "Bach and his wife," writes Franklin, "do not age, since the viewer should be aware that these people are only representing Bach and his wife" (85).

6. Richard Roud recounts that Straub first approached Helene Weigel about the role of Johanna. According to Roud, the filmmaker abandoned the idea due to the actress's Viennese Jewish accent, unsuitable for the narrative set in Rhineland, but also because he wanted to thwart the possibility of the actress's premeditating the role and imposing on him an undesired acting style (53).

7. See, for example, James Monaco's *How to Read a Film* (2000) and Ian Aitken's *European Film Theory and Criticism* (2001).

8. *Machorka-Muff* includes other shots that feature ponderous pans of little narrative significance. In the sequence of scenes showing Machorka-Muff in a walk through the city, for example, we see the Rhine with a few ships and boats on its surface. The camera then pans to the left to reveal the protagonist in a medium shot. Leaned against a fence, Machorka-Muff straightens up and goes away from the camera. In the film's penultimate scene, the camera performs the same movement in the opposite direction after Inniga declares that she "always feel[s] this . . . when [she is] a bride," to reveal a hazy landscape. Both images are of low contrast, with the kind of photographic inexpressivity associated with

newsreels. This seems precisely the point: potentially earth-shattering processes (such as the rearmament of West Germany) commence peacefully. Some other Straub and Huillet films, however, reverse the suggested relation between cause and effect. Thus, in *Fortini/Cani* (1976), the camera pans over a tranquil landscape where civil populations were once massacred by the Fascists. No evidence of the crime is visually perceptible to the viewer: it is the testimony of Franco Fortini, the writer of the film on which the book is based, to which we need to turn for the grim truth of the landscape. The film thus directs us to the human-inscribed, literary aspect of an image.

9. Of course, the novel only simulates the contingency: every detail it includes was invented, or at least selected from historical material, by its writer. Straub and Huillet's presence in the described scenes, and in *History Lessons* in general, is less overt than that of Brecht in *The Business of Mr. Julius Caesar*—a possibility granted to the filmmakers by the medium's photographic nature.

10. As the second ride scene unfolds, the viewer conversant with film technology will likely guess that its duration, too, as well as the running time of the anticipated similar scenes, will approximate ten minutes (the length of a standard film reel when exposed at twenty-four frames per second). By adjusting its aesthetics to an industrial standard, the film points to its materiality.

11. The scene where the otherwise silent character tells the banker an anecdote of Caesar's capture by the pirates as he walks alongside him further suggests the association of moving through space and agency, or at least of the mentioned activity and the young man.

12. The parallelism between the viewer and the young man is promoted by the film's other instances of self-referentiality. Aside from the use of a reformulated shot-countershot syntax—to be discussed shortly—perhaps the most prominent of these is the use of black leader to break the banker's monologue in the third scene featuring the character.

13. Böll comments on the subject as follows: "I think Herr Straub's weakness is that he needs other people's material to realize his own cinematic ideas" (qtd. in Böser 25; translation mine).

14. Perhaps significantly, the writing of "Small Organon for the Theatre," a key programmatic text of epic/dialectical theater, coincided with the staging of *The Antigone of Sophocles.*

15. Besides the Brecht-written prologue, the play contains also a series of additions of verses by other authors, including Pindar and Goethe. For an analysis of the Pindar quotations in the adaptation, see Pohl 1988.

16. The only deviation from the original in terms of the delivery concerns the elders. By not distinguishing between this group of characters and invariably using the plural form of the noun when indicating their lines, Brecht's adaptation suggests that these segments should be delivered in unison. The film, however, often assigns portions of this material to individual members of the group, thereby dynamizing the dialogue's rhythm.

17. Referred here are Warhol's early 1960s plotless films of extreme length (for instance, nearly six hours for *Sleep* [1963] and nearly nine for *Empire* [1964]), photographed in static, long takes (their duration equaling that of a 16 mm film

roll), within which little movement occurs (for example, the occasional wiggling of a sleeping man in *Sleep*, and the passing of airplanes through the frame in *Empire*), showing no variation in shot scale.

18. See, for example, Heiney's discussion of the subject (159).

19. See Heiney 161 and Potter 79.

20. The second schema in Brecht's "*Vergnügungstheater oder Lehrtheater*" ("Theatre for Entertainment or Theatre for Learning," 1935) contains formulations similar to the above in terms of both content and style.

21. It is this dramaturgical decision that facilitated the subsequent incarnation of *Sicily!* as a theatrical show. Produced at the Teatro Francesco Batolo in Buti in April 1998, the show employed some of the actors from the film, minimalistic setting consisting mainly of white blocks, and colored lighting.

22. The comparison would not be worth making if Straub and Huillet themselves did not contrast their approach to cinema with Godard's, along with expressions of respect and admiration for their peer. See Manfred Blank's 1984 film *Wie will ich lustig lachen: Danièle Huillet und Jean-Marie Straub und ihr Film Klassenverhältnisse* (How Merrilly Shall I Laugh: Danièle Huillet and Jean-Marie Straub and Their Film *Class Relations*). Godard has made a similar gesture in *Hélas pour moi* (Oh, Woe Is Me, 1993), where a character searches for the version of Straub and Huillet's *Antigone* that features a lizard in the background.

23. For a crucial example, see Robbe-Grillet.

24. Later in the text, the painter makes a less ambiguous remark on the subject, included also in the film: "And my eyes, you know, my wife tells me that they jump out of my head, they get all bloodshot" (Gasquet 125).

25. Rauschenbach calculates that the Renaissance perspective distorts fifteen out of twenty-seven parameters, whereas the alternative system distorts nine out of twenty-seven (30).

Chapter 4

1. For an insightful discussion of the two trends in British cinema, see, for example, Hill 127–76.

2. An older version of the statement was translated into French and published as *The Media Crisis* (2004).

3. While Watkins's criticism falls upon the mass audiovisual media in general, he condemns for the global media crisis the aggressively dominant American MAVM, which—in his view—"now hold precisely the same position regarding Washington, as Dr. Goebbels' propaganda machinery held vis-à-vis the Reich Chancellery in Berlin, and the Nazi Party" ("American MAVM").

4. For an account of the similarly unfortunate distribution and reception histories of *The War Game* and *La Commune*, see the pages dedicated to the films on the filmmaker's website ("Peter Watkins: Filmmaker/Media Critic").

5. An example would be the inclusion of *Punishment Park* on *Rolling Stone*'s list of the most important films of 1971.

6. See, for example, Nichols 87 and Goodall 8.

7. It should be mentioned as a side note that Jacopetti and Prosperi do not share Eisenstein's political orientation. In case one misses the condescension that pervades their portrayal of the indigenous peoples of various Western colonies and developing countries where they filmed a number of their scenes—but one example of the Italian filmmakers' rightist leanings—Jacopetti repeatedly implies what his politics are in his programmatic essay "Considerations on the Documentary Film" (1966), where he responds to his "partisan" critics (Goodall 146–53).

8. Six out of the twenty-five films included in Mark Goodall's mondo filmography were made by Italian filmmakers.

9. A perfunctory Internet search conducted on the day of this writing (December 16, 2013) has retrieved several forums where fans debate the authenticity of deaths in mondo.

10. See, for example, Goodall 7.

11. See, for example, Méranger; Wayne.

12. Watkins himself testifies to the sense of biographical kinship he felt between Munch and himself as being a decisive factor in his pursuit of the project. He recalls that he decided to make a film about Munch after seeing his work at the artist's museum in Oslo, knowing that this would be a way to make a film also about himself (Welsh 169).

13. Strindberg and Munch were also acquaintances, as acknowledged by *Edvard Munch*, where Strindberg is featured as an episodic character.

14. A reminder seems apt here that Watkins has expressed disbelief in the possibility of objectivity in cinema, as a medium of artistic, and therefore personal expression, and adds that all the filmmaker can aim for is a responsible subjectivity ("Public").

15. The following entry from Munch's diaries is typical of their style, marked by syncopated verses and, often, unfinished sentences that display an arbitrary use of punctuation:

> 39
> O my dear ladies bohemians and pigs
> . . . What have you gone and done
> Yes I must say that
> I have sh t . . .
>   a hell of a trick habit
>   a fanfare of virtue
>   the act was (Munk 69)

16. In addition to the identified methods of editing, *Edvard Munch* extensively utilizes what Eisenstein refers to as vertical editing—the term denoting (primarily) the sound-image relationship. Many of the film's dialectical juxtapositions are predicated on the use of the two different aspects of film shot. To give but one example, the sound of Munch's crying, and the occasionally murmured expressions of his inability to "go on," accompanies the montage consisting of scenes that feature Munch and his fellow painters, as well as his encounter with

a prostitute. For an extensive discussion of editing in relation to Eisenstein's own *Alexander Nevsky* (1938), see Eisenstein "Vertical."

17. The middle one in the former group of scenes represents the most conspicuous example of *Munch*'s use of continuity editing techniques. Its ten shots—showing Munch and Mrs. Heiberg in the woods—the film's longest stretch that shows consistency in figure position, direction, and speed of movement. The scene's voiceover, however, somewhat ruptures the continuity established by the visuals. The ending of its second part heard in the scene ("Later in his life, Edvard Munch is to express a deep disillusionment that all his father could do as a doctor for his dying mother, and his dying sister, and for himself, was to put his hands together and pray") coincides with a close-up of Mrs. Heiberg and Munch. At once a thematic match and a disruption of the narrative's spatial and temporal continuity, the combination of elements exemplifies one of the film's many uses of vertical editing.

18. Both organic and constructivist metaphors pervade Eisenstein's writings. For an insightful discussion of the dynamic between these, see Andrew, *Major Film Theories* (60–63, 64–67).

19. The film's original, TV version—from which the analysis was made—is 5 hours and 45 minutes in length, while the shorter, cinema version runs for 3 hours and 30 minutes.

20. These are *Der Flug des Lindbergs* (Lindberg's Flight, later retitled to *Der Ozeanflug* [The Ocean Flight], 1929), *Der Jasager* (*The One Who Says Yes*, 1929–1930) and its variant *Der Neinsager* (The One Who Says No, 1929–1930), *The Measures Taken*, *Die Ausnahme und die Regel* (The Exception and the Rule, 1930–1937), *Die Horatier und die Kuriatier* (Horatii and Curiatii, 1934), and the play fragments *Der böse Baal der asoziale* (The Evil Baal, the Asocial One, published in 1968) and *Fatzer* (Steinweg 15).

21. The play's narrative is characteristic of the play type's pedagogical nature. Disregarding the Party's directives to refrain from emotionally reacting to the injustices toward workers that he witnesses, the Young Comrade inadvertently contributes to the premature beginning of a revolutionary protest. He also accidentally discloses his identity, enabling the authorities to trace him. Neither able to take him nor to leave him without further endangering the mission, the Four Agitators decide that the only solution for the problem would be Young Comrade's execution. The characters' disguising themselves by masks before entering China, where their mission of organizing workers is to take place, emphasizes the play's focus on the subservience of individualism to a common motive. Once they put on masks, the Party Secretary tells them they "are all without name and mother, blank pages on which the Revolution writes its instructions" (Brecht, qtd. in Friedrich, "Brecht and Postmodernism" 56).

22. Friedrich attributes the political group's enthusiasm for *Jasager I* to the play's supposed hostility to the subject, antirationalism and antihumanism (ibid., 54).

23. Watkins here repeats the strategy used in *Punishment Park*, whose performers "held views at least approximated those of their characters" (Rapfogel 22).

24. The sometimes questionable results of Watkins's method of directing the dialogues are easier to accept when considered in relation to the democratic stance that underlies it. Scott MacDonald's commentary of *The Journey* applies here too: "The focus of *The Journey* . . . is the thoughts and experiences of average people, and Watkins' commitment to the people who agreed to talk with him was nearly absolute: he would give them an opportunity to respond to his questions and would treat their responses with respect, not simply in a metaphoristic sense, but in terms of the allocation of screen time" (MacDonald, "Filmmaker" 367).

25. This, and the other translations of the film's lines, are borrowed from the First Run Features DVD edition of the film.

26. The lines are not accompanied by the names of their respective speakers, as the narrative fails to identify all characters in the scene.

27. The film includes an exception to this rule, notable mainly for its singularity. It occurs after the scene where the Polish members of the National Guard are interviewed by a TV Commune journalist. One of them declares the following: "If you want to change Europe, you must change its unjust social order. It's our goal." Next, the film cuts for about a second and a half to black screen, which is followed by an image of the TV Versailles anchor. He lifts his eyes from the sheets of paper on the desk before him to the camera, smiles coyly for a moment, and looks down again. As in the famous Kuleshov experiment, the film codes the otherwise "neutral" smile (presumably shot before "action" was called) as an expression of mocking irony.

28. See also Welsh 345–46.

Chapter 5

1. For an articulation and explanation of Brecht's position regarding the aesthetics of shock, see *Werke* 22.2: 824–25.

2. Behind the reasoning that informs Badley's suggestion that Brecht "forbade" such response is the lack of distinction between the notions of *Gefühl* and *Einfühlung* in Brecht, previously mentioned in relation to Murray Smith's critique of "Brechtianism."

3. Brecht's position that the individual is never autonomous but inherently conditioned by a web of societal factors allowed for the poststructuralist linking of his thought with the described conception. Still, the reasons for classifying Brecht within the preceding cultural paradigm are more numerous.

4. For examples, consult "Lars von Trier's Depression" and *Chaos Reigns at the Cannes Film Festival.*

5. For an early example, see Forst; for a recent one, see Bainbridge.

6. Hypnosis is a recurring theme in von Trier's cinema. For an extensive discussion of this topic, see Stewart.

7. This view of pastiche is put forward by Fredric Jameson's "Postmodernism and Consumer Society" (1984).

8. The board that issued the certificates included, beside the authors of the manifesto, Danish filmmakers Kristian Levring and Søren Kragh-Jacobsen.

9. See, for example, Mackenzie "Manifest"; Gaut; Bainbridge. Jan Simons's expression of surprise that the movement is often discussed in terms of realism, "on which the manifesto is altogether silent," is itself surprising, as the techniques resulting from the obligations and restrictions imposed by the "Vow of Chastity" have been traditionally mobilized toward realist aesthetics.

10. This principle is famously betrayed in numerous neorealist films, due to the inability of reconciling the cinematographic style that filmmakers associated with the movement favored—a style predicated on the use of elaborate camera movements and artificial lighting—with space limitation that is often intrinsic to location shooting.

11. Caroline Bainbridge describes the manifesto's style as "playful and highly ironic" (87). For an insightful discussion of the relationship between the latter two attitudes in the context of postmodernism, see Hutcheon.

12. For an explanation of the role of Gilles Jacob, the programming director of the Cannes Film Festival, in von Trier's career, see Stevenson 154–55.

13. In 1968, for example, a group of filmmakers led by François Truffaut attempted to shut down the festival in support of the student protests.

14. The broad application of the terms evokes Godard's Dziga Vertov group the "Vow of Chastity," thereby meriting Schepelern's comparison between the two (58).

15. The choice of digital video as a format for most *Dogme 95* films can be partly explained by the near-concurrence of the manifesto's launching and the commercialization of low-cost digital video technology. In 1995, Sony started to market the DCR-VX1000 digital camera. The relatively inexpensive device was directly connectable to a home computer, enabling the nonprofessional to post-produce image and sound without quality loss. The camera used three-chip technology, which gave sharper and more vibrant colors than its analog counterpart, and its capacity for time base correction allowed for a greater stabilization of the image. Smaller than a VHS camcorder, the camera had nearly two times the resolution of the amateur format, sufficient to meet the broadcasting standards. It was this camera that von Trier went on to use for *The Idiots* (Vinterberg's *Dogme 95* film, which premiered earlier, was shot with a yet simpler camera, Sony's PC-7E one-chip handycam).

16. The censor bars covering the genitalia of the male characters in the version of the film distributed theatrically, as well as in the VHS format, in North America aid the result. As the culmination of the narrative—the slap Karen receives from her husband—lends itself to be interpreted as an assertion of patriarchal power, the mentioned interventions of the distributor of the film for the countries where films are still censored perhaps appropriately transform the penises into phalluses.

17. Friedrich's associating *Baal* and postmodernism on the basis of "espousal of selflessness" as a common denominator for the play and the cultural trend is reasonable, if not entirely original: it is this play and *In the Jungle of the Cities*, 1924 that Elisabeth Wright uses as examples to provocatively construct a postmodern Brecht in her 1989 study that uses the phrase for the title. Wright's omission of

the *Lehrstücke* from her (exceedingly few) cases in point seems well founded in light of the many demarcation points between the principles of operation and the respective goals of the Artaudian theater of cruelty on the one hand, and the Brechtian learning-plays on the other.

18. The same argument is put forward in Friedrich's "Brecht and Post-modernism," commented upon in the previous chapter.

19. The prominence of the film's metafilmic aspect has been noted also by other commentators, such as Müller (245, 250) and Gaut (94–96).

20. "It is not solely out of aesthetic revulsion that [the Dogme 95 brethren] aim to make antibourgeois films," writes Walters, "but they are surely equally motivated by a recognition that the hegemony in whose interests such films operate is itself a thing to be challenged and changed" (Walters 43).

21. Here, a reminder seems useful that the key technique of Stanislav-ski's method is not simply antithetical to Brecht's. The latter's method of actor preparation includes three stages, comprehensively described by John Rouse (239–41). In the first stage, the actor gets acquainted with the character through asking herself about the reasons for the character's actions. The second phase "continues the work . . . but in an antithetical direction" (239): in accordance with the key Stanislavski principle, the actor here searches for the character's truth in a subjective sense and explores her or him "in all the detail demanded by the most naturalistic director" (240), while remaining tied to the Brechtian theater's broad goal of social change by using the character's social behavior as a criterion for selection among her discoveries. The final phase entails an examination of the character from the society's point of view, and attempts to bring back the "mistrust and astonishment of the first phase" (Brecht, qtd. in Rouse 240). Rouse concludes his commentary on the tripartite process of the Brechtian actor's preparation by referring to an appendix to the *Organon* where "a dialectical unity between the gestural presentation of the character in his social relationships and a realistic emotional foundation won through identification" (Rouse 240) is the actor's ultimate goal in performance.

22. Murray Smith offers an interesting, and entirely different, interpretation of the scene. In this view, the couple "appear to sustain, mutually, the spassing act, as they embrace each other and make love; but as with Stoffer's outbursts, Josephine's state of being slips imperceptibly into what now seems an authentic state of nervous breakdown" ("Lars" 117).

23. Examples include Forst; Koutsourakis.

24. The topics of economy and religion are subtly brought together by the motto "*Dictum ac factum*: No sooner said than done" (as translated in Nobus 24) above the entrance to the town's mine. In the narrative context premised on a principal dialectic of the Bible, these words seem an allusion to John's "In the beginning was the Word" (1:1).

25. For example, Hermes; Kothenschulte.

26. To a considerably smaller extent, the same applies to the dialogue. In a conversation with the film's director of photography, von Trier discloses that he instructed the translator from Danish (in which the screenplay was originally

written) not to entirely adjust the text to English, the language of the film's production. The choice of not "smoothing the seams" of the translation—to use the Brechtian phrase—is presumably aimed at producing an estranging effect.

27. Although this does not necessarily have to hold also for 3D cinema, which is currently experiencing a revival, in practice it does: the world of *Avatar* (2009), for example, emphasizes the audiovisual differences and not the similarities, between the spatio-temporal coordinates of the auditorium and itself: the audience is still paying to see a world different from theirs, and not for possible use of the technology for blurring the boundary between the two.

28. For a comprehensive, richly illustrated volume on Brecht's theater productions, see Berliner Ensemble and Weigel.

29. Von Trier recounts that during the pre-production he decided that the film should not look like they were filming a theater stage, but should have a sense of theater to it (Björkman 246).

30. Despite the similarity of the overall impressions given by the two films' respective cinematographic styles, the differences between them are worth acknowledging. *Dogville* shows consistency within a given scene in terms of color temperature and aperture value, and seems to employ the manual focus mode. More importantly, the image possesses a greater sharpness, suggesting the use of a fully professional camera, as opposed to *The Idiots*' "prosumer" VX-2000. All these qualities make the cinematography of *Dogville* appear more controlled, that is, professional, than that of *The Idiots.*

31. The pop song is as central a structural element in von Trier's cinema as it is in Brecht's dramatic artworks. He is the lyricist for many of the original ones amongst these (*Epidemic*, *Europa*, *Dancer in the Dark*.)

32. Nixon was, of course, one of the most fiercely anti-communist presidents of the United States. The following succession of lines from Bowie's song is of relevance for this chapter's purposes, hinting at Nixon and the House Un-American Activities Committee, which investigated Eisler and Brecht among many others: "Do you remember your president Nixon? / Do you remember the bills you have to pay? / Or even yesterday? / Have you been an un-American?"

Chapter 6

1. For the sake of brevity, what follows does not concern itself with the many thematic resonances between Brecht's own theater and the cinema of Straub and Huillet, Watkins, and von Trier, which have been intermittently pointed to throughout the book. Some of them, however, need to be reiterated: the fascination with America of both the young Brecht and von Trier, the shared topic of Brecht's *Days of the Commune* and Watkins's *La Commune (Paris 1871)*, and—most obviously—the use of Brecht's texts as bases for Straub and Huillet's *Antigone* and *History Lessons*.

Works Cited

46-okunen no koi (Big Bang Love, Juvenile A). Dir. Takashi Miike. 2006. Perf. Ryûhei Matsuda and Masanobu Andô. Shochiku Films. Film.

À bout de soufflé (Breathless). Dir. Jean-Luc Godard. 1959. Perf. Jean Seberg and Jean-Paul Belmondo. Criterion Collection, 2010. DVD.

Adorno, Theodor. *Aesthetic Theory*. 1970. Minneapolis: U of Minnesota P, 1997. Print.

The Adventures of Robin Hood. Dir. Michael Curtiz and William Keighley. 1938. Perf. Errol Flynn and Olivia de Havilland. Warner Bros. Film.

Africa addio (Farewell Africa). Dir. Gualtiero Jacopetti and Franco Prosperi. 1966. Cineriz. Film.

Aitken, Ian. *European Film Theory and Criticism*. Bloomington: Indiana UP, 2001. Print.

Albera, François. "Sickle and Hammer, Cannons, Cannons, Dynamite." *Die Früchte des Zorns und der Zärtlichkeit*. Ed. Astrid Johanna Ofner. Vienna: Viennale, 2004. Print.

Alice in den Städten (Alice in the Cities). Dir. Wim Wenders. 1974. Perf. Yella Rottländer and Rüdiger Vogler. Filmverlag der Autoren. Film.

An American Family. Prod. Jacqueline Donnet, Craig Gilbert, and Susan Lester. 1973. Perf. Patricia Loud and Bill Loud. PBS. Television.

L'Amérique insolite (America as Seen by a Frenchman). Dir. François Reichenbach. 1960. Les Films de la Pléiade. Film.

Andrew, Dudley. *Mists of Regret: Culture and Sensibility in Classic French Film*. Princeton, NJ: Princeton UP, 1995. Print.

Andrew, J. Dudley. *The Major Film Theories*. London: Oxford UP, 1976. Print.

Antichrist. Dir. Lars von Trier. 2009. Perf. Willem Dafoe and Charlotte Gainsbourg. Criterion Collection, 2010. DVD.

Die Antigone des Sophokles in der hölderlinschen Übertragung für die Bühne bearbeitet von Brecht (Sophocles' Antigone in Hölderlin's Translation as Reworked by Brecht). Dir. Jean-Marie Straub and Danièle Huillet. 1991. Perf. Astrid Ofner and Ursula Ofner. *Danièle Huillet et Jean-Marie Straub: Volume 3*. Editions Montparnasse, 2007. DVD.

Apocalypse Now. Dir. Francis Ford Coppola. 1979. Perf. Marlon Brando, Martin Sheen, and Robert Duvall. Paramount, 2004. Videocassette.

Aristotle. *Poetics*. New York: Hill and Wang, 1962. Print.

Armes, Roy. "Jean-Marie Straub: Strict Counterpoint." *The Ambiguous Image*. London: Secker and Warburg, 1976. 208–15. Print.

Arrowsmith, S.M.J. "Peter Watkins." *British Television Drama*. Ed. George W. Brandt. Cambridge: Cambridge UP, 1981. 217–38. Print.

Arthur, Paul. "The Troublemaker." *Film Comment* 40.3 (2004): 58–65. Print.

Austin, J. L. *How to Do Things with Words*. 1955. Cambridge, MA: Harvard UP, 1962. Print.

Avatar. Dir. James Cameron. 2009. Perf. Sam Worthington and Zoe Saldana. Twentieth Century Fox. Film.

The Baby of Macon. Dir. Peter Greenaway. 1993. Perf. Julia Ormond and Ralph Fiennes. Allarts /UGC/La Sept. Film.

Badley, Linda. *Lars von Trier*. Urbana: U of Illinois P, 2010. Print.

Bainbridge, Caroline. *The Cinema of Lars Von Trier: Authenticity and Artifice*. London: Wallflower, 2007. Print.

Baltic Deputy. Dir. Iosif Kheifits and Aleksandr Zarkhi. 1937. Perf. Nikolai Cherkasov and Marta Domasheva. Film.

Barish, Jonas. *The Antitheatrical Prejudice*. Berkeley: U of California P, 1981. Print.

Barthes, Roland. "Diderot, Brecht, Eisenstein." *Screen* 15.2 (1974–75): 33–40. Print.

———. *Image—Music—Text*. Ed. and trans. Stephen Heath. New York: Hill and Wang, 1977. Print.

Baudrillard, Jean. *Simulacra and Simulation*. 1981. Trans. Sheila Faria Glaser. Ann Arbor: U of Michigan P, 1994. Print.

Baudry, Jean Louis. "Ideological Effects of the Basic Cinematographic Apparatus." 1970. *Film Theory and Criticism*. Ed. Leo Braudy and Marshall Cohen. Oxford: Oxford UP, 1999. 345–55. Print.

Bazin, André. *What Is Cinema? (1958–1962)*. Ed. Hugh Gray. Berkeley: U of California P, 1967–1972. Print.

Becker, Florian. "Towards an Understanding of 'Gestus': Five Theses on Brecht's Conception of Realism." *Brecht Yearbook / Das Brecht Jahrbuch 33* (2008): 25–50. Print.

Beckett, Samuel. *Waiting for Godot*. 1952. New York: Grove Press, 1970. Print.

Befrielsesbilleder (Images of a Relief). Dir. Lars von Trier. 1982. Perf. Edward Fleming and Kirsten Olesen. Film.

Beneath the Valley of the Ultravixens. Dir. Russ Meyer. 1979. Perf. Kitten Natividad and Ann Marie. RM Films International. Film.

Benjamin, Walter. "A Small History of Photography." 1931. *One Way Street*. Ed. Susan Sontag. London: Verso,1985. 240–57. Print.

———. *Understanding Brecht*. 1966. London: Verso, 2003. Print.

Berliner Ensemble and Helene Weigel, eds. *Theaterarbeit: 6 Aufführungen des Berliner Ensembles*. 2nd rev. and enlarged ed. Berlin: Henschel, 1961. Print.

Bhushan, Nyay. "Lars von Trier's Sex Epic 'Nymphomaniac' Can't Compete at Cannes, Says Thierry Fremaux." *Hollywood Reporter*, November 22, 2013. Web.

Björkman, Stig, ed. *Trier on von Trier*. London: Faber and Faber, 2003. Print.

Blackburn, Simon. *Oxford Dictionary of Philosophy*. 2nd ed. New York: Oxford UP, 2008. Print.

Bogdal, Klaus-Michael. "Eine Metaphysik des Sichtbaren? Fragen zum Montagebegriff." *Alternative* 117.20 (1977): 259–64. Print.

Böll, Heinrich. "Bonn Diary." *Stories, Political Writings, and Autobiographical Works*. Ed. Martin Black. New York: Continuum, 2006. Print.

Bordwell, David. "The Idea of Montage in Soviet Art and Film." *Cinema Journal* 11.2 (1972): 9–17. Print.

———. *Narration in the Fiction Film*. Madison: U of Wisconsin P, 1985. Print.

———. *The Way Hollywood Tells It: Story and Style in Modern Movies*. Berkeley: U of California P, 2006. Print.

Bordwell, David, Janet Staiger, and Kristin Thompson. *The Classical Hollywood Cinema: Film Style and Mode of Production to 1960*. New York: Columbia UP, 1985. Print.

Böser, Ursula. *The Art of Seeing, the Art of Listening: The Politics of Representation in the Work of Jean-Marie Straub and Danièle Huillet*. Frankfurt am Main: Peter Lang, 2004. Print.

Brady, Martin. "Brecht and Film." *The Cambridge Companion to Brecht*. Ed. Peter Thomson and Glendyr Sacks. Cambridge: Cambridge UP, 2006. 297–317. Print.

Der Bräutigam, die Kömodiantin und der Zuhälter (The Bridegroom, the Comedienne, and the Pimp). Dir. Jean-Marie Straub and Danièle Huillet. 1968. Perf. James Powell and Lilith Ungerer. *Love Is Colder than Death*. Fox Lorber, 2003. DVD.

Breaking the Waves. Dir. Lars von Trier. 1996. Perf. Emily Watson and Stellan Skarsgård. Artisan Entertainment, 2000. DVD.

Brecht, Bertolt. *Brecht on Theatre*. Ed. John Willett. London: Methuen & Co., 1964. Print.

———. *Collected Plays, Volume 8*. Ed. Tom Kuhn and David Constantine. London: Methuen, 2003. Print.

———. *The Days of the Commune*. Trans. Clive Barker and Arno Reinfrank. London: Eyre Methuen, 1978. Print.

———. *Gesammelte Werke in 20 Bänden*. Frankfurt am Main: Suhrkamp Verlag, 1967. Print.

———. *The Messingkauf Dialogues*. London: Methuen, 1978. Print.

———. "The Monster." *Collected Short Stories*. New York: Methuen, 1983. Print.

———. *Saint Joan of the Stockyards*. Trans. Frank Jones. London: Eyre Methuen, 1976. Print.

———. "Theatre for Learning." Trans. Edith Anderson. *Brecht Sourcebook*. Ed. Henry Martin and Carol Bial. London: Routledge, 2000. 21–28. Print.

———. *Werke: Grosse kommentierte Berliner und Frankfurter Ausgabe*. Berlin and Frankfurt: Aufbau-Verlag and Suhrkamp, 1988. Print.

Brewster, Ben, and Colin MacCabe. "Making Kuhle Wampe: An Interview with Georg Hoellering." *Screen* 15.4 (1974–75): 71–79. Print.

Browne, Nick, ed. *Cahiers du cinéma, 1969–1972: The Politics of Representation*. Ed. Nick Browne. Cambridge, MA: Harvard UP, 1990. Print.

Bruck, Jan. "Brecht's and Kluge's Aesthetics of Realism." *Poetics 17* (1988): 57–68. Print.

Buehler, George. *Bertolt Brecht—Erwin Piscator: ein Vergleich ihrer theoretischen Schriften*. Bonn: Bouvier, 1978. Print.

Byg, Barton. "Brecht, New Waves, and Political Modernism in Cinema." *A Bertolt Brecht Reference Companion*. Ed. Siegfried Mews. Westport, CT: Greenwood Press, 1997. 220–37. Print.

———. *Landscapes of Resistance: The German Films of Danièle Huillet and Jean-Marie Straub*. Berkeley: U of California P, 1995. Print.

Carroll, Nöel. "Anti-Illusionism in Modern and Postmodern Art." *Leonardo* 21.3 (1988): 297–304. Print.

———. *Mystifying Movies: Fads & Fallacies in Contemporary Film Theory*. New York: Columbia UP, 1988. Print.

Carlson, Marvin. "The Resistance to Theatricality." *SubStance* 31.2 (2002): 238–50. Print.

Cézanne. Dir. Jean-Marie Straub and Danièle Huillet. 1989. Prod. Le Musée d'Orsay, La Sept, Diagonale and Straub-Huillet. *Danièle Huillet et Jean-Marie Straub: Volume 4*. Editions Montparnasse, 2009. DVD.

Chaos Reigns at the Cannes Film Festival. Prod. Zentropa Entertainments 23 Aps, 2009. *Antichrist*. Criterion Collection, 2009. DVD.

Chapaev. Dir. Georgi Vasilyev and Sergei Vasilyev. 1935. Perf. Boris Babochkin and Leonid Kmit. Film.

Charlotte etc. Dir. Christophe Goffettte. M6 Vidéo. 2009. *Antichrist*. Criterion Collection, 2009. DVD.

Chaudhuri, Shohini. "Dogma Brothers: Lars von Trier and Thomas Vinterberg." *New Punk Cinema*. Ed. Nicholas Rombes. Edinburgh: Edinburgh UP, 2005. 153–67. Print.

Un chien andalou (An Andalusian Dog). Dir. Luis Buñuel. 1929. Perf. Pierre Batcheff and Simone Mareuil. Luis Buñuel and Pierre Braunberger. Film.

Chronik der Anna Magdalena Bach (Chronicle of Anna Magdalena Bach). Dir. Jean-Marie Straub and Danièle Huillet. 1967. Perf. Gustav Leonhardt and Cristiane Lang-Drewanz. *Danièle Huillet et Jean-Marie Straub: Volume 3*. Editions Montparnasse, 2008. DVD.

La commune (Paris, 1871). Dir. Peter Watkins. 1999. Perf. Aurélia Petit and Gerald Watkins. New York: First Run Features, 2001. DVD.

Comolli, Jean-Luc, and Jean Narboni. "Cinema / Ideology / Criticism." 1968. *Movies and Methods, Volume 1*. Ed. Bill Nichols. Berkeley: U of California P, 1976. 22–30. Print.

Confessions about Anxiety. Prod. Electric Parc Aps. *Antichrist*. Criterion Collection, 2009. DVD.

The Cook, the Thief, His Wife and Her Lover. Dir. Peter Greenaway. 1989. Perf. Richard Borringer and Michael Gambon. Elsevier-Vendex. Film.

Corneille-Brecht. Dir. Jean-Marie Straub and Cornelia Geiser. 2009. Perf. Cornelia Geiser. Film.

Culloden. Dir. Peter Watkins. 1964. Perf. Olivier Espitalier-Noel and George McBean. Project X, 2006. DVD.

Curran, Angela. "Bertolt Brecht." *The Routledge Companion to Film and Philosophy*. Ed. Paisley Livingstone and Carl Plantinga. London: Routledge, 2009. 323–32. Print.

Currie, Gregory. "Film, Reality, and Illusion." *Post-theory: Reconstructing Film Studies*. Madison: U of Wisconsin P, 1996. 325–34. Print.

Dalla nube alla Resistenza (From the Clouds to Resistance). Dir. Jean-Marie Straub and Danièle Huillet. 1978. *Danièle Huillet et Jean-Marie Straub: Volume 2*. Editions Montparnasse, 2008. DVD.

Les Dames du Bois Boulogne. Dir. Robert Bresson. 1945. Perf. Paul Bernard and María Casares. Les Films Raoul Ploquin. Film.

Damisch, Hubert. *A Theory of /Cloud/: Toward a History of Painting*. 1972. Trans. Janet Lloyd. Stanford: Stanford UP, 2002. Print.

Dancer in the Dark. Dir. Lars von Trier. 2003. Perf. Björk and Catherine Deneuve. New Line Home Video, 2001. DVD.

Davis, Tracy C., and Thomas Postlewait, eds. *Theatricality*. Cambridge: Cambridge UP, 2003. Print.

Debord, Guy. *Society of the Spectacle*. 1967. Trans. Donald Nicholson-Smith. New York: Zone Books, 1995. Print.

Deleuze, Gilles. *Cinema 2: The Time Image*. 1985. Trans. Hugh Tomlinson and Robert Galeta. New York: Continuum, 2005. Print.

"Dialectic." *Random House Webster's Unabridged Dictionary*. 2nd ed. New York: Random House, 2000. 547. Print.

Diamond, Elin. "Brechtian Theory / Feminist Theory: Toward a Gestic Feminist Criticism." *TDR* 32.1 (1988): 82–94. Print.

The Diary of an Unknown Soldier. Dir. Peter Watkins, 1959. *Punishment Park*. Doriane Films, 2010. DVD.

Direktøren for det hele (The Boss of It All). Dir. Lars von Trier. 2006. Perf. Jens Albinus and Peter Gantzler. IFC, 2007. DVD.

Dogme # 1—Festen (The Celebration). Dir. Thomas Vinterberg. 1998. Perf. Ulrich Thomsen and Henning Moritzen. Universal Studios Home Video, 2004. DVD.

Dogme #2—Idioterne (The Idiots). Dir. Lars von Trier. 1998. Perf. Bodil Jørgensen and Jens Albinus. October Films / USA Films, 2000. Videocassette.

Dogville. Dir. Lars von Trier. 2003. Perf. Nicole Kidman and Paul Bettany. Lions Gate Entertainment, 2004. DVD.

Dupuy, Jean-Pierre. *On the Origins of Cognitive Science: The Mechanization of the Mind*. Cambridge, MA: MIT Press, 2009. Print.

Eckhardt, Juliane. *Das epische Theater*. Darmstadt: Wissenschaftliche Buchgesellschaft, 1983. Print.

Edvard Munch. Dir. Peter Watkins. 1974. Perf. Geir Westby and Gro Frass. New York: New Yorker Video; Toronto: Distributed by Project X, 2006. DVD.

Egginton, William. *How the World Became a Stage*. Albany: State U of New York P, 2003. Print.

Einleitung zu Arnold Schönbergs Begleitmusik zu einer Lichtspielszene: Introduction to Arnold Schoenberg's 'Accompaniment for a Cinematographic Scene.' Dir.

Jean-Marie Straub and Danièle Huillet. 1972. Editions Montparnasse, 2007. DVD.

Eisenstein, Sergei. *Film Form: Essays in Film Theory*. 1949. San Diego: Harcourt Brace Jovanovich, 1977. Print.

———. "The Montage of Attractions." 1923. S. M. Eisenstein: *Selected Works. Volume 1: Writings, 1922–34*. Ed. Richard Taylor. London: BFI, 1988. 33–38. Print.

———. "Montage of Attractions: For *Enough Stupidity in Every Wiseman*." *Drama Review* 18.1 (1974): 77–85. Print.

———. "Vertical Montage." *Selected Works: Volume 2: Towards a Theory of Montage*. Ed. Michael Glenny and Richard Taylor. London: BFI, 1991. 327–400. Print.

Eisenstein, Sergei, Vsevolod Pudovkin, and Grigori Alexandrov. "Statement on Sound." *S. M. Eisenstein: Selected Works: Volume 1: Writings, 1922–34*. Ed. Richard Taylor. London: BFI, 1988. 113–14. Print.

Elbeshlawy, Ahmed F. "Dogville: Lars Von Trier's Desexualized America." *Scope: An Online Journal of Film Studies 10* (2008): n.p. Web.

The Element of Crime. Dir. Lars von Trier. 1984. Perf. Duke Addabayo and Gotha Andersen. Criterion Collection, 2000. DVD.

Elsaesser, Thomas. "From Anti-Illusionism to Hyper-Realism: Bertolt Brecht and Contemporary Film." *Re-Interpreting Brecht: His Influence on Contemporary Drama and Film*. Ed. Pia Kleber and Clin Visser. Cambridge: Cambridge UP, 1990. 170–85. Print.

———. *New German Cinema: A History*. New Brunswick, NJ: Rutgers UP, 1989. Print.

———. *Weimar Cinema and After: Germany's Historical Imaginary*. London: Routledge, 2000. Print.

Epidemic. Dir. Lars von Trier. 1986. Perf. Alland De Waal and Ole Ernst. Home Vision Entertainment, 2004. DVD.

Esslin, Martin. *Brecht: A Choice of Evils*. London: Methuen, 1984. Print.

———. *Brecht: The Man and His Work*. New York: Doubleday, Anchor Books, 1961. Print.

———. *Brecht. Das Paradox des politischen Dichters*. Frankfurt: Athenäum, 1962. Print.

Europa (Europe). Dir. Lars von Trier. 1991. Perf. Jean-Marc Bar and Barbara Sukowa. Criterion Collection. 2008. DVD.

Fairfax, Daniel. "Jean-Marie Straub and Danièle Huillet." *Senses of Cinema* 52 (2009): n.p. Web.

Faster, Pussycat! Kill! Kill! Dir. Russ Meyer. 1965. Perf. Tura Satana, Haji. Eve Productions. Film.

Féral, Josette. "Theatricality: The Specificity of Theatrical Language." *SubStance* 31.2 (2002): 94–108. Print.

Fibiger, Bo. "A Dog Not Yet Buried—Or Dogville as a Political Manifesto." Trans. Lisbet Fibiger. *p.o.v: A Danish Journal of Film Studies* 16 (2003): 56–65. Print.

Fischer, Matthias-Johannes. *Brechts Theatertheorie: Forschungsgeschichte, Forschungsstand, Perspektiven.* New York: Peter Lang, 1989. Print.

Fischer-Lichte, Erika. *The Semiotics of Theater.* Bloomington: Indiana UP, 1992. Print.

The Five Obstructions. Dir. Jørgen Leth and Lars von Trier. 2004. Koch Lorber Films, 2004. DVD.

Forst, Achim. *Breaking the Dreams: Das Kino des Lars von Trier.* Marburg: Schüren, 1998. Print.

Fortini/Cani. Dir. Jean-Marie Straub and Danièle Huillet. 1976. Perf. Franco Lattes. *Danièle Huillet et Jean-Marie Straub: Volume 2.* Editions Montparnasse, 2008. DVD.

Fradkin, Ilja. *Bertolt Brecht: Weg und Methode.* Frankfurt am Main: Röderberg-Verlag, 1977. Print.

Franklin, James. "Jean-Marie Straub / Danièle Huillet." *New German Cinema: From Oberhausen to Hamburg.* Boston: Twayne, 1983. 74–88. Print.

The Freethinker. Dir. Peter Watkins. 1994. Perf. Yasmine Garbi and Anders Mattsson. Project X, 2006. DVD.

Freud, Sigmund. "Two Encyclopaedia Articles." *Collected Papers: Volume 5; Miscellaneous Papers, 1888–1938.* London: Hogarth Press, 1949. 107–36. Print.

Fried, Michael. *Absorption and Theatricality: Painting and Beholder in the Age of Diderot.* Berkeley: U of California P, 1980. Print.

———. *Art and Objecthood: Essays and Reviews.* Chicago: U of Chicago P, 1998. Print.

Friedrich, Rainer. "Brecht and Postmodernism." *Philosophy and Literature* 23.1 (1999): 44–64. Print.

———. "The Deconstructed Self in Artaud and Brecht: Negation of Subject and Antitotalitarianism." *Forum for Modern Language Studies* 26.3 (1990): 282–95. Print.

———. "On Brecht and Eisenstein." *Telos* 31 (1977): 155–64. Print.

Fuegi, John. *Brecht and Company: Sex, Politics, and the Making of Modern Drama.* New York: Grove, 1994. Print.

Furmanov, Dmitri. *Chapaev.* 1924. Moskva: Gos. Izd-vo Khudozh. Lit-ry, 1947. Print.

Galt, Rosalind. "Back Projection: Visualizing Past and Present Europe in *Zentropa*." *Cinema Journal* 45 (2005): 3–21. Print.

Gasquet, Joachim. "What He Told Me . . ." 1921. Trans. Julie Lawrence Cochran. *Conversations with Cézanne.* Ed. Michael Doran. Berkeley: U of California P, 2001. Print.

Gaut, Berys. "Naked Film: Dogma and Its Limits." *Purity and Provocation: Dogma 95.* Ed. Mette Hjort and Scott Mackenzie. London: BFI, 2003. 89–101. Print.

Genette, Gérard. "Flaubert's Silences." *Figures of Literary Discourse.* New York: Columbia UP, 1982. 183–202. Print.

Gersch, Wolfgang. *Film bei Brecht.* München: Hanser, 1975. Print.

Gerstenkorn, Jacques. "Lever de rideau" (Curtain Raiser). *Cinéma et théâtralité*. Ed. Christine Hamons-Siréjols, Jacques Gerstenkorn, and André Gardies. Lyon: Aléas, 1994. 13–18. Print.

Geschichtsunterricht (History Lessons). Dir. Jean-Marie Straub and Danièle Huillet. 1972. Perf. Gottfried Bold and Johann Unterpertinger. *Danièle Huillet et Jean-Marie Straub: Volume 3*. Editions Montparnasse, 2008. DVD.

Gidal, Peter. *Materialist Film*. London: Routledge, 1989. Print.

Gluckstein, Donny. *The Paris Commune: Revolution in Democracy*. London: Bookmarks Publications, 2006. Print.

Goffman, Erving. *The Presentation of Self in Everyday Life*. Garden City, NY: Doubleday Anchor Books, 1959. Print.

Golem. Dir. Paul Wegener. 1920. Perf. Paul Wegener and Albert Steinrück. Kino on Video, 2002. DVD.

Gomez, Joseph A. *Peter Watkins*. Boston: Twayne Publishers, 1979. Print.

Goodall, Mark. *Sweet & Savage: The World through the Shockumentary Film Lens*. London: Headpress, 2006. Print.

"Grace." *Random House Webster's Unabridged Dictionary*. 2nd ed. New York: Random House, 2000. 826. Print.

Gran, Anne-Britt. "The Fall of Theatricality in the Age of Modernity." *SubStance* 31.2 (2002): 251–64. Print.

The Great Gatsby. Dir. Baz Luhrmann. 2013. Perf. Leonardo DiCaprio and Tobey Maguire. Warner Bros. Film.

Greene, Doyle. *Lips Tits Hips Power: The Films of Russ Meyer*. London: Creation, 2004. Print.

Grimm, Reinhold. "Bertolt Brecht and Antonin Artaud: Some Comparative Remarks." *Perspectives and Personalities: Studies in Modern German Literature Honouring Claude Hill*. Ed. Ralph Ley, Maria Wagner, Joanna M. Ratych, and Kenneth Hughes. Heidelberg: Carl Winter Universität, 1978. 118–24. Print.

———. *Strukturen: Essays zur deutschen Literatur*. Göttingen: Sachse & Pohl, 1963. Print.

Gunning, Tom. "The Cinema of Attractions: Early Film, Its Spectator and the Avant-Garde." *Early Cinema: Space, Frame, Narrative*. Ed. Thomas Elsaesser and Adam Barker. London: BFI, 1990. 56–62. Print.

———. "What's the Point of an Index? or, Faking Photographs." *Nordicom Review* 25.1–2 (September 2004): 39–49. Print.

Hamon-Sirejols, Christine, Jacques Gerstenkorn, and André Gardies, eds. *Cinéma et Théatralité*. Lyon: Aléas, 1994. Print.

Handke, Peter. "Antigone." *Die Früchte des Zorns und der Zärtlichkeit*. Vienna: Viennale, 2004. Print.

Hanoi, Martes 13 (Hanoi, Tuesday 13). Dir. Santiago Alvarez, 1968. Instituto Cubano del Arte e Industrias Cinematogràficos (ICAIC). Film.

Happel, Reinhold. " 'Kuhle Wampe oder Wem gehört die Welt'—eine exemplarische Analyse." *Film und Realität in der Weimarer Republik*. Ed. Helmut Korte. München: Carl Hanser Verlag, 1978. 169–212. Print.

Harsin, Jayson. "On Manderlay." *Bright Lights Film Journal* 51 (February 2006): n.p. Web.

Harvey, Sylvia. "Whose Brecht? Memories for the Eighties." *Screen* 23.1 (1982): 45–59. Print.

Hauptmann, Gerhart. *The Weavers*. London: Methuen, 1980. Print.

Heath, Stephen. "God, Faith and Film: Breaking the Waves." *Literature & Theology: An International Journal of Theory, Criticism and Culture* 12.1 (March 1998): 93–107. Print.

———. "Lessons from Brecht." *Screen* 15.2 (1974): 103–28. Print.

Hegel, Georg Wilhelm. 1807. *Phenomenology of Spirit*. Oxford: Clarendon Press, 1977. Print.

Heiney, Donald. *Three Italian Novelists: Moravia, Pavese, Vittorini*. Ann Arbor: U of Michigan P, 1968. Print.

Hemingway, Ernest. *The Sun Also Rises*. 1926. New York: Charles Scribner's Sons, 1954. Print.

Henry V. Dir. Adrian Noble. Perf. Kenneth Branagh. Royal Shakespeare Company, 1984. Theater.

Hermes, Manfred. "Schule der Erbarmungslosigkeit." *Der Freitag* 44, October 24, 2003: 11. Print.

Hertofer, Astrid. "Brecht: An Aesthetics of Conviction?" *German Monitor: Bertolt Brecht: Centenary Essays*. Ed. Steve Giles and Rodney Livingstone. Amsterdam: Rodopi, 1998. 211–26. Print.

Hill, John. *Sex, Class, and Realism: British Cinema 1956–1963*. London: BFI, 1986. Print.

Hillier, Jim, ed. *Cahiers du cinéma, the 1950s: Neo-realism, Hollywood, New Wave*. Cambridge, MA: Harvard UP, 1985. Print.

———. *Cahiers du cinéma, 1960–1968: New Wave, New Cinema, Re-evaluating Hollywood*. Cambridge, MA: Harvard UP, 1986. Print.

Hinck, Walter. "Kamera als Soziologe." *Brecht heute: Brecht Today* 1 (1971): 68–79. Print.

Hjort, Mette. "Dogma 95: A Small Nation's Response to Globalisation." *Purity and Provocation: Dogma 95*. Ed. Mette Hjort and Scott Mackenzie. London: BFI, 2003. 31–47. Print.

Hölderlin, Friedrich. *The Death of Empedocles*. 1797–1800. Trans. David Farrell Krell. Albany: State U of New York P, 2008. Print.

Hollier, Bloch. *A New History of French Literature*. Cambridge, MA: Harvard UP, 1989. Print.

Holub, Robert C. *Reception Theory: A Critical Introduction*. London: Methuen, 1984. Print.

Hutcheon, Linda. "Irony, Nostalgia, and the Postmodern." *Methods for the Study of Literature as Cultural Memory, Studies in Comparative Literature* 30 (2000): 189–207. Print.

The Idiots (Idioterne). Dir. Lars von Trier. 1998. Perf. Bodil Jørgensen and Jens Albinus. Zentropa Entertainments et al. Film.

In the Year of the Pig. Dir. Emile de Antonio. 1968. Emile de Antonio Productions and Turin Film Productions. Film.

Innes, C. D. *Erwin Piscator's Political Theatre: The Development of Modern German Drama*. Cambridge: Cambridge UP, 1972. Print.

Intolerance. Dir. D. W. Griffith. 1916. Perf. Mae Marsh and Robert Harron. Kino International Corp., 1990. Videocassette.

Italian for Beginners. Dir. Lone Scherfig. 2000. Perf. Andres W. Berthelsen and Anette Støvelbæk. Walt Disney Video, 2002. DVD.

Jakobson, Roman. "The Dominant." *Poetry of Grammar and Grammar of Poetry. Selected Writings: Volume 3*. The Hague: Mouton, 1981. 751–56. Print.

Jameson, Fredric. *Brecht and Method*. New York: Verso, 1998. Print.

———. "Postmodernism and Consumer Society." 1984. *Studies in Culture: An Introductory Reader*. Ed. Ann Gray and Jim McGuigan. London: Arnold, 1997. 192–205. Print.

Jestrovic, Silvija. *Theatre of Estrangement: Theatre, Practice, Ideology*. Toronto: U of Toronto P, 2006. Print.

———. "Theatricality as Estrangement of Art and Life in the Russian Avant-garde." *SubStance* 31 (2–3): 2002. 42–56. Print.

Jeune et jolie (Young and Beautiful). Dir. François Ozon. 2013. Perf. Marine Vacth and Géraldine Pailhas. Mandarin Films et al. Film.

Joachim Gatti. Dir. Jean-Marie Straub and Danièle Huillet. *Danièle Huillet et Jean-Marie Straub: Volume 6*. Editions Montparnasse, 2011. DVD.

Julius Caesar. Dir. Deborah Warner. Barbican Theatre, 2005. Theater.

Kaiser, Georg. *The Coral*. 1914. New York: Ungar, 1963. Print.

———. *Gas I*. 1918. New York: Ungar, 1963. Print.

———. *Gas II*. 1920. New York: Ungar, 1963. Print.

Kapla, Marit. "Lars von Trier in Dogville." *Lars von Trier: Interviews*. Ed. Jan Mumholdt. Jackson: UP of Mississippi, 2003. 205–12. Print.

Keffer, Kyle, and Tod Linafelt. "The End of Desire: Theologies of Eros in the Song of Songs and *Breaking the Waves*." *Journal of Religion and Film* 2.1 (April 1998): n.p. Web.

Kim, Hyung-Ki. *Eine vergleichende Untersuchung zu Brechts Theatertheorien im 'Messingkauf' und im 'Kleinen Organon für das Theater*. Frankfurt am Main: Peter Lang, 1992. Print.

Kitses, John. *Horizons West*. Bloomington: Indiana UP, 1969. Print.

Klassenverhältnisse (Class Relations). Dir. Jean-Marie Straub and Danièle Huillet. 1983. Perf. Christian Heinisch and Reinald Schnell. *Danièle Huillet et Jean-Marie Straub: Volume 4*. Editions Montparnasse, 2009. DVD.

Knopf, Jan. *Brecht-Handbuch: Theater*. Stuttgart: J.B. Metzlersche Verlagsbuchhandlung, 1980. Print.

———, ed. *Brecht-Handbuch Band 3: Prosa, Filme, Drehbücher*. Stuttgart: Verlag J.B. Metzler, 2001. Print.

Knudsen, Peter Øvig. "The Man Who Would Give Up Control." *Lars von Trier: Interviews*. Ed. Jan Lumholdt. Jackson: UP of Mississippi, 2003. 117–24. Print.

Kothenschulte, Daniel. "Brechter als Brecht." *Frankfurter Rundschau* 246, October 22, 2003. 17. Print.

Koutsourakis, Angelos. *Politics as Form in Lars von Trier: A Post-Brechtian Reading.* London: Bloomsbury, 2013. Print.

Kuhle Wampe. Dir. Bertolt Brecht and Slatan Dudow. 1932. Perf. Hertha Thiele, Martha Wolter, and Lilli Schönborn. DEFA Film Library, 2008. DVD.

Laak, Lothar van. *Medien und Medialität des Epischen in Literatur und Film des 20. Jahrhunderts.* München: Wilhelm Fink, 2009. Print.

Laakso, Hanna. "Idioterne / The Idiots." *The Cinema of Scandinavia.* Ed. Soila Tytti and Jacob Neiiendam. London: Wallflower, 2005. 203–12. Print.

Lachmann, Renate. "Die 'Verfremdung' und das 'Neue Sehen' bei Viktor Šklovskij." *Verfremdung in der Literatur.* Ed. H. Helmers. Darmstadt: Wissenschaftliche Buchgesellschaft, 1984. 321–51. Print.

Lajtha, Terry. "Brechtian Devices in Non-Brehctian Cinema: Culloden." *Literature/Film Quarterly* 9.1 (1981): 9–14. Print.

Lang, Joachim. *Episches Theater als Film: Bühnenstücke Bertolt Brechts in den audiovisuellen Medien.* Würzburg: Königshausen & Neumann, 2006. Print.

"Lars von Trier's Depression Could Finish His Filmmaking." CBC News. Saturday, May 12, 2007. Web.

Le Dantec, Mireille Latil. "Bresson, Dostoevsky." *Robert Bresson.* Ed. James Quandt. Toronto: Toronto International Film Festival Group, 1998. 325–38. Print.

Lellis, George. *Bertolt Brecht: Cahiers du Cinéma and Contemporary Film Theory.* Ann Arbor: UMI Research Press, 1982. Print.

Lenin, V. I. *Materialism and Empirio-Criticism: Critical Comments on a Reactionary Philosophy.* 1908. New York: International Publishers, 1927. Print.

Lesage, Julia. "The Films of Jean-Luc Godard and Their Use of Brechtian Dramatic Theory." PhD diss., Indiana University, 1975. Print.

Lessard, Bruno. "Digital Technologies and the Poetics of Performance." *New Punk Cinema.* Ed. Nicholas Rombes. Edinburgh: Edinburgh UP, 2005. 102–12. Print.

Little Big Man. Dir. Arthur Penn. 1970. Perf. Dustin Hoffman and Faye Dunaway. Cinema Center Films and Stockbridge-Hiller Productions. Film.

Loin du Viêt-nam. Dir. Joris Ivens et al. Societe pour le Lancement des Ouevres Nouvelles, 1967. Film.

Loong Boonmee raleuk chat (Uncle Boonmee Who Remembers His Past Lives). Dir. Apichatpong Weerasethakul. 2010. Perf. Thanapat Saisaymar and Jenjira Pongpas. Strand Releasing. DVD.

Lukács, György: *Geschichte und Klassenbewußtein. Studien über materialistische Dialektik.* Berlin: Neuwied, 1970. Print.

Lumholdt, Jan, ed. *Lars von Trier: Interviews.* Jackson: UP of Mississippi, 2003. Print.

Lyotard, Jean-François. *The Postmodern Condition: A Report on Knowledge.* 1979. Minneapolis: U of Minnesota, 1984. Print.

MacCabe, Colin. "Realism and the Cinema: Notes on Some Brechtian Theses." *Screen* 15.2 (1974): 7–27. Print.

MacDonald, Scott. "The Filmmaker as Global Circumnavigator: Peter Watkins' The Journey and Media Critique." *Documenting the Documentary: Close Readings of Documentary Film and Video*. Ed. Barry Keith Grant and Jeannette Sloniowski. Detroit: Wayne State UP, 1998. 360–68. Print.

———. "Peter Watkins." *A Critical Cinema 2*. Ed. Scott MacDonald. Berkeley: U of California P, 1992. 402–22. Print.

Machorka-Muff. Dir. Jean-Marie Straub and Danièle Huillet. 1962. Perf. Erich Kuby and Renate Langsdorff. *Danièle Huillet et Jean-Marie Straub: Volume 1*. Editions Montparnasse, 2007. DVD.

MacKenzie, Scott. "Direct Dogma: Film Manifestos and the fin de siècle." *p.o.v.* 10 (2000): n.p. Web.

———. "Manifest Destinies: Dogma 95 and the Future of the Film Manifesto." *Purity and Provocation: Dogma 95*. Ed. Mette Hjort and Scott Mackenzie. London: BFI, 2003. 48–57. Print.

Man with a Movie Camera. Dir. Dziga Vertov. 1929. Kino Video, 2003. DVD.

Manderlay. Dir. Lars von Trier. 2005. Perf. Bryce Dallas Howard and Isaach De Bankolé. IFC, 2006. DVD.

Mandolfo, Carleen. "Women, Suffering and Redemption in Three Films of Lars von Trier." *Literature & Theology: An International Journal of Religion, Theory and Culture* 24.3 (September 2010): 285–300. Print.

Manovich, Lev. *The Language of New Media*. Cambridge, MA: MIT Press, 2001. Print.

Martig, Charles. "Weibliche Christusse im Werk Lars von Triers: von *Medea* bis *Dogville*." *Dogville* aus der Perspektive theologischer Anthropologie." *Dogville—Godville: Methodische Zugänge zu einem Film Lars von Triers*. Ed. Stefan Orth, Michael Staiger, and Joachim Valentin. Marburg: Schüren, 2008. 141–58. Print.

Martin, Carol, and Henry Bial, eds. *Brecht Sourcebook*. New York: Routledge, 2000. Print.

Marx, Karl, and V. I. Lenin. *Civil War in France*. New York: International Publishers, 1988. Print.

McCabe and Mrs. Miller. Dir. Robert Altman. 1971. Perf. Warren Beatty and Julie Christie. David Foster Productions and Warner Bros. Film.

Méranger, Thierry. "Entretein avec Peter Watkins: Mon cinéma met en cause le cinéma." *Cahiers du Cinéma* 598 (2005): 82–86. Print.

Mercadante, Linda. "Bess the Christ Figure? Theological Interpretations of *Breaking the Waves*." *Journal of Religion and Film* 5.1 (April 2001): n.p. Web.

Merrell, Frank. "Charles Sanders Peirce's Concept of the Sign." *The Routledge Companion to Semiotics and Linguistics*. Ed. Paul Cobley. New York: Routledge, 2001. Print.

Metropolis. Dir. Fritz Lang. 1928. Perf. Alfred Abel and Gustav Frölich. Kino on Video, 2002. DVD.

Metz, Christian. *Langage et cinéma*. Paris: Larousse, 1971. Print.

———. "Photography and Fetish." *The Critical Image: Essays on Contemporary Photography*. Ed. Carol Squiers. Seattle: Bay Press, 1990. 155–64. Print.

Michelson, Annette, ed. *Kino-Eye: The Writings of Dziga Vertov*. Berkeley: U of California P, 1984. Print.

Möbius, Hanno. *Montage und Collage*. München: Wilhelm Fink Verlag, 2000. Print.

Monaco, James. *How to Read a Film*. New York: Oxford UP, 2000. Print.

Mondo cane (A Dog's World). Dir. Gualtiero Jacopetti, Paolo Cavara, and Franco Prosperi. 1962. Cineriz. Film.

Moses und Aron (Moses and Aaron). Dir. Jean-Marie Straub and Danièle Huillet. 1974. Perf. Günter Reich and Louis Devos. *Danièle Huillet et Jean-Marie Straub: Volume 1*. Editions Montparnasse, 2007. DVD.

Moulin Rouge. Dir. Baz Luhrmann. 2001. Perf. Nicole Kidman and Ewan MacGregor. Twentieth Century Fox. Film.

Mueller, Roswitha. *Bertolt Brecht and the Theory of Media*. Lincoln: U of Nebraska P, 1989. Print.

Müller, Klaus-Detlef. *Die Funktion der Geschichte im Werk Bertolt Brechts: Studien zum Verhältnis von Marxismus und Ästhetik*. Tübingen: Niemeyer, 1967. Print.

Müller, Marion. *Vexierbilder: die Filmwelten des Lars von Trier*. St. Augustin: Gardez!, 2000. Print.

Munk, Edvard. *The Private Journals of Edvard Munch: We Are Flames Which Pour Out of the Earth*. Ed. Gill J. Holland. Madison: U of Wisconsin P, 2005. Print.

Murphy, G. Ronald, S.J. *Brecht and the Bible*. Chapel Hill: U of North Carolina P, 1980. Print.

Mutter Courage und ihre Kinder (Mother Courage and Her Children). Dir. Peter Palitzsch and Manfred Wekwerth. 1961. Perf. Helene Weigel and Angelika Hurwicz. DEFA. Videocassette.

Mysteries of a Hairdressing Salon. Dir. Erich Engel and Bertolt Brecht. 1923. Perf. Blandine Ebinger and Karl Valentin. Film.

Nichols, Bill. *Introduction to Documentary*. Bloomington: Indiana UP, 2001. Print.

Nicht Versöhnt oder Es hilft nur Gewalt, wo Gewalt herrscht (Not Reconciled or Only Violence Helps Where Violence Rules). Dir. Jean-Marie Straub and Danièle Huillet. 1964. Perf. Heinrich Hargesheimer and Karlhein Hargesheimer. *Danièle Huillet et Jean-Marie Straub, Volume 1*. Editions Montparnasse, 2008. DVD.

Nietzsche, Friedrich. *The Birth of Tragedy*. 1872. Garden City, NY: Doubleday, 1956. Print.

Nobus, Dany. "The Politics of Gift-Giving and the Provocation of Lars von Trier's *Dogville*." *Film-Philosophy* 11.3 (2007): 23–37. Print.

La notte di San Lorenzo (The Night of the Shooting Stars). Dir. Paolo Taviani and Vittorio Taviani. 1982. Perf. Omero Antonutti and Margarita Lozano. RAI—Radio Televisione Italiana. Film.

O somma luce. Dir. Jean-Marie Straub and Danièle Huillet. 2009. Perf. Giorgio Passerone. *Danièle Huillet et Jean-Marie Straub: Volume 6*. Editions Montparnasse, 2011. DVD.

October. Dir. Sergei Eisenstein. 1927. Perf. Vladimir Popov and Vasili Nikandrov. Tartan Video, 1997. Videocassette.

Oesmann, Astrid. *Staging History: Brecht's Social Concepts of Ideology*. Albany: State U of New York P, 2005. Print.

Oh, Seong-Kyun. *Die materialistisch-dialektische Fundierung des epischen Theaters Brechts als eines zweidimensionalen theatralischen Kommunikationssystems*. Frankfurt am Main: P. Lang, 1998. Print.

Orth, Stefan. "Gnade, wem Gnade gebührt?: *Dogville* aus der Perspektive theologischer Anthropologie." *Dogville—Godville: Methodische Zugänge zu einem Film Lars von Triers*. Ed. Stefan Orth, Michael Staiger, and Joachim Valentin. Marburg: Schüren, 2008. 179–94. Print.

The Osbournes. Dir. Donald Bull, CB Harding, Sarah Pillsbury, and Todd Stevens. Perf. Ozzy Osbourne and Sharon Osbourne. MTV Channel, 2002–2005. Television.

Padre Padrone (Father and Master). Dir. Paolo Taviani and Vittorio Taviani. 1977. Perf. Omero Antonutti and Saverio Marconi. Rai 2. Film.

Païni, Dominique. "Straub, Hölderlin, Cézanne." *Senses of Cinema* 39: May 2006. Web.

Parmalee, Patty Lee. *Brecht's America*. Columbus: Ohio State UP, 1981. Print.

Pat Garrett & Billy the Kid. Dir. Sam Peckinpah. 1973. Perf. James Coburn and Kris Kristofferson. MGM. Film.

Pavis, Patrice. "Brechtian Gestus and its Avatars in Contemporary Theatre." *Brecht 100 < = > 2000: Brecht Yearbook / Das Brecht Yahrbuch* 24 (1999): 176–90. Print.

———. *Dictionary of the Theatre: Terms, Concepts, and Analysis*. 1980. Toronto: U of Toronto P, 1998. Print.

Penzendorfer, Anneliese. *Lars von Triers DOGVILLE: ein Fusion Film vs. Brechts episches Theater: Eine Filmanalyse in 13 Kapiteln und einem Prolog*. VDM Verlag Dr. Müller, 2010. Print.

Perez, Gilberto. *The Material Ghost: Film and Their Medium*. Baltimore: Johns Hopkins UP, 1998. Print.

Pettifer, James. "Against the Stream—Kuhle Wampe." *Screen* 15.2 (1974): 49–63. Print.

Phelan, Peggy. *Unmarked: The Politics of Performance*. London: Routledge, 1993. Print.

Plato. *The Republic*. New York: Basic Books, 1968. Print.

Pohl, Rainer. "Strukturelemente und Pathosformen in der Sprache." *Brechts Antigone des Sophokles*. Ed. Werner Hecht. Frankfurt am Main: Suhrkamp, 1988. 245–60. Print.

Polan, Dana. "Brecht and the Politics of Self-Reflexive Cinema." *Jump Cut* 17 (1974): 29–32. Print.

———. "A Brechtian Cinema? Towards a Politics of Self-Reflexive Film." *Movies and Methods: Volume II*. Ed. Bill Nichols. Berkeley: U of California P, 1985. 661–71. Print.

Potter, Joy Hambuechen. *Elio Vittorini*. Boston: Twayne Publishers, 1979. Print.

Prédal, René. "Robert Bresson: L'Aventure intérierure." *Robert Bresson*. Ed. James Quandt. Toronto: Toronto International Film Festival Group, 1998. 73–116. Print.

Prince, Stephen. "True Lies: Perceptual Realism, Digital Images, and Film Theory." *Film Quarterly* 49.3 (1996): 27–37. Print.

Privilege. Dir. Peter Watkins. 1967. Perf. Paul Jones and Jean Shrimpton. New Yorker Video, 2008. DVD.

Pudovkin, V. I. *Film Technique and Film Acting*. Ed. and trans. Ivor Montagu. New York: Grove Press, 1960. Print.

Pummer, Claudia Alexandra. "Elective Affinities: The Films of Danièle Huillet and Jean-Marie Straub." PhD diss., U of Iowa, 2011. Print.

Quandt, James. "Introduction." *Robert Bresson*. Ed. James Quandt. Toronto: Toronto International Film Festival Group, 1998. 1–16. Print.

Quantum of Solace. Dir. Marc Forster. 2009. Perf. Daniel Craig and Olga Kurylenko. MGM. Film.

Rapfogel, Jared. "Cautionary Tales and Alternate Histories: The Films of Peter Watkins." *Cineaste* 32.2 (2007): 20–25. Print.

Rauschenbach, Boris V. "Perceptual Perspective and Cézanne's Landscapes." *Leonardo* 15.1 (Winter 1982): 28–33. Print.

Reader, Keith. "'D'où cela vient-il?' Notes on Three Films by Robert Bresson." *Robert Bresson*. Ed. James Quandt. Toronto: Toronto International Film Festival Group, 1998. 283–98. Print.

Reich, Bernard. *Im Wettlauf mit der Zeit*. Berlin: Henschelverlag, 1970. Print.

Reimer, Robert C., and Carol J. Reimer. *The A to Z of German Cinema*. Lanham, MD: Scarecrow Press, 2010. Print.

Reinelt, Janelle. "The Politics of Discourse: Performativity Meets Theatricality." *SubStance* 31.2 (2002): 201–15. Print.

Riget (Kingdom I). Dir. Lars von Trier. 1994. Perf. Ernst-Hugo Järegård and Kirsten Rolffes. Koch Lorber Films, 2005. DVD.

Riget II (Kingdom II). Dir. Lars von Trier. 1997. Perf. Ernst-Hugo Järegård and Kirsten Rolffes. Zentropa Entertainment, 1997. Film.

Rissing, Michaela, and Thilo Rissing. "Kino auf den Spuren Kierkegaards." *Dogville—Godville: Methodische Zugänge zu einem Film Lars von Triers*. Ed. Stefan Orth, Michael Staiger, and Joachim Valentin. Marburg: Spüren, 2008. 195–212. Print.

Robbe-Grillet, Alain. *For a New Novel: Essays on Fiction*. 1963. Trans. Richard Howard. Evanston, IL: Northwestern UP, 1989. Print.

Roberts, John. "Dogme 95." *New Left Review* 238 (1999): 141–49. Print.

Robin Hood: Men in Tights. Dir. Mel Brooks. 1993. Perf. Cary Elwes and Richard Lewis. Brooksfilms and Gaumont, 1993. Film.

Rodowick, D. N. *Elegy for Theory*. Cambridge, MA: Harvard UP, 2014. Print.

Rogers, Joel. "Jean-Marie Straub and Danièle Huillet Interviewed: *Moses und Aron* as an Object of Marxist Reflection." *Jump Cut* 12/13 (1976): 61–64. Print.

Römers, Holger. "'Colorado Death Trip': The Surrealist Recontextualisation of Farm Security Administration Photos in Dogville." *Senses of Cinema* 34 (2004). Web.

Rosenbaum, Jonathan. "Mother Courage and Her Children and History Lessons." Web.

Roud, Richard. *Jean-Marie Straub*. London: Secker and Warburg in association with the BFI, 1971. Print.

Rouse, John. "Brecht and the Contradictory Actor." *Acting (Re)Considered*. Ed. Phillip B. Zarrilli. London: Routledge, 1995. Print.

Rozik, Eli. "Acting: The Quintessence of Theatricality." *SubStance* 31.2 (2002): 110–24. Print.

Rüllicke-Weiler, Käthe. *Die Dramaturgie Brechts: Theater als Mittel der Veränderung*. Berlin: Henschel, 1966. Print.

Sandler, Willibald Sandler. "Die pervertierte Gabe: Dogville aus der Perspektive dramatischer Theologie." *Dogville—Godville: Methodische Zugänge zu einem Film Lars von Triers*. Ed. Stefan Orth, Michael Staiger, and Joachim Valentin. Marburg: Schüren, 2008. 213–28. Print.

Saturday Night, Sunday Morning. Dir. Karel Reisz. 1961. Perf. Albert Finney and Shirley Anne Field. Continental Distributing, 2002. DVD.

Savage, Robert. "The Precedence of Citation: On Brecht's The Antigone of Sophocles." Colloquy: *Text Theory Critique* 11 (May 2006): 99–126. Print.

Schacherreiter, Christian. "Bertolt Brecht und Karl Korsch: Untersuchungen zur Subjekt-Objekt-Dialektik in realistischer Literatur und marxistischer Philosophie." *Sprachkunst* 19 (1988): 59–78. Print.

Schatz, Thomas. *Hollywood Genres: Formulas, Filmmaking, and the Studio System*. Philadelphia: Temple UP, 1981. Print.

Schepelern, Peter. "'Kill Your Darlings': Lars von Trier and the Origin of Dogma 95." *Purity and Provocation: Dogma 95*. Ed. Mette Hjort and Scott Mackenzie. London: BFI, 2003. 58–69. Print.

Schmidt, Hugo. "Epic Theater and the Antigone Versions by Anouilh and Brecht." *Hypatia: Essays in Classics, Comparative Literature, and Philosophy Presented to Hazel E. Barnes on Her Seventieth Birthday*. Ed. William M. Calder, Ulrich K. Goldsmith, and Phyllis B. Kevevan. Boulder: Colorado Associated UP, 1985. 199–211. Print.

Schoeps, Karl-Heinz. "From Distancing Alienation to Intuitive Naiveté: Bertolt Brecht's Establishment of a New Aesthetic Category." *Monatshefte* 81.2 (1989): 186–98. Print.

Schöttker, Detlev. *Bertolt Brechts Ästhetik des Naiven*. Stuttgart: Metzler, 1989. Print.

Schrader, Paul. *Transcendental Style in Film: Ozu, Bresson, Dreyer*. New York: Da Capo Press, 1988. Print.

Schwarze Sünde (Black Sin). Dir. Jean-Marie Straub and Danièle Huillet. 1990. Perf. Andreas von Rauch, Vladimir Baratta, and Howard Vernon. Straub-Huillet, Dominique Païni, and Hamburg Radio. Film.

Shafer, David A. *The Paris Commune: French Politics, Culture and Society at the Crossroads of the Revolutionary Tradition and Revolutionary Socialism*. New York: Palgrave Macmillan, 2005. Print.

Shafto, Sally. "Artistic Encounters: Jean-Marie Straub and Danièle Huillet and Paul Cézanne." *Senses of Cinema* 52 (September 2009): n.p. Web.

Shklovsky, Viktor. "Art as Technique." 1917. *Russian Formalist Criticism: Four Essays*. Ed. Lee T. Lemon and Marion J. Reis. Lincoln: U of Nebraska P, 1965. 3–24. Print.

———. "Sterne's Tristram Shandy: Stylistic Commentary." 1921. *Russian Formalist Criticism: Four Essays*. Ed. Lee T. Lemon and Marion J. Reis. Lincoln: U of Nebraska P, 1965. 25–57. Print.

Shoard, Catherine. "Lars von Trier Makes Vow of Silence after Cannes Furore." *The Guardian*, October 5, 2011. Web.

Sicilia! (Sicily!). Dir. Jean-Marie Straub and Danièle Huillet. 1998. Perf. Gianni Buscarino and Angela Nugara. *Danièle Huillet et Jean-Marie Straub: Volume 2*. Editions Montparnasse, 2008. DVD.

Silberman, Marc. "Brecht and Film." *A Bertolt Brecht Reference Companion*. Ed. Siegfried Mews. Westport, CT: Greenwood Press, 1997. 197–219. Print.

———, ed. *Brecht on Film and Radio*. London: Methuen, 2000. Print.

———. "Brecht's Gestus or Staging Contradictions." *Brecht Yearbook / Das Brecht Jahrbuch 31* (2006): *Young Mr. Brecht Becomes a Writer*. 319–35. Print.

———. *German Cinema: Texts in Context*. Detroit: Wayne State UP, 1995. Print.

Simons, Jan. *Playing the Waves: Lars von Trier's Game Cinema*. Amsterdam: Amsterdam UP, 2007. Print.

Smith, Greg M. *Film Structure and the Emotion System*. Cambridge: Cambridge UP, 2003. Print.

Smith, Henry Nash. *Virgin Land: the American West as Symbol and Myth*. Cambridge, MA: Harvard UP, 1950. Print.

Smith, Murray. "Lars von Trier: Sentimental Surrealist." *Purity and Provocation: Dogma 95*. Ed. Mette Hjort and Scott Mackenzie. London: BFI, 2003. 111–21. Print.

———. "The Logic and Legacy of Brechtianism." *Post-Theory: Reconstructing Film Studies*. Ed. David Bordwell and Noël Carroll. Madison: U of Wisconsin P, 1996. 130–48. Print.

Solano, Jeanette Reedy. "Blessed Broken Bodies: Exploring Redemption in Central Station and Breaking the Waves." *Journal of Religion and Film* 8.1 (April 2004): n.p. Web.

Soldovieri, Stefan. "War-Poetry, Photo(epi)grammetry: Brecht's *Kriegsfibel*." *A Bertolt Brecht Reference Companion*. Ed. Siegfried Mews. Westport, CT: Greenwood Press, 1997. 139–67. Print.

Stein, Gertrude. *Lectures in America*. 1935. Boston: Beacon Press, 1985. Print.

Steinweg, Reiner. *Lehrstück und episches Theater: Brechts Theorie und die theaterpädagogische Praxis*. Frankfurt: Brandes & Apsel, 1995. Print.

Stevenson, Jack. *Lars von Trier*. London: BFI, 2002. Print.

Stewart, Elizabeth. "Hypnosis, Identification, and Crime in Lars von Trier's European Trilogy." *Film Journal* 12 (2005): n.p. Web.

Stifters Dinge (Stifter's Things). Dir. Heiner Goebbels. Theatre Vidy Lausanne, T&M Nanterre Paris, Schauspielfrankfurt, Berliner Festspiele—Spielzeit Europa, Grand Theatre Luxembourg, Teatro Stabile Turino, 2007. Print.

Straub, Jean-Marie. "Filmcritica: Eisenstein, Brecht." *Filmkritik* 7 (September 1973): 300–303. Print.

Stroszek. Dir. Werner Herzog. 1977. Perf. Bruno S. and Eva Mattes. Skellig Edition. Film.

Sud pralad (Tropical Malady). Dir. Apichatpong Weerasethakul. 2004. Perf. Banlop Lomnoi and Sakda Kaewbuadee. Strand Releasing, 2005. DVD.

Tassi, Marguerite A. *The Scandal of Images*. Selinsgrove: Susquehanna UP, 2005. Print.

A Taste of Honey. Dir. Tony Richardson. 1961. Perf. Dora Bryan and Robert Stephens. Continental Distributing. Videocassette.

This Is America. Dir. Romano Vanderbes. 1977. Pace Films. Film.

This Is America 2. Dir. Romano Vanderbes. 1980. Pace Films. Film.

Three Colors: Blue. Dir. Krzystof Kieślowski. 1993. Perf. Juliette Binoche and Benoît Régent. Eurimages, France 3 Cinéma and Canal + Film.

TMZ on TV. Created by Harvey Levin and Jim Paratore. 2007–present. Perf. Harvey Levin. TMZ.com and Harvey Levin Productions. Television.

Der Tod des Empedokles (The Death of Empedocles). Dir. Jean-Marie Straub and Danièle Huillet. 1986. Perf. Martina Baratta and Vladimir Baratta. Janus Film and les Films du Losange. Film.

Todorov, Tzvetan, and Arnold Weinstein. "Structural Analysis of Narrative." *NOVEL: A Forum on Fiction* 3.1 (1969): 70–76. Print.

Tout va bien. Dir. Jean-Luc Godard and Jean-Perre Gorin. 1972. Perf. Yves Montand and Jane Fonda. Criterion Collection and Home Vision Entertainment, 2005. DVD.

Toy Story. Dir. John Lasseter. 1995. Perf. Tom Hanks and Tim Allen. Pixar Animation Studios and Walt Disney Pictures. Film.

Trier, Lars von, and Anthony Dod Mantle. "Audio Commentary." *Dogville*. Lions Gate Entertainment, 2004. DVD.

Triumph des Willens (Triumph of the Will). Dir. Leni Riefenstahl. 1935. Leni Riefenstahl Produktion and Reichspropagandaleitung der NSDAP. Synapse Film, 2001. DVD.

Troilus and Cressida. Dir. Mark Wing-Davey. Perf. Neal Huff and Elizabeth Marvel. Delacorte Theater, 1995. Theater.

Trop tot, trop tard (Too Early, Too Late). Dir. Jean-Marie Straub and Danièle Huillet. 1981. Perf. Bahgat Elnadi and Danièle Huillet. Straub-Huillet. Film.

Turim, Maureen. "Jean-Marie Straub and Danièle Huillet: Oblique Angles on Film as Ideological Interventiolns." *New German Filmmakers: From Oberhausen through the 1970s*. Ed. Klaus Phillips. New York: Ungar, 1984. 335–58. Print.

———. "Textuality and Theatricality in Brecht and Straub/Huilllet: 'History Lessons' (1972)." *German Film and Literature: Adaptations and Transformations*. Ed. Eric Rentschler. New York: Methuen, 1986. 231–45. Print.

Turovskaia, Maia. *Na granitse iskusstv: Brekht i kino*. Moskva: Iskusstvo, 1985. Print.

Vaßen, Florian. "Bertolt Brechts 'Learning-play': Genesis und Geltung des Lehrstücks." *Brecht Then and Now / Brecht damals und heute*. Ed. Marc Silberman et al. Madison: International Brecht Society, 1995. 201–15. Print.

Vertov, Dziga. "WE: Variant of a Manifesto." *Kino Eye: The Writings of Dziga Vertov*. Ed. Annette Michelson. Trans. Kevin O'Brian. Berkeley: U of California P, 1984. 5–9. Print.

La vie d'Adèle—Chapitres 1 et 2 (Blue Is the Warmest Color). Dir. Abdellatif Kechiche. 2013. Perf. Léa Seydoux and Adèle Exarchopoulos. Quat'sous Films et al. Film.

Une visite au Louvre (A Visit to Louvre). Dir. Jean-Marie Straub and Danièle Huillet. 2004. *Danièle Huillet et Jean-Marie Straub: Volume 4*. DVD. Editions Montparnasse, 2009.

Vittorini, Elio. *Conversazione in Sicilia: In Sicily*. Trans. Wilfrid David. New York: New Directions, 1949. Print.

Von Heute auf Morgen (From Today Till Tomorrow). Dir. Jean-Marie Straub and Danièle Huillet. 1996. Perf. Christine Whitlesey and Richard Salter. *Danièle Huillet et Jean-Marie Straub: Volume 1*. Editions Montparnasse, 2007. DVD.

Walsh, Martin. *The Brechtian Aspect of Radical Cinema*. Ed. Keith M. Griffiths. London: BFI, 1981. Print.

Walters, Tim. "Reconsidering *The Idiots*: Dogme 95, Lars Von Trier, and the Cinema of Subversion?" *Velvet Light Trap* 53 (2004): 40–54. Print.

Wannamaker, Annette. "'Marking Time': Bertolt Brecht's Antigone as Tragedy of Revolution and Exile." *Brecht Yearbook / Das Brecht-Jahrbuch 31* (2006): 336–52. Print.

The War Game. Dir. Peter Watkins. 1965. Toronto: Project X Distribution. New York: New Yorker Video, 2006. DVD.

Watkins, Peter. "The Fear of Commitment." *Literature / Film Quarterly* 11.4 (1983): 221–33. Print.

———. *The Media Crisis*. Homnisphères: Paris, 2004. Print.

———. Peter Watkins: Filmmaker / Media Critic. "Media Crisis." 2009. Web.

———. Peter Watkins: Filmmaker / Media Critic. "Introduction to the Listing of My Films." 2009. Web.

———. Peter Watkins: Filmmaker / Media Critic. "*La Commune (de Paris, 1871)*." 2009. Web.

———. Peter Watkins: Filmmaker / Media Critic. "Media Statement." 2009. Web.

———. Peter Watkins: Filmmaker / Media Critic. "Public-alternative Processes and Practices." 2009. Web.

———. Peter Watkins: Filmmaker / Media Critic. "Punishment Park." 2009. Web.

———. "Peter Watkins Self Interview on Punishment Park." "Alienated in Vancouver." Allan Macinnis. 2006. Web.

———. *The War Game*. BBC TV, 1965. Print.

Wayne, Michael. "The Tragedy of History: Peter Watkins's La Commune." *Third Text* 16.1 (2002): 57–69. Print.

The Web. Dir. Peter Watkins. 1956. Film.

Weill, Kurt. "Gestus in Music." 1929. *The Brecht Sourcebook*. London: Routledge, 2000. 61–65. Print.

Weisberg, Neils. "Great Cry and Little Wool." *p.o.v.* 10 (2000). Web. February 3, 2011.

Weiss, Peter. *The Investigation: oratorio in 11 cantos*. 1965. Trans. Alexander Gross. London: Calder & Boyars, 1966. Print.

Weisstein, Ulrich. "Imitation, Stylization, and Adaptation: The Language of Brecht's Antigone and Its Relation to Hölderlin's Version of Sophocles." *German Quarterly* 46.4 (1973): 581–604. Print.

Welsh, James Michael. "Narration and Authorship in the Cinema of Peter Watkins." PhD diss., U of Kansas, 1996. Print.

White, Hayden. "Manifesto Time." *Manifestos for History*. Ed. Keith Jenkins, Sue Morgan, and Alun Munslow. New York: Routledge, 2007. 222–31. Print.

White, John J. *Bertolt Brecht's Dramatic Theory*. Rochester: Camden House, 2004. Print.

Wie will ich lustig lachen: Danièle Huillet und Jean-Marie Straub und ihr Film Klassenverh Klassenverhältnisse (How Merrily Shall I Laugh: Danièle Huillet and Jean-Marie Straub and Their Film Class Relations). Dir. Manfred Blank. 1984. Film.

Willett, John. "Brecht and the Motion Pictures." *Brecht in Context: Comparative Approaches*. London: Methuen, 1984. 107–28. Print.

———. *The Theatre of Bertolt Brecht*. London: Methuen, 1964. Print.

———. *The Theatre of Erwin Piscator*. London: Eyre Methuen, 1978. Print.

William Shakespeare's Hamlet. Dir. Kenneth Branagh. 1996. Perf. Kenneth Branagh and Derek Jacobi. Warner Bros. 2007. DVD.

Williams, Mark. "Real-Time Fairy Tales: Cinema Prefiguring Digital Reality." *New Media: Theories and Practices of Digitextuality*. 159–78. New York: Routledge, 2003. Print.

Wilson, David, ed. *Cahiers du cinéma. Volume 4, 1973–1978: History, Ideology, Cultural Struggle: An Anthology from Cahiers du cinéma, nos. 248–292, September 1973–September 1978*. Ed. David Wilson. London: Routledge & Kegan Paul, 2000. Print.

Winter, Jessica. "Is Lars von Trier a Misogynist? Maybe Not!" *Slate*, October 22, 2009. Web.

Witt, Michael. *Jean-Luc Godard, Cinema Historian*. Bloomington: Indiana UP, 2013. Print.

Witte, Karsten. "Brecht und der Film." 1972. *Text und Kritik: Bertolt Brecht I*. München, 2006. 62–83. Print.

Wollen, Peter. "Godard and Counter Cinema: *Vent d'est*." *Movies and Methods, Volume 2*. Ed. Bill Nichols. 1972. Berkeley: U of California P, 1985. Print.

———. " 'Ontology' and 'Materialism' in Film." *Readings and Writings: Semiotic Counter-Strategies*. London: Verso, 1982. 189–207. Print.

Wood, Robert E. *Placing Aesthetics*. Athens: Ohio UP, 1999. Print.

Woods, Barbara Allen. "The Function of Proverbs in Brecht." *Monatshefte für deutschen Unterricht* 61.1 (1969): 49–57. Print.

———. "Perverted Proverbs in Brecht and *Verfremdungsprache*." *Germanic Review* 43 (1968): 100–108. Print.

Woolf, Virginia. *The Captains' Death Bed*. London: Hogarth Press, 1950. Print.

Wright, Elizabeth. *Postmodern Brecht: A Re-presentation*. London: Routledge, 1989. Print.

Les yeux ne veulent pas en tour temps se fermer ou peut-être qu'un jour Rome se permettra de choisir à son tour ou Othon (Eyes Do Not Want to Close at All Times or Perhaps One Day Rome Will Permit Herself to Choose in Her Turn or Othon). Dir. Jean-Marie Straub and Danièle Huillet. 1969. Perf. Adriano Apra and Anne Brumagne. Janus Film. Film.

Zemplén, Gábor Á. *The History of Vision, Colour, & Light: Theories Introductions, Texts, Problems*. Bern: Bern Studies in the History and Philosophy of Science, 2005. Print.

Index